Emotions at Work
Normative Control, Organizations, and Culture in Japan and America

Harvard East Asian Monographs, 213

Emotions at Work

Normative Control, Organizations, and Culture in Japan and America

Aviad E. Raz

Published by the Harvard University Asia Center
and distributed by Harvard University Press
Cambridge (Massachusetts) and London 2002

Printed in the United States of America

The Harvard University Asia Center publishes a monograph series and, in coordination with the Fairbank Center for East Asian Research, the Korea Institute, the Reischauer Institute of Japanese Studies, and other faculties and institutes, administers research projects designed to further scholarly understanding of China, Japan, Vietnam, Korea, and other Asian countries. The Center also sponsors projects addressing multidisciplinary and regional issues in Asia.

Library of Congress Cataloging-in-Publication Data
Raz, Aviad E., 1968–
    Emotions at work : normative control, organizations, and culture in Japan and America
    / Aviad E. Raz.
        p. cm. -- (Harvard East Asian monographs ; 213)
    Includes bibliographic references and index.
    ISBN 0-674-00858-8
        1. Psychology, Industrial--Cross-cultural studies. 2. Emotions--Cross-cultural studies.
    3. Corporate culture--Cross-cultural studies. I. Title. II. Series.
    HF5548.8. R293 2002
    158.7--dc 21   2001051968

Index by the author

⊗   Printed on acid-free paper

Last figure below indicates year of this printing
12 11 10 09 08 07 06 05 04 03 02

For Nira, my mother

People constantly experience emotions, yet in organizational theory, as in organizational life, the exploration of emotions has been largely de-emphasized, marginalized, or ignored.

   —American sociologist Joanne Martin (et al. 1998: 429)

Japanese industrial relations are not concerned with the exact definition of the rights of parties in a dispute . . . but turn rather on a kinship-type relationship within the enterprise-family and on emotional understanding. . . . Subordinates are not supposed to express disagreement or to state their grievances openly; they are expected to endure hardships in anticipation of the benevolent consideration of the superior.

   —Japanese legal scholar Hanami Tadashi (1979: 54, 57)

Japanese strikes were essentially emotional affairs rather than economic struggles.

   —American historian of Japan Thomas Smith (1984: 595)

[In the United States] emotion has been regarded as a disruptive, rather than productive force in work groups. . . . Groups expressing emotion have typically been treated as escaping work.

   —British sociologist Amanda Sinclair (1992: 617)

Always extend your antenna of understanding and consideration. Respond in both a rational and emotional way.

   —From *Lectures on Cheerful Manners*, a women's junior
   college workbook for office ladies in Japan

Can anyone doubt that organizations are emotional cauldrons? Only perhaps those who have been schooled in a particular analytical approach.

   —British sociologist Martin Albrow (1992: 326)

Contents

Tables and Figures

Tables

Figures

Abbreviations

AFL	American Federation of Labor
GM	General Motors
MBS	management by stress
NUGW	National Union of General Workers
NUMMI	New United Motors Manufacturing, Inc.
OL	office lady
QCC	quality control circle
TQM	total quality management
UAW	United Auto Workers

Emotions at Work
Normative Control, Organizations, and Culture in Japan and America

Introduction

Our work life is filled with emotions. How we feel on the job, what we say we feel, and what feelings we display—all these are important aspects of organizational behavior and workplace culture. Many jobs demand that the employee display a certain range of emotions; in other environments workers are expected to suppress all emotion. Common to both extremes and the points in between is the emphasis on the management of emotions. Rather than focusing on the psychology of personal emotions at work, however, I will concentrate on emotions as role requirements, on workplace emotions that combine the private with the public, the personal with the social, and the authentic with the masked. Perhaps a few exemplary workplace scenarios, selected from my interviews and participant observations in Tokyo during 1995–96 and 2000, will better frame this focus.

After finishing an important presentation to the company president, a section manager in a large Japanese organization bumped into his superior, a division manager, on the way back to his office. Originally the division manager had been scheduled to make the presentation but had delegated the task to the section manager on the excuse that he had to attend an important meeting in another part of Tokyo. Recounting the story to me, the section manager said:

I felt angry with my superior because he lied to me. . . . I mean, couldn't he just come to me and discuss the matter? At least this would have shown that he cares. I didn't mind doing the presentation—I think it was good for my career—but I was really furious about the guy when I saw him standing there trying to avoid me. He often says that he is an American-style manager, because he can approach the president directly. I think it also means that he is not so good at teamwork.

A young *sarariiman* (salaryman; a common term in Japan for a regular office employee) complained that OLs (office ladies; that is, young female office workers) in his section were spreading gossip about him. He was particularly annoyed that the gossip centered on what he saw as petty things; for example, "I heard that one OL accused me, during her lunch break with her friends, of throwing MY trash in HER wastebasket." The gossip, he complained, was becoming more and more emotional and less and less logical; the OLs were "spoiled children" who had to be indulged. An OL from the same office told me, in contrast, that she and the other OLs always needed to be attentive to the orders and whims of their male co-workers and bosses. In her words, an OL is trained and disciplined "to reach out and guess the other's request before he even utters it."

The time was 7 P.M., and six male employees of a Japanese manufacturing company were just sitting down to dinner in a restaurant located in one of the company's buildings. The six had come to the restaurant straight from work, and the dinner was a regular event in company life. As conversation turned to their children, they handed around photos. One man who had no photo was humorously reproached and told not to forget to put a picture of his kids in his wallet for the next dinner. Another man spoke about his troubles with a daughter who was dating a foreigner. The others offered consolation and advice. "You see," one of the men said to me as well as the others, "we are exactly like Americans, talking about our families at work."

These examples speak of emotions. And we react to them with our own emotions: we experience anger, or boredom, or empathy, or delight as we read about such people. Such emotional reactions are part of our socialization, and the personal experience of emotion reflects a larger cultural context. The Americans and Japanese to whom I have told these stories have, for example, reacted with different emotions. The subject of *displayed* emotions is a related, yet different issue. Imagine being told these stories at work, while sitting with a group of co-workers; the emotions you display may be different from those you actually feel. The interpersonal display of emotion also reflects the social situation. These observations invoke the tension that is central to this study—the tension between internal and socially prescribed emotion and, more broadly, between "emotionality" and "rationality" in organizations.

The rhetoric of collective emotionality, which is pervasive in Japan, provides a common socio-cultural framework for emotional experience and display in organizations. This rhetoric ranges from managerial descriptions of the firm-as-family to the calls of enterprise-based unions for respect and mutual trust. The stories I told above are typical examples of that rhetoric, however extraordinary they may seem to Western observers or, for that matter, Western sociologists of organizations. In a recent international convention on industrial relations held in Tokyo, a representative of Japan's National Union of General Workers (Zenkoku ippan rōdō kumiai) bantered about the "parent-child" relationship of employers and enterprise-based unions. If they are the "big family," he said, then we are outsiders and strangers. Foreign conference participants listening to the simultaneous English translation nodded to each other at this point, as if acknowledging a password. The paternalism of "Japanese-style management" has indeed become a conventional stereotype in the West. But is it still, or has it ever been, an accurate representation of workplace reality?

The workplace scenarios that open this book introduce its major dramatis personae: management, the union, and employees. Sometimes these parties constitute ideal dyads, such well-known pairs as management-union or salaryman-OL. The relationships among these parties also represent social distance—for example, between regular and temporary workers. Such relationships designate core (*uchi*) and periphery (*soto*), inside and outside. They can stand for both solidarity and antagonism, familiarity and otherness.

These scenarios also depict the relationship between emotions and workplace culture. There are organizational practices that deal with emotions; they promote certain feelings and emotional behaviors and suppress others according to the requirements of the company. Emotions such as mutual trust and responsibility are built into industrial arrangements such as quality control circles and work teams. Organizations have also instituted practices that center on the emotions of individual workers, such as self-evaluation and personnel counseling. One of the most blatant of these practices is the manual for emotion management—the sincere display of smiles and cheerfulness, for example—that is used to select and train service workers in Japan and the United States.

These scenarios also throw into relief the two ways in which emotions are manifested at work: namely, the practical and the ideological. The practical aspects of emotions center on the personal feelings of employees as expressed in the various social procedures of the shop floor, the office, or the service encounter. Emotions at work also have an ideological manifestation. Japanese-style management as an ideological regime is said, for example, to be based on broad emotional scripts of paternalism (*onjōshugi*) and mutual trust (*sōgo shinrai*).

The use of emotions at work has become fashionable recently. Although traditionally emphasized by the human relations school in the United States, the value of emotionality on the job has nevertheless been denied under the influence of dominant models such as "scientific management" and "open systems" theory. Recently, the American-led "discovery" of organizational culture as a managerial recipe has blended Western-style design with Japanese-style devotion. Proponents of organizational culture have premised their models on the distinction between values and norms, declared philosophy and real life. The difference between the ideological and the practical is the difference between the "dreamt-of" and the "lived-in." It is up to management to decide on the "dream" and make it a part of employees' life. Here I study this new organizational training by locating it in the context of normative control.

Finally, these scenarios portray an aspect of the complex relationship between "Japan" and "America." The scenarios focus on Japanese workers because my fieldwork was done in Japan, and I use Japanese organizations as the reference point, with comparisons made to the United States as a model and mirror. These vignettes represent practices that take place, to various extents, in both Japanese and American workplaces. The American discourse on emotions at work is no less intensive than its Japanese counterpart, although some of the premises are different. In the American discourse, for example, emotions that would weaken the organization—for example, stress—are to be especially managed. A more "Japanese-style" emphasis on "love and sympathy" as organizational goals has, however, recently been preached by American management gurus such as Tom Peters and Nancy Austin (1986). The management of emotions has become part of the personnel-training agenda in both the United States and Japan. New concepts such as "emotional intelligence" are part of this trend and are thought to provide companies with instrumental criteria for measuring the "emotional personality" of job applicants and the "emotional performance" of workers. Recently, many American writers have capitalized on the growing legitimacy of emotional manipulation in organizations and written practical guides for survival in the "office jungle" that purport to teach the worker, in his or her free time, how "not to hate your job," "how to handle stress," "how to deal with your boss and other difficult people," "how to lie effectively," and "how to market yourself in the office."

The interest in emotions at work also reflects cultural differences. Although normative control takes place in both American and Japanese organizations, practices, ideologies, and forms of reception are very different. These differences are, however, evolving within a global framework of mutual observation. Japanese managers regard assertiveness on the job as "American" and bemoan its negative repercussions in the form of "bad teamwork." Japanese workers may consider "family talk" as being American, yet they ignore the fact that American employees would go home much earlier and actually spend time *with* their children rather than talk about them with co-workers. The scenarios therefore represent both the models and their local appropriation. Japan has looked to the United States for models as much as the United States has looked to Japan for that purpose. Much has been written in this context about the cross-cultural flow of management models. The examples that immediately come to mind are scientific management (Taylorism) in Japan and "total quality management" (TQM) in the United States. In contrast, the cross-cultural flow of normative control, or the comparative study of emotions at work, has been ignored.

The Study of Organizational Cultures

This is a study about organizational culture. Emotions are part of culture, and therefore emotions at work are part of organizational culture. There is a broad sociological interest in emotions at work and normative control that goes beyond the particular field of organizational culture, however. Writing on the lives of office workers in 1951, the eminent American sociologist C. Wright Mills prophetically observed that "in the movement from authority to manipulation . . . exploitation becomes less material and more psychological" (Mills 1951: 110). This study deals with the institutionalization of "psychological manipulation" across workplaces and cultures. The literature on organizational culture sprung from the study of Japanese companies, and much of what scholars of organizational culture tell us is based on their comparison of "Japan" and "America." However, this study is not a conventional analysis of organizational culture. The view presented in this book sees organizational and workplace cultures as two different entities that can be influenced by a local, surrounding culture. The concept of "culture" is extended here to serve as an independent variable. A similar analysis is performed by contingency theory in regard to the "cultural fit" in Japan between tradition and organizational models such as "paternalism," "teamwork," or "the firm-as-family." Contingency theory holds that organizations, in different institutional and cultural settings, seek to maximize their "fit" with those environments and thereby enhance their viability (Scott 1987).

From the perspective of "cultural contingency" (Lincoln & Kalleberg 1990: 18), organizations are fitted to the norms and values of their cultural habitat. In Japan, the company is regarded as a microcosm of Japanese society. The Japanese company is the arena in which one learns proper "human relations." The company is comparable to the army in prewar and wartime Japan as an important agency of adult socialization in national values (Yoshino 1992). However, although values may constitute management's favorite rhetoric, it is through labor disputes and status conflicts that "ideologies" are translated into (or resisted by) shop-floor norms. In addition, the rhetoric of values may be a facade that masks shop-floor realities. The "fit" that contingency theory speaks of can therefore be part of the ideological facade maintained by management.

Novel managerial ideologies are often sold as "participatory systems" in a way that conceals their authority structure. The reactions of employees to such ideologies and practices are both intriguing and revealing. My leading questions, then, are What are the expressed values and practices of normative control in the organizational cultures of Japanese and American companies? Which workplace cultures promote emotional subjugation, and what sort of "shop-floor kingdoms" encourage emotional resistance? Since I am interested here in cross-cultural comparison, a third form of culture enters the picture—the "surrounding local culture." This encompasses such broader spheres of life as schooling, gender roles, politics, and national culture. The values and norms of employees are not merely those ordained by the organizational culture. They are also influenced by values and norms of the local surrounding culture.

This threefold view of culture—organizational, workplace, and surrounding—can be modeled by three overlapping circles (see Fig. 1). Each circle denotes analytically different yet practically interrelated discursive fields. There is no order of precedence here, but rather a dynamic interplay. The first circle represents organizational culture: the ideology of management and its top-down messages, systems, norms, and artifacts. It is highlighted in the figure because organizational culture often serves as the reference point or the point of departure for the study of emotions at work. The second circle encompasses workplace culture—the everyday practices of organizational life as seen from the workers' point of view. These two circles only partially overlap. The common part designates areas of congruity and acceptance, or "devotion," in management parlance. The second circle also provides room for "countercultures" and for workers' subversion of managerial ideology. The third circle stands for the surrounding local culture, whose values, norms, and socialization can influence both acceptance of and resistance to organizational culture. Although Figure 1 depicts a particular situation of partial overlapping of all three circles, in reality the relations among the three circles are dynamic and their borders depend on the situation being studied.

The three-circle model can be applied to both inter- and intracultural analyses. In the case of transplanted organizational culture, for example, the top circle of organizational culture represents the original, global managerial system (for example, Toyotism). The circle on the lower right is the workplace culture in the transplant (for example, selection and training procedures in a Toyota-GM transplant in the United States and workers' views of these practices). The circle on the lower left stands for the influences of local culture (rural, midwestern American culture). In each circle, different facets of emotions at work might be stressed. For example, managers usually stress emotion as social glue (as, for example, in the case of paternalism) and as positive motivation (mutual trust through teamwork). Workplace cultures may reproduce this emphasis, or conversely they may subvert it through an emphasis on negative motivation (soldiering or sabotage).

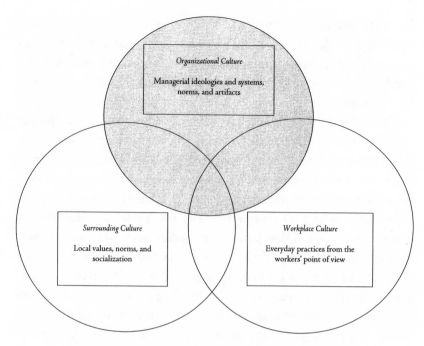

Fig. 1   A three-circle model of the triangulation of organizational, workplace, and surrounding cultures

The surrounding culture represents broader institutions and scripts that influence the emotions of workers (the nature of unions, the American discourse of individualism).

The model contains multi-variable and complex interactions and is implemented here in an inductive and ethnographic way rather than in a deductive and statistical manner. I use this model as a framework that enhances analysis of case studies and allows for comparison among cases. One of the most ubiquitous cases of emotion management in the service industry, for example, is "smile training," in which front-line employees are trained to express kindness, courtesy, and friendliness to customers. In my analysis of smile training, the first circle (organizational culture) represents the American management system of smile training, which has become part of a global service culture. In terms of emotions at work, this circle contains at least three facets of emotion management: (1) emotion as an objective expression—the smile; (2) emotion as motivation—the subjective role-playing of the front-line employee (a smiling air hostess, for example); and (3) emotion as social structure—smile training as an institutionalized practice of human resource management.

The second circle (workplace culture) may involve the Japanese domestication and implementation of service training. As an expression, the smile is universally reproduced; yet its mediating social structures are domesticated. An OL's manual for smile training differs from its American counterpart. The motivation of Japanese employees is made to fit local considerations of the "smile" as public performance. One result is that Japanese front-line employees are less concerned, compared with their American counterparts, about "being phony." They are more accepting in general of the concept of "show" and "keeping up appearances." The third circle, that of surrounding local culture, encompasses the local construction in Japan of the "smile" as a primary emotion mask; this construction also involves expression, social glue, and motivation. The cultural construction of emotional masks such as the smile implies that Japanese culture might be a source of positive socialization for emotion management at work.

The three-circle model is an analytical tool whose boundaries are flexible and dynamic. Its aim is to promote an understanding of cultures within organizations as negotiated orders. This model also promotes a culture-sensitive sociology of emotions. I will illustrate this claim by comparing my own study of service training in Japan to other, American studies, mainly to Arlie Hochschild's (1983) study of service training at Delta Air Lines. Hochschild's path-breaking study was the first to use the term "emotion management." Yet Hochschild's study (in a manner that is typical of the literature) did not include cross-cultural comparison. Some of her generalizations, although presented as universal, were nevertheless biased toward the surrounding, local culture of the United States.

My questions require both analysis and comparison. This study therefore focuses, first, on pinpointing central mechanisms of normative control in which emotional scripts are at work. The analysis begins by describing these mechanisms and their elements as objective practices of human resource management. It then presents the subjective meanings that such practices have for managers and workers. In cases in which meanings are in conflict—for example, in work teams that are presented as examples of industrial democracy, although team leaders are not elected but appointed by management—the emerging emotional interplay is particularly intriguing.

In addition, these questions will be asked from a comparative perspective. "America" and "Japan" provided the twentieth century with its dominant managerial models. These models have traditionally been framed within an all-embracing dichotomy: Fordism versus Toyotism, scientific management versus lean production, "Theory A" versus "Theory Z." This study presents an alternative view that seeks to collapse such dichotomies and to unearth the parallels between the two imaginaries of "America" and "Japan." "Japan" and "America" have been so entangled in a mutual web of innovation and importation that there is no clear-cut division between the two. Each country has, at various stages, been both a model for and a mirror of the other. Moreover, the debates regarding American or Japanese management models have usually been conducted within the mainstream organizational discourse of rationalization, which is limited in scope.

I offer the study of emotions at work as an alternative vantage point onto organizational and workplace cultures, a means of estrangement through which the familiar "America" and the exotic "Japan" can be reconsidered. As I hope to show, sociological constructs of emotions at work, such as "emotional dissonance" and the "false self," are not universal responses to the commercialization of human feelings in late-stage capitalism. Rather, they are cultural responses conditioned on earlier forms of socialization and civilizing processes.

There is a twofold rationale for this project of putting emotions to work and using the sociology of emotions to study organizations. First, the emotional script of many organizational practices often goes un-noticed. When it is noticed, it is usually in the form advocated by management. Focusing on the emotional component can throw into relief the normative control built into such "rational" practices as work teams, quality circles, service manuals, and self-declaration forms. Second, the sociology of emotions as employed in this study is critical of seductive ideologies that mask exploitation and conflict. Japanese-style management, for example, has long been viewed as an emotional discourse founded on Japanese cultural tradition. Historical analysis sensitive to the use of emotional scripts as political facades can show that the ideology of Japanese-style management is largely a matter of lip service. Small group activities, hailed in Japan and the United States as a hallmark of the emotional culture of Japanese-style man-agement, can be unveiled as intricate mechanisms of normative and remunerative control. Conversely, a comparative reading of workplace ethnographies shows that when small group activities are used to give workers a voice in managing their own work, American workers can overcome their declared disposition to individualism.[1]

"Japan" Meets "America": A Journey for Real Between Two Imaginaries

Japanology has, in many cases, consisted of the study of "Japan" as a fictive Other. This is certainly not a novel assertion, but it is useful to mention it every time one deals with "Japan." Many of our popular and academic notions of "Japan" are based on projecting our "selves"

---

1. Positive reactions to small group activities such as quality control circles were found among Japanese as well as American workers. Lincoln and Kalleberg (1990: 236), for example, found that "[quality control] membership is linked to greater commitment in both samples [the U.S. and Japan] . . . and to a lesser degree, satisfaction." They (1990: 244) also found similar positive attitudes in both countries toward welfare programs and conclude that "the effective-ness of these structures is by no means confined to Japanese workers; they produce returns in worker loyalty to U.S. firms as well." However, the artificial framework of the questionnaire may have acted as yet another organizational practice in eliciting "proper" attitudes.

(or ideas about "America") onto the Other (the way we perceive "Japan"); thus we frame the other within pre-existing categories such as model or mirror, foe or friend (to borrow the convenient set found in the title of Schodt's 1994 book). Some of these stereotypes have become domesticated in Japan and then sold back to foreigners. Furthermore, "Japan" has been essentialized by many interpreters claiming to have found the key to its economic success or modernization or social solidarity.

In contrast, I see Japan and America as entangled in a cultural flow, and I delineate specific streams within that flow from three broad perspectives. These perspectives are interrelated, and they are distinguished here solely for analytical purposes. The first perspective is the interplay between particularism (localization, uniqueness) and universalism (globalization, isomorphism). The second consists of the distinction between the economy (the bureaucratic spheres of labor and industry) and culture (as conventionally translated into the normative side of work and workplace identities). The third deals with the organizational dynamics of rationality and emotionality. I use these three perspectives to focus, respectively, on three themes: managerial discourses, workplace cultures, and emotions at work. The oppositions of global and local, economy and culture, and rationality and emotion have become clichés of interpretation, and "America" and "Japan" have become entangled in these oppositions. "America" has been imagined as the apex of globalization and economic rationality, whereas "Japan" has often been essentialized through the image of cultural uniqueness and emotionality. My intention is to show the power of these generalizations and to go beyond them. The following description is therefore intended not to provide answers but to unsettle and disturb.

The Global and the Local

As model, as mirror, and sometimes as monster, Japan has long captured the Western imagination. Today, a bewildering array of studies, books, films, academic programs, comics, television shows, plays, and

organized tours purport to explicate and unmask "Japan."[2] In the early
1970s, the popular view, for many Americans, was that modernizing
Japan proved the global superiority of capitalism and the faults of the
communist model (see Miyoshi & Harootunian 1991).[3] The trope of
"un-Marxist Japan," whose traditions of "vertical society" negated class
conflict, revived the old rhetoric of American nativism that "America"
was a society free of social distinctions. In the 1980s and until the
bubble economy burst in the early 1990s, the popular trope of "Japan"
as a unique superpower propelled by particularistic interests[4] suggested that Japan was quickly filling the vacuum created by the collapse of the Soviet Union and that the "yellow peril" (a phrase coined
in 1905) was replacing communism as the menacing Other. As one
observer noted, "America needs a credible enemy, and Japan may
eventually prove the best candidate around" (Ahmad 1991: 27).

The mutual importation of management systems by America and
Japan has both reaffirmed and blurred the global/local interplay. The
study of management systems is conventionally the subject of organizational theory, whose terminology, worldview, and analysis are supposed to be global and universal (see, for example, Scott 1987). The
universality of the organizational gaze precedes and obliterates, in the
eyes of its followers, any other contextual (cultural) mode of interpretation: "Looking at culture alone obscures the fact that business

---

2. Different countries have produced different images of "Japan" (see Befu & Kreiner 1992).
On the symbolic interplay between "America" and "Japan" as a bipolar relationship of attraction and competition, see Iriye 1975 and Johnson 1988. On how the academic study of Japanology in the United States and elsewhere has legitimated essentializing images of "Japan," see
Dale 1986.

3. Successful modernization was also the organizing ideological framework for representing the Japanese in *National Geographic*. The efflorescence of Japan began there at the same
time (1967–68) that Vietnam and Southeast Asia suddenly disappeared from the pages of the
magazine because of the Vietnam War. Positive images of the Japanese could therefore serve
as an antidote to the "bad Asians," and the Japanese were constructed as the civilized alien as
opposed to the savage alien, the Vietnamese (see Lutz & Collins 1994: 130–31).

4. The popular trope of "Japan" as a menacing Other is captured in Michael Crichton's
successful 1992 novel (and film) *Rising Sun* (see Raz & Raz 1996).

organizations, no matter how well they accord with cultural beliefs, are fundamentally responses to market opportunities and conditions. Enterprise may be culturally informed, but it remains enterprise. Moreover, cultural variables are insufficiently distinguishable . . . to have clear explanatory force" (Hamilton & Biggart 1988: S53).

Local organizational cultures are regarded in organizational theory as stages in the universal narrative of rational systematization.[5] The master narrative of organizational development is constructed not as culturally specific or even culturally oriented but as universal. Since the rise of modern organizational forms in the mid-nineteenth century, social scientists have generally treated organizations as instrumental structures little affected by culture. Organizations were thought to conform to general rules of efficiency rather than to local cultural dictates. However, the view of what is universal in organizational evolution was developed in a specific cultural context. This "view from nowhere" is specifically American because neo-classical economic and rationalist organizational theories are based on generalizations from the American case. As the neo-institutional approach argues, "American organizational practices have been treated by theorists as ideal-typical and pure, while the diverse organizational practices found in other countries were treated as adjustments to government meddling" (Dobbin 1994: 127). This view emphasizes the globalization of American-born management systems, such as Taylorism and, later, open systems. Taylorite thought, also termed "scientific management," was introduced to Japan around 1913 and later influenced the Japanese "efficiency movement" of the 1920s, the Depression-era "industrial rationalization," the postwar drive for productivity,

---

5. Placed in the universalistic rubrics of organizational theory, the (very different) industrial histories of "Japan" and "America" can be contrasted with a third, European model. In this logic, "large, capital-intensive firms had developed in Japan and the U.S. before unionism had a chance to sink strong roots. . . . America shares with Japan limited public regulation of the workplace and, in the case of large nonunion U.S. companies, a common approach to organizing internal labor markets" (Jacoby 1993: 211, 241).

and, later, TQM (see Tsutsui 1998; Warner 1994). In this view, Japanese-style management is neither particularly novel nor even especially Japanese.

Japanese-style management, however, is also celebrated for its "three pillars"—the seniority system, lifetime employment, and enterprise-based unionism. These practices, which are often explained as emanations of a culture of age-sets, groupism, and paternalism, are hailed by their proponents as the complete opposites of "scientific management." A large and influential group of Japanese scholars and managers has promoted a local view of Japanese-style management as a unique organizational culture based on Japanese tradition (Hazama 1964, 1978; Hayashi 1988). This approach views "global" American-style management as an ideology that alienates the workforce and is doomed to fight a losing battle with Japanese corporations.

My point is that both "global" and "local" explanations are artificial and that reality is full of hybrids and crisscrossing modifications. This should not surprise readers familiar with Japan's distinctive bent for mixing Western ways with local practices. For example, one can describe, following scholars such as Andrew Gordon (1985, 1998) and William Tsutsui (1998), the pragmatic domestication of Taylorism into an illusive "Japanese-style management," whose paternalistic ideology was actually lip service. Taylorism co-exists with Japanese-style management in the world of part-time workers, in Japan and elsewhere, where union membership, promotion, and lifetime employment have no practical relevance (see Raz 1999a). "Welfare corporatism," a hallmark of Japanese-style management, was in part modeled after the corporate welfare plans that proliferated in the United States in the 1920s.[6] Also, some central ideas of Japanese-style manage-

---

6. Henry Ford, known for his implementation of standardization and systematization on the assembly line, was also one of the pioneers of welfare plans. Ford experimented with programs of "welfare work" such as inexpensive meals, music at meal times, dances, fashion shows, group discounts, an employee health fund, savings, pensions, and loans in order to stabilize the workforce and reduce the prevalence of "five-day men" (those who quit after receiving one paycheck). Furthermore, in order to survey the potential loyalty of workers, Ford's investigators examined employees' personal conduct and housing arrangements

ment—such as company philosophy, managers as guides, bottom-up decision making, participatory suggestion schemes, and commitment to teamwork—were inculcated through seminars held in 1949–50 by the American Occupation Forces (see Okazaki-Ward 1993: 28).

Another example of the global/local interplay is the globalization of quality control. A distinct practice of Japanese management, quality control was in part inspired by American management seminars and by the American statistician W. Edward Deming. Japanese engineers who argued that quality control required the cooperation and understanding of all the members of an organization were also inspired by the writings of General Electric quality guru Armand Feigenbaum, who was the first to coin the term "total quality control." These various cases form a now-familiar dialectic of the local (cultural exceptionalism) and the global (management models and fads).

The Public and the Private

The second perspective views the workplace as a meeting place for the opposite poles of public and private, bureaucracy and feelings, and most broadly—the economy and culture. Although taken for granted, these oppositions are the product of social construction. Norbert Elias (1978, 1982, 1983) has described the development of European society in the Middle Ages in the direction of curbing passions and adhering to more refined behavioral standards. According to Elias's historical scheme, it was only in European court societies that the control of one's emotions was defined as a source of power. Such emotional control gradually diffused from the courtly aristocracy through lower levels of society. The constraining of emotions and their management have become signs of modernity. Elias (1978: 182) also emphasized the increas-

---

(Jacques 1996: 121–22). Such practices later declined, in part because they were viewed by workers as interference in their privacy and a violation of their civil rights. See Tone 1997 on the origins, development, and legacy of American welfare work from 1900 to 1920. See also Garon 1987: 170–71 on the early Japanese importation of American welfare corporatism. For a critical account of the original American programs, see Meyer 1981.

ing privatization of emotion, as adults "privatized all their impulses (particularly sexual ones)." Increasing emotional control was associated with sharper distinctions between the private and the public.

Elias described modernity as a shift from uncontrolled passion to emotional protocols in court societies. Max Weber traced a similar process in the institutionalization of charisma, and Michel Foucault wrote about a complementary process of repressing sexuality. All these processes contributed to a growing distinction between private and public, and all are grounded in Western history. The Western discourse about modernity and civil society is indeed underpinned by the liberal differentiation of public and private, work and home,[7] career and family life. The modern workplace has been constructed as the site of instrumental rationality, and the affective life is relegated to the domestic sphere.[8] Emotion, defined in the West as something private (inside the individual; see Lutz 1990), was banished from the workplace. Moreover, since the individual expression of emotion might challenge authority, it thus legitimated the need for control. This is, for example, how the human relations school has typically regarded emotion at work.

The Western separation of public and private has made it seem natural to American social scientists to worry about the conflict between "instrumentality" and "affectivity." Neo-Marxist studies of the

---

7. To take the differentiation of "work" and "home" for granted is, moreover, to buy into *malestream* discourse. As Pringle (1989: 169) and other feminists have shown, whereas male bosses can decide for themselves the extent to which they will keep home and work apart, female office workers such as secretaries do not have this luxury. Male bosses often have their secretaries do personal chores for them and do not hesitate to call them at home, something women do not do unless specifically asked to.

8. Michel Crozier (1965) argued that the impersonal and bureaucratic workplace culture in the French office reflects the fact that the office worker expects to find satisfaction and fulfillment in the private spheres of life rather than in his work or with his fellow workers. The opposite example would be Thomas Rohlen's (1974) account of the fusion of private (home) and public (work) in a Japanese office. Similarly, William Ouchi (1981: 10) attacks American culture by claiming that "the notion that productivity may be dependent upon trust, subtlety, and intimacy, probably seems strange to most people."

labor process, including Hochschild's (1983) analysis of emotion management, have adopted a similar distinction that separates the public and the private into artificial extremes. Such separation arguably follows Marx's view of objective exploitation and subjective alienation, which are the flip sides of capitalism. Those who believe in the separation of work and home are thus inclined to perceive the relations between capitalists and workers as inevitably adversarial. In such a worldview, the "public" use of emotions is associated with capitalism and instrumentality, and emotions become either tools for compliance or instruments of resistance.

Japan, however, is held not to have experienced the same differentiation of the economy and culture that has characterized Western civil society. "Worker society" in Japan has conversely formed a quasi-autonomous culture revolving around emotional ideologies in which the company takes the form of a family and the work or age group has the characteristics of a primary social unit. The concept of the traditional household (*ie*) illustrates Japan's integration of public and private and its blurring of the distinction between the economy and culture. The *ie* is both an enterprise/work organization and a domestic unit of kinship. The "company" and the "family" are therefore inseparable in a way unfamiliar to members of cultures in which "household" has a different history.[9]

Japan does, however, have well-known distinctions between the private and the public, captured in pairs such as *uchi/soto* and *honne/tatemae*, to mention the most famous. Reality is too complex to be affixed to a parsimonious model. Alongside existing cultural distinctions between private and public, the Japanese have developed an important and pervasive work ethic that (stated simply) stresses devotion to duty and self-discipline as leading in time to self-development

---

9. There is a vast literature, in Japan and the United States, that regards the *ie* as the basic component of traditional Japanese society (and economy). The culturalist approach behind Japanese-style management argues that following industrialization, the *ie* became the template for the firm-as-family pattern. See, e.g., Murakami 1980, Nakane 1970, and Mito 1994.

20   *Introduction*

and harmony.[10] Devotion to duty (the public and socially appropriate) is seen as the road to self-fulfillment (the private and personally felt).

In Japan, a chorus of social psychologists tells us, emotional behavior is governed to a great extent by shared rules of feeling that constrain the public display of individuals in one common manner (Matsumoto 1996). Emotions are a social, not just personal, resource that families, schools, and firms entice and exploit in their members. This contrasts with the generally greater variations in behavior allowed by American society. Furthermore, because emotion is constructed as relatively ordered and controlled, its individual (and group) expression vindicates rather than challenges authority and is thus a legitimate means of social and organizational control. This is how Japanese-style management has typically regarded emotions at work.[11] But in terms of union activity, for example, one sees a reversal of the stereotype. American trade unions are more collectivist than Japan's "enterprise-based unions," which may actually compete with one another. As Japanese labor scholar Kumazawa Makoto (1996: 24) argues, "One must abandon the deeply-rooted and ubiquitous notion that in their basic mode of thinking western workers are individualistic and Japanese are group-oriented."

---

10. The work ethic of self-fulfillment, which has strong roots in Confucianism, is subsumed by Rohlen (1974: 52) under the general Japanese tradition of "spiritualism" (*seishin-shugi*). It also occupies a major role in Dorinne Kondo's (1990) attempt to explain the work ideology of "*katachi de hairu*," to enter (i.e., to realize oneself) through the rules of the prescribed form. Thomas Smith (1984) provides a historical account of how manual workers appropriated the new concept of self-realization (*jiko jitsugen*) as part of their "quest for dignity." At the turn of the twentieth century, the interests of workers and employees were, according to Smith, combined to form a new rhetoric of identity that shaped workers' consciousness and became symbiotically enmeshed in managerial paternalism.

11. In Japan, the primary functional unit of the organization is often said to be not the individual worker but the work group. These groups are the emotional seedbeds of cohesion and loyalty, according to the "Great Tradition" of many ethnographic studies (Cole 1971; Dore 1984; Rohlen 1974). Not surprisingly, these studies focus on the industrial sector and the established business world—the factory and the bank. More recent ethnographies, however, shed new light on work groups as territories of control and conflict (Kondo 1990; Lo 1990; in Japanese, see Gunji 1982 on NHK).

The Rational and the Emotional

In "Japan" (so the story goes; see the epigraphs in the front matter), emotionality has been the basic component of Japanese-style management. In "America," in contrast, rationality has been at the heart of managerial systematization. Using this binarism as a framework for the interplay of the global and the local, various organizational narratives have shown how Japanese-style management appropriated "rational" systems from America, and how American management incorporated human relations and, more recently, even began a process of "Japanization."

The dichotomy of rational/emotional also has a gendered subtext. Rationalism, in Western culture, is stereotypically masculine, and emotionalism is considered feminine. These binary components color the opposite "languages" spoken by men and women. The traditional dominance of rationality over emotionality in the West is tied to the appropriation of rationality as a stereotypical masculine trait. Women are preferred for relatively low-paying and low-status service positions since recruiters consider them to have the greater propensity for emotional labor. When asked to label the subjective experience of the average man and the average woman in a problematic situation (such as a bad argument with a co-worker), Americans tend to say that the average female would feel "emotional" and the average male "stressed."[12] Psychologists have therefore explained stress, a widely used buzzword in recent years, as a result of men's inability to get "in touch" with their emotions.

Of course, rationalization was an inherent part of Japanese-style management from the start, and welfare capitalism and industrial betterment often preceded the adoption of scientific management in the United States. Recently, emotionality has become popular in manage-

---

12. The gender stereotypes of emotionality and stress are invoked in Robinson & Johnson 1997. Good points of departure into the vast literature on gender stereotypes of emotionality and stress are provided in Lazarus 1993.

rial literature in the United States. Managers, for example, are offered emotional catalogues and "relationship theories" as keys to attracting and keeping customers (Fournier 1998; Mick & Fournier 1998); "emotional intelligence" is sold as an upgrade for management, since "many of today's managers fail due to rigidity and poor relationships" (Miller 1999: 25); and scientific studies hail successful companies such as the Body Shop for developing a unique culture of "bounded emotionality" for its primarily female workforce (Martin et al. 1998). Despite these recent bursts of managerial interest in emotionality, American management and labor lag behind their counterparts in Japan in this respect. This study will analyze the development of emotionality as a key idiom in the discourse of both management and labor in Japan and its persistence even in today's diversified and global forms of employment, unionization, and management.

Rationality has a neat organizational definition. It is intentional, reasoned, goal-directed behavior aimed at maximizing gains. In an ideal scenario, organizational actors presented with options select the optimal alternative for reaching their goal. Herbert Simon (1976) introduced the concept of *bounded* rationality to suggest that choice is limited because individuals act with incomplete information and explore only a limited number of alternatives. Simon's criticism was directed primarily at the individual. His remedy for individual limitations was the organization. Whereas individual rationality is bounded, the organization can transcend these bounds.

Simon (1976) therefore urged the organization to reduce complexity and uncertainty by relegating routine decisions to its lower levels (the manual) and by making decisions about the nonroutine the preserve of the upper levels of the hierarchy. Bounded rationality justified the deskilling of workers and called for complete control by management. In Simon's words (1976: 101), "Human rationality . . . gets its higher goals and integration from the institutional setting in which it operates and by which it is molded." Management is the mind of the organization and develops its goals and plans its work tasks, which are then executed by the body, or the workers (see also Braverman 1974).

Simon (1989) depicted holistic forms of reasoning, such as intuition, as *nonrational* and decisions based on emotions as *irrational*. Simon's work has promoted a Cartesian split inherent in organizational theory from the start—rationality versus emotionality, mind versus body, and management versus labor.[13]

Devalued and appropriated, the emotions of the "body," or the workers, became instruments for achieving such organizational goals as efficiency, profit, and productivity. Emotions in the American workplace were co-opted and alienated in the form that Arlie Hochschild (1979, 1983) termed *emotional labor*. The mainstream organizational discourse of rationality provided the mental framework through which emotions were put to work. Although "bounded rationality" is actually a recipe for domination, it was sold as neutral and objective.

The leading Japanese idiom for describing the organizational person, "bounded emotionality," although apparently the reverse of bounded rationality, works toward the same ends. Japanese-style management has replaced—at least ideologically and rhetorically—fragmented labor with the company-as-family, external supervision with self-monitoring, hierarchical order (Simon's ends-means chain) with teamwork and group decision making, the mind-body dualism with concentric self-identity, and maximization of profits with "goodwill."[14] Dennis Mumby and Linda Putnam (1992: 474) present these traits as examples of how organizational life can be freed of the direct control of management, once managerial rationalism is replaced with an emotional disposition. Bounded emotionality is for these authors an imagined, theoretical *remedy* to the managed heart of real employees.

---

13. Simon's bounded rationality converges with scientific management. Both warrant the division between management and labor: the worker must give up control to management of how the work is to be done. This condition, as Braverman (1974) argues, was a general trend in the twentieth century.

14. "Goodwill" is a term employed by Ronald Dore to explain the unique Japanese culture of economic transactions. In Dore's words, "Transaction costs in Japan may be lower than elsewhere; 'opportunism' may be a lesser danger in Japan. This is because of the explicit encouragement, and actual prevalence, in the Japanese economy of what one might call moralized trading relationships of mutual goodwill" (1984: 463). In other words, Japanese business firms can be seen as emotionally bounded by goodwill not to change transaction costs independently.

My point is, in contrast, that bounded emotionality provides the company with an equally stringent means of *normative* control. Ironically, Mumby and Putnam entirely miss the dark side of bounded emotionality, as exemplified in Japanese stories of *karōshi* (death from overwork). Japanese workers can be emotionally bounded by managerial paternalism and by their expected devotion to their company, group, and peers. They are emotionally bounded by the social expectation that they will cultivate their self through work and their identity through managerial spiritual guidance. Japanese-style management has taken the premises of bounded emotionality and put them to work. The power of these stereotypes is illustrated in Table 1, which presents a symmetrical opposition between two managerial discourses of control.

Employment security, workplace unionism, the seniority system, and company welfare programs became part of the Japanese management system as a means of promoting loyalty. Japanese unions emphasized, to borrow Robert Cole's terminology, "job security over the control of job opportunities" (1985: 576). A worker's willingness to offer his or her ideas for free depends in part on a sense of "belonging" to the firm. The ability of the firm to mobilize such feelings is what Ronald Dore (in his introduction to Kamata 1982: xxviii) terms "membership motivation." (The opposite is "market motivation," namely, being propelled by one's career prospects and being willing to consider new job offers and better individual employment terms.) Finally, in-house company education in Japan also involves special training courses and sessions to implant the proper image of the company person. Japanese-style management comprises both spiritual guidance and self-realization. The Japanese manager is ideally not an "expert" but a "guide." It is tempting to match "America" and "Japan" with the opposition between bounded rationality and bounded emotionality, and many scholars (particularly William Ouchi in his *Theory Z*) have done so. Yet to resort to such a categorization would be to embrace the stereotypes. The two managerial discourses need to be tested against workplace realities.

Table 1
Rational and Normative Ideologies of Control
in U.S. and Japanese Managerial Discourses

Bounded rationality Taylorism/Fordism	Bounded emotionality Japanese-style management/ human relations
Coercion, direct control	Normative, indirect control
External supervision	Self- and peer supervision
Hierarchical order, managerial ladder	Teamwork, group decision making
Individual wage incentives	Collective bonuses
Individual promotion based on merit	Seniority system
Income security	Job security
Market motivation	Membership motivation
Fragmented labor	The company-as-family
Piecemeal work, deskilling	Reskilling, "job enhancement"
Display rules, behaviorism	Emotion management, social psychology
Production efficiency	Self-realization
Stress	Emotionality

Furthermore, there is some "America" and some "Japan" in each of the two opposing columns in Table 1. The mechanisms of bounded emotionality are not unique to Japanese-style management; they are also part of the American school of human relations.[15] In general, normative control is never completely devoid of rational control, and vice versa. The most prevalent form of emotion management (regarded as normative control) in the service sector, for example, is the service manual, in which behavior protocols and time-and-motion checklists are written down in the most formalistic and rational of manners.

According to Michael Burawoy (1985), companies in advanced capitalism organize their systems of control in one of two ways—as

---

15. As Robert Cole (1985: 572) argues, "Japanese managers are far more likely than their American counterparts to think of solutions to managerial problems as coming from the area of human relations rather than technical relations." Japanese and American managers, however, have practiced normative control within different ideologies, market conditions, and labor-management relations, differences that the following chapters set out to analyze.

despotic or as hegemonic regimes. The despotic company uses direct coercion to control its workforce. The hegemonic approach is more wide-ranging, subtle, and indirect and manufactures consent through normative control. Burawoy regards the latter as the more powerful of the two. Table 1 begins with the notion of these two systems of control and outlines their different elements. These two systems should not, however, be regarded as mutually exclusive. Organizations do not confront an either/or choice between rational and normative control. Rather, in many historical contexts, both in the United States and Japan, these two systems have been used to complement each other.

The concepts of bounded rationality and bounded emotionality are reminiscent of Stephen Barley and Gideon Kunda's (1992) contrasting of "design" and "devotion." The rational rhetoric of design is utilitarian and stresses the streamlining of production processes and an appeal to the worker's self-interest. According to Barley and Kunda (1992), this rhetoric characterized the managerial ideologies of scientific management and systems rationalism (1955–80). The normative rhetoric of devotion emphasizes that by "winning the hearts and minds" of the workforce, managers could achieve moral authority. This rhetoric emerged in the United States with "industrial betterment" (1870–1900), became prominent with the human relations movement (1923–55), and was carried over into the most recent surge of normative control, namely, organizational culture (1980–present). By articulating this succession of managerial ideologies, Barley and Kunda argue that managerial discourse appears to have alternated between ideologies of normative and rational control.[16]

---

16. The emphasis on normative control as a form of managerial ideology is itself a relatively recent addition to organizational theory. Previously, the canon of organizational theory—the body of knowledge studied in business schools—has argued for a progressive evolution of organizational thought in which rationalization features prominently and "normative control" plays a very minor role. Within this traditional view, the American literature on organizations started with a "closed system" approach focusing on the internal administrative affairs of organizations; this was later replaced with an "open system" perspective that took into consideration the broader environment (Scott 1987; see Shenhav 1999 for criticism). Organizational theory starts with scientific management and describes it, together with the writings of Henry Fayol and Max Weber, as being concerned with organizations as closed sys-

This view misses an important point. In various places and times, managers have mouthed the ideology of devotion while practicing the methods of design. In prewar Japan, for example, the articulation of paternalism had little practical content and in fact masked and enabled the domestication of scientific management. Similarly in the United States, design and devotion co-existed and reinforced each other. Personnel management was sold by human relations experts to management as a device that complemented rather than replaced scientific management. By emphasizing the emotional side of working from a perspective of normative *control*, my aim in this book is to collapse such dichotomies as design/devotion, showing their co-existence as historical bundles (not strands) of ideology and practice.

The bounded emotionality of the "company as family" should therefore also be seen as a rational program designed by capitalists to "induce workers to join the pseudo-community of the firm" (Kumazawa 1996: 39).[17] The three pillars of Japanese-style management are a postwar package deal that served to maximize workers' commitment. Such work structures, though no doubt taking advantage of pre-existing cultural patterns, represent internal labor markets linked to

---

tems. According to the organizational theory narrative, it was only with the open systems perspective, introduced in the 1950s and the 1960s, that the broader environment entered as a source of uncertainty. This transformation from "closed systems" in the early 1900s to "open systems" in the mid-twentieth century provides organizational theory with a clear-cut evolutionary account of theorizing and treating organizations.

17. Kumazawa Makoto (1996) convincingly develops the argument that in contrast to the ideological claim of the cultural basis of the Japanese "company as community," this claim in fact represents a form of management-induced "false consciousness." Traditional Japanese communities were egalitarian in nature, whereas the company-as-community is basically hierarchical. Traditional community was organic; the company is mechanic. In reality, Kumazawa (1996: 39–40) argues, Japanese workers reluctantly joined the "company as family" because they had been forced out of traditional communities and into the city. In the countryside where the traditional community still existed, managerial paternalism was weaker. It could grow stronger in the city, where community had broken down. However, even though this argument stresses the rupture between tradition (community) and modernization (management), it also inadvertently makes a case for continuation, since modern Japanese management in fact appropriated norms and bases of control from traditional Japanese culture.

organizations' drive for control of the motives and behaviors of their
members (Burawoy 1979; Edwards 1979).

Japan's Organizational Cultures Today

No one organizational culture characterizes Japan today. The once-
dominant model of the three pillars of Japanese-style management,
which was, in any case, reserved for a minority of regular male employees from the start, seems less dominant now. The seniority system (a complex mixture of both seniority and merit components in
the first place) is increasingly under attack from the proponents of the
now more fashionable performance pay. Only about 15 percent of the
labor force now enjoys lifetime employment, and that practice is per-
sistently being undermined by "corporate restructuring." In October
2001, Japan's unions said that in the upcoming year, the *shuntō* (bonus
negotiations) would focus on jobs not raises. The estimated rate of
unionization fell to about 22 percent in 1999 after a long and steady
decline.[18] The once-celebrated core of Japan's labor force is gradually
shrinking, as the periphery of contingent workers becomes larger.

Having entered the post-industrial stage about twenty years ago,
Japan now has a large service sector consisting mainly of part-timers
and temporary workers. The organizational culture of this sector does
not follow the once-dominant culture of Japanese-style management.
Or, more accurately, the service sector may subscribe to the organizational culture of Japanese-style management, but its workplace culture
is split between a minority of regular workers and an overwhelming
majority of contingent workers. Paradoxically, the service industry is
also the sector that seeks to inculcate, produce, and sell "emotions" in
the most commercialized way. What means of normative control are
employed within the workplace cultures of the service industry in

---

18. The decline in the estimated unionization rate is even stronger when considered
against the continuously growing number of employees (Japan Institute of Labor 2000: 42).
The main factors behind the decline in the unionization rate are probably the burgeoning of
employment in the service sector and the increase in part-time and temporary workers.

Japan and America, and how are they related to the ideological facades of organizational culture, on the one hand, and the templates of surrounding local culture, on the other?

In order to discuss such questions, this book employs a comparative approach, as it moves from the relationships between employers and unions to relations between management and workers. The structure of the book therefore roughly corresponds to the history of Japan's labor relations. The employer-union relationship provides a context for an analysis of the emotional ideology of Japanese-style management. This context has already been documented by scholars writing on paternalism in Japanese industrial relations, but I try to complicate the picture of present-day labor relations by describing other types of unions in Japan and their appropriation of the emotionalist discourse. I use this context to discuss the more contemporary relationship of white-collar managers and their work partners (such as OLs, contracted employees, and part-timers), especially in the service sector. The service sector provides the major examples for the analysis of emotion management.

This study is based on both original and derivative research. The analysis builds on previous ethnographies of the workplace that have addressed practices and ideologies of normative control and emotion management, often without actually using these concepts. This study sets out to discuss and analyze in an integrative manner the increasing volume of workplace ethnographies from Japan as well as the United States, in addition to cross-cultural ethnographies (particularly on Japanese management in American factories). This cross-cultural and multi-sector perspective permits a reflexive reading of the cultural agendas of the sociology of emotion management. The book's integrative goal is thus complemented by a critical attempt to situate social theories of emotion management within the cultural context of their production.

My own ethnographic work is based on participant observation in Japan during 1995–96 and again in 2000. I build on my 1995–96 fieldwork at Tokyo Disneyland (Raz 1999a) to construct a fuller analysis of service culture in Japan today. I draw for this purpose on ethnographic materials not used in the original Tokyo Disneyland study. A visit to Japan in 2000 provided an opportunity for participant observation, interviews, and textual analysis. These were done in several key settings. First, I updated my research on the Tokyo Dome company by analyzing its service manuals and observing the training that took place before the opening of the new Tokyo Dome Hotel (opened June 1, 2000). Second, I collected materials on alternative forms of management and unionization in present-day Japan, which can shed light on the formerly dominant organizational culture of male regular workers in enterprise-based unions. My analysis focuses on co-partnership management as it is currently practiced in three Japanese medium-size companies and on the case of the National Union of General Workers.

"Japan" is therefore approached in this study from two major directions. First, it provides a location where various cultures of emotion management can be described. When compared to the situation in the United States, this description provides a historical perspective and a viewpoint from which to analyze emotion management as cultural flow, whose manuals undergo both globalization and domestication. Second, the cross-cultural comparison of Japan and the United States generates reflexivity. For example, the concept of emotion management was originally defined and studied by Arlie Hochschild in an American service firm (Delta Air Lines) and was later further developed in the American context. My argument is that the American study of emotion management in U.S. workplaces is culturally biased. Questions regarding emotion management as *necessarily* leading to a "false self" are, for example, preconditioned by the American culture of authentic individualism. It is perhaps not surprising that the major criticism of Hochschild's original conceptions came from a European sociologist (Cas Wouters; see their extensive 1989 correspondence in the British journal *Theory, Culture & Society*). I hope to show that not only our emotions but also our sociology/ies of emotion are managed by our culture. The nature of our sociological thinking about emotion management is, to varying extents, culture-dependent.

CHAPTER ONE

Design, Devotion, and Defiance: The Study of Organizational Cultures in Japan and America

In the 1980s, the introduction of Japan into discussions of organizational culture proved to be a timely and fertile challenge to the study of this subject. Analysis of the Japanese context promises similar rewards for research on the sociology of emotions, a topic of increasing interest not only to sociologists of organizational behavior but also to scholars in the social sciences and the humanities in general as well as in cultural and gender studies in particular. During the past fifteen years or so, a steady stream of workplace ethnographies, published in English, has attempted to probe the consciousness of Japanese workers employed in such diverse settings as factories, offices, shops, households, department stores, and amusement parks. Each of these studies has concentrated on its own setting, yet all have addressed—to some extent—the same questions: How does the Japanese model involve both harmonious collaboration of management and workers and normative control? How is it both a new development in human resource management and a logical, cultural adaptation of Fordism and Taylorism? This chapter and the book as a whole are intended as a road map for an informed reading of this growing scholarly corpus. By integrating the concerns of these studies and showing their underlying themes, I hope to point to some possible future directions for research.

There are three major strands in the relevant literature, which I discuss here under the rubrics of design, devotion, and defiance.[1] The first strand consists of the conventional organizational theory that began with Taylor. This framework stresses "design": rationalization, productivity, and systematization. Emotions are discarded as irrational and are best left outside the workplace. This frame of reference has its roots in mechanical engineering and focuses on organizations as systems (Scott 1987).

The second strand, like the first, is part of the discourse of management.[2] However, it does not discard emotion; rather, it inserts the study and manipulation of emotion into the managerial agenda. This strand emphasizes "devotion" in the form of human relations, industrial psychology, and strong organizational culture and stresses that managers should be attuned to emotion. The two strands—one emerging from Frederick Taylor's scientific management and the other, in the U.S. context at least, from Elton Mayo's human relations—are two forms of a managerial ideology of control.

Within the strand of "devotion," social scientists, who have often served as management consultants, strive to insert emotions into management recipes and appropriate emotions for the managerial discourse of rationalization and systematization. Emotions that might

---

1. The term "defiance" puts the focus more on a denial of existing theory than on the positive contribution the new theory is making. I have considered other terms, such as "alternative" (which retains, however, a focus on denial) or "anti-managerial" (although theories put under the rubric of defiance can go beyond anti-managerialism). I therefore use "defiance" for the lack of a better term. It is also possible that not all the people I put under this rubric would recognize themselves as "defiant." The spectrum of defiance ranges from the moderate to the extreme.

2. Management systems are discourses, or ideologies, in the sense that they promulgate a set of assumptions and values that paves the way for the rhetorical construction of taken-for-granted objects. These objects, in the case of managerial discourse, are typically corporations, employees, and managers. The concept of "managerial discourses" or management systems as ideology goes back to Reinhard Bendix (1963). It was later developed by Guillen (1994) and Shenhav (1999), among others.

damage the organization—for example, stress—are a particular concern. Management gurus Tom Peters and Nancy Austin (1986), for
example, emphasize love and sympathy as organizational goals. Love
is equated with loyalty and teamwork and respect for the individual;
the manager needs "passion, zest, energy, care, love and enthusiasm"
(Austin 1986: 292). The management of emotions becomes part of the
personnel-training agenda (Giacalone and Rosenfeld 1991). The use
(and popularity) of new concepts such as "Emotional Intelligence"
(Goleman 1995) can be seen as part of this strand.

The third perspective, defiance, defies and transcends the managerial discourses of design and devotion; it arose in critical studies conducted by historians and social scientists. In contrast to design and
devotion, this third strand defies the functionalist premises of management and its (either rationalized or emotionalized) goals and
devices.

Table 2 summarizes the American and Japanese literatures on organizational behavior under the three paradigms of design, devotion,
and defiance. That studies conducted in the United States and Japan
can be grouped according to the same categories is in itself interesting.
It points to the interplay between the global and the local or the dialectic of "modeling" and "mirroring." The human relation theorists
and managers of mid-century, for example, would feel at home with
the American discovery of Japanese-style management in the 1980s.
Theory Z and *The Art of Japanese Management*, both popular management texts of the 1980s, used an approach to organizations similar to
the one found in Mayo's works. The business firm in these texts was a
community, and the buzzwords were "involvement," "participation,"
"loyalty," "commitment," "sense of belonging," and "team spirit."

Table 2 reveals the deep epistemological split between emotionality
and rationality; no strand of scholarship crosses the line between them.
Most of the literature reproduces, rather than questions, the binary
narratives of global/local, public/private, and rational/emotional. To
judge from the table, the binarism emotionality/rationality appears
to be what a structuralist would regard as mental structure. As I hope

Table 2
Paradigms for the Study of Organizational Behavior in the United States
and Japan and in the Context of Japanese-Style Management (JSM)

	Design	Devotion	Defiance
United States	Scientific management, systematization, post-Taylorism	Human relations, post-Mayoism, organizational culture	Neo-Marxist, neo-institutional, feminist & labor studies. Hochschild's emotion management
Japan	Professional publications of practitioners, consultants, & engineers	JSM literature; The "Great Tradition"	The "Little Tradition"
JSM in American eyes	FILM* theory; importation of U.S. management systems	"Theory Z" literature	Workplace ethnographies in Japan & in U.S. transplants

*Firm industrial labor markets.

to show, however, the "mental structure" of emotionalism (Japanese-style management) versus rationality (American-style management) is not a reflection of an innate cognitive schema[3] but builds on and reproduces an ideological debate. In the United States, "rationality" was legitimized as the modern remedy for uncertainty and labor unrest (a form of "emotionality"). In Japan, "rationality" (*gōrisei*) was contrasted with "Japanese-style" management and its "emotionalism."

Devotion and Design in the Japanese Context

The American-born managerial gospel of design is subverted in an interesting way in the Japanese context. Mainstream Japanese scholarship assumes that management in Japan is constructed on local traditions of hierarchy, group responsibility, and emotionalism. The ortho-

---

3. The argument in favor of "two brains, two minds, two different kinds of intelligence: rational and emotional," is advanced, for example, by Daniel Goleman (1995: 28).

dox interpretation is that all the distinctive features of Japanese-style management—lifetime employment, the seniority system, welfare capitalism, employee loyalty, teamwork, and workplace unionism— are expressions of traditional Japanese culture.[4]

Unlike the American version of scientific management, this perspective does not discard emotion. On the contrary, Japanese-style management fully appropriates emotion into its worldview. It is, like American human relations theory, a perspective of devotion that stresses normative control. Japanese and American managerial doxa therefore seem to be reversed. In the United States, orthodox managerial thinking was built on rationalist and anti-emotional premises; in Japan, however, emotionalism, familialism, and spiritual training were presented as part and parcel of Japanese-style management.

The ideology of "design" found in the United States therefore contrasts, in its ideal type at least, with the local Japanese ideology of "devotion." The gospel of design did, however, reach Japan at various periods and in various forms and left its rationalist mark on the development of Japanese management. Besides the implementation of rational systems by managers and engineers, there are Japanese scholars whose analysis of industrial relations in Japan is premised on design rather than devotion. Such scholars view Japanese industrial relations as progressive not because they build on a culturalist tradition of trust but because they bring about relative stability and efficiency for both capital and labor. According to Koike Kazuo (1988), Shirai Tai-shirō (1983), Nitta Michio, and their like-minded colleagues, pragmatic Japanese workers cooperated with postwar management to establish what we now know as Japanese-style management. In this version, Japanese teamwork is framed by worker competition over appraisal and promotion. Japanese workers are not emotional creatures

---

4. The impressive list of scholars who support the emotionalist or culturalist view of Japanese-style management includes Odaka Kunio (1984), Hazama Hiroshi (1964, 1978, 1989), Hanami Tadashi (1979, 1981), Mito Tadashi (1994), Hayashi Shuji (1988), and Nakane Chie (1970). For a more recent anthropological perspective, which nevertheless repeats the culturalist paradigm, see Nakamaki 1992, 1997; and Nakamaki & Hioki 1997.

but rational individuals who make long-range cost-benefit calculations; this explains the organizational use of lifetime employment.[5]

The discourse of emotionalism should therefore not be exaggerated or taken at face value. Managers often mouth emotionalism while practicing rationalization. Studies and publications that revolve around "design" have been produced in Japan in large quantities by, for example, Japanese management practitioners, consultants, and engineers. Japanese engineering associations actively promote systematization for quality control, which was started with a clear design rationale. Engineering publications publicize rational arrangements of the production line, such as, notably, the "just-in-time system" in Toyota and the U-shape assembly line. Japanese engineers and managers have also promoted rational systems of work performance, authority, workflow, and payment as techniques for controlling labor. Even the hallmark of Japanese human relations, the quasi-autonomous work group, is underpinned by personnel appraisal (*satei*) that translates into personal remuneration—just as in Taylor's scientific management.

Japanese-Style Management in American Eyes

Looking at Japanese-style management as both a model and a mirror, American literature on Japanese management can also be subsumed under the heading of either devotion or design. Management studies thus reinforce the epistemological split between the global and the local, the rational and the emotional; indeed, many management studies have looked at the other ("Japan") for the purpose of seeing the "true America." The culturally oriented approach has adopted the mainstream model of Japanese-style management and by so doing reinforced it. The many Western scholars who stress the cultural exceptionalism of Japan have made this approach the orthodoxy in Japanese studies as well as in the popular American imagination.[6] Because of this, many business guides paint an overly emotional picture of how to

---

5. Interview with Professor Koike Kazuo, June 3, 2000.
6. See, e.g., Abegglen 1958, Rohlen 1974, Ouchi 1981, and Pascale & Athos 1981a, b.

negotiate with the Japanese. A prestigious MIT guide, for example, claims that "Japan is an insider/outsider society, in which one must build connection and trust. . . . To do so requires passing through four key stages—from 'Know Me' to 'Trust Me' to 'Believe Me' to 'Marry Me'" (Gercik 1996: 3).

The second approach replaces cultural exceptionalism and devotion with a Japan that mirrors global processes of industrial design (see, e.g., Nakayama 1974). This approach seeks to explain Japanese-style management as a by-product of labor market systems (see, e.g., Lincoln & McBride 1987). A complementary view relates the takeoff of postwar Japanese-style management to the labor laws and industrial democratization imposed by the American occupation (see, e.g., Okazaki-Ward 1993: 27–31; and Morita 1986). The strand of design also includes a group of American engineers and management scholars who stress Japan's successful importation of American methods, such as scientific management, Fordism, and Deming's quality control (see Wren 1994; and Eberts & Eberts 1995).

Defying the Hegemony of Design and Devotion

A third approach to the history of Japanese management challenges the epistemological splits between global and local and between the rational and the emotional. This approach, "defiance," can serve as an umbrella concept that brings together several research agendas on both sides of the Pacific. Inspired by Arlie Hochschild's work, defiant sociological studies in the United States share a critical view of the rational manipulation of emotions in and by organizations. A critical sociology of emotions at work focuses on the subjective, and intersubjective, construction of emotions within power structures of gender, hierarchy, and micro-politics. Hochschild's study has inspired a growing list of studies on organizational practices such as recruitment, selection, socialization, promotion, and performance requirements.[7]

---

7. See, e.g., Rafaeli & Sutton 1989, 1990; Van Maanen & Kunda 1989; Albrow 1992; Fineman 1993; Leidner 1993; and Pierce 1995.

This strand grows out of a critical Marxist approach. Like Marx, the practitioners of this line of inquiry focus on the exploitation and alienation inherent in capitalism. Exploitation is the objective, institutional facet and consists of the growing division of labor, the wage system with its surface value, and work conditions. Alienation, on the other hand, represents the subjective, personal facet, which is located in workers' responses and in their consciousness. Hochschild's concept of "emotion management" opened up a new research agenda because it combined the institutional and the personal in a critical manner. It joined (objective) training and its (personal) internalization and execution. The concept of emotion management seeks to defy and to subvert the normative order of organizations by exposing the managerial design of emotions at work and workers' reactions to such imposed devotion.

Another defiant strand that extends from neo-Marxism has been developed within labor studies. One of the central works was Harry Braverman's *Labor and Monopoly Capital* (1974), which drew on Marx's concept of alienation. Other key works in this tradition were written by Michael Burawoy (1979), Richard Edwards (1979), and David Montgomery (1979). Labor scholarship has traditionally provided a defiant alternative to managerial declarations. Recent labor scholarship in the United States has played a central role in exposing managerial facades in the American auto transplants. Labor researchers such as Mike Parker (1993), Laurie Graham (1995), and Steve Babson (1993) have critically described American workers' resistance to and subversion of American-style Japanization.

Yet another strand of defiance characterizes the neo-institutional perspective. Neo-institutional approaches to organizations are part of a wider intellectual endeavor that "problematizes modernity, and questions the social origins of the whole constellation of institutions" (Dobbin 1994: 123). Neo-institutionalists examine organizations as embedded in culture, although they have not specifically studied emotions at work. However, this approach is significant for questioning the managerial view of "organizational culture."

In Japan, the paradigm of defiance is generally adopted by social scientists and historians working in the Marxist tradition. There are still no Japanese studies of emotion management, however; this American concept has not yet been domesticated in Japan, for cultural reasons that will be discussed below. Ross Mouer and Sugimoto Yoshio (1986: esp. chap. 3) provide an overview of the Marxist tradition in Japanese social science. Interestingly, these authors frame the Marxist approach as the "Little Tradition" (which stresses conflict and class interests), in contrast to the "Great Tradition" in Japanese studies (which emphasizes cohesion and uniformity in Japanese society).[8]

There is now a critical mass of defiant interpretations of Japanese work practices, for example, in Japanese, the works of Kamata Satoshi (1974, 1980) on Toyota and on shipbuilding yards and Ueno Eishin (1960, 1985a–e) on coalmining; and in English, Kamata Satoshi (1982), Dorinne Kondo (1990), and Matthew Allen (1994). Against the sizable and dominant literature in Japan on labor-management relations that tends to stress the commitment and devotion of the Japanese worker, some Japanese scholars have consistently argued for a careful reappraisal of this myth (see, e.g., Nishimura 1970 and Fujita 1972). Tokunaga Shigeyoshi (1983) provides a Marxist interpretation of Japanese industrial relations. Endō Koshi (1989) represents the view that Japanese labor relations policy was grounded in the Occupation of Japan and developed from the new American-imposed labor laws rather than in some depoliticized cultural tradition. Another study by Endō (1994) defies the myth of the Japanese worker as born for teamwork by showing how team attitudes are measured and remunerated. Finally, Kumazawa Makoto's *Portraits of the Japanese Workplace* (1996) provides an excellent doorway for the Western reader into the dark side of Japanese workplace culture.

---

8. Other Little Traditions of dissent include the liberal modernists (of which Maruyama Masao is a leading example), feminists, and advocates of "people's history" (*minshūshi*) such as Irokawa Daikichi (see Andrew Gordon's overview of these strands in his foreword to Kumazawa 1996). Taken together, these critical traditions are perhaps not so "little."

In the specific context of Japanese-style management, two key historical studies utilizing a paradigm of defiance are Andrew Gordon's (1985, 1998) accounts of the evolution of labor relations in heavy industry in Japan. Gordon is suspicious of both overly emotional depictions of Japanese-style management and overly rationalistic views of the managerial urge to systematize production and stabilize the workforce. He shows how much of the culture of the firm-as-family and the paternalistic ideology of management was originally nothing more than lip service. Conversely, in Gordon's reconstruction, management gradually and often reluctantly instituted welfare programs, promotion and tenure tracks, and company councils only in response to labor disputes and labor-market problems. This approach rejects the idea, championed by such representatives of the Japanese management system approach as Hazama Hiroshi and William Ouchi, that already in the 1920s and 1930s Japanese managers in large firms "thought of themselves as looking after all aspects of their employees' lives" and that the employees had the "deeply engrained attitude of committing themselves to the care of the managers of the firm" (quoting Gordon's criticism of Hazama, in Gordon 1985: 471*n*135).

The critical literature also shows a clear-cut gender stratification. Monographs on female workers, particularly ethnographic studies, have been written—to the best of my knowledge—mostly by female researchers. A few prominent examples of that literature are, for example, Dorinne Kondo (1990) on female artisans, Jeannie Lo (1990) on OLs and female workers in factories, Glenda Roberts (1994) on blue-collar women in the textile industry, and Mary Brinton (1993) in a more general account of gender and work.[9] A similar phenomenon can be found in the United States, for example, the work of Jennifer Pierce (1995) on paralegals and attorneys, Mary Romero (1992) on female domestic labor, Rosemary Pringle (1988) on (Australian) secre-

---

9. See also the British anthologies *Women in the Japanese Workplace* and *Japanese Women Working*, edited, respectively, by Mary Saso (1990) and Janet Hunter (1993).

taries, and obviously Hochschild's foundational study (1983) on air hostesses.

This book adopts a defiant perspective in tracing the roles of emotion as a social structure in the workplace and of rules on feeling as enforcers of commitment. My theoretical disposition is to analyze emotion as an institutionalized "social fact" that objectively (so to speak) exists within the organizational system of control. Such emotional themes underlie, for example, the Japanese-style institutions of firm-as-family and welfare capitalism. My aim here is to uncover the actual practices and mechanisms through which emotional scripts are institutionalized by examining such organizational practices as TQM, just-in-time delivery, quality control, service manuals, annual self-declarations, promotion protocols, and so on. Studying the flip side of emotion, on the other hand, requires a different methodology. In tracing the role of emotion in conflict and subversion, I emphasize the consciousness of employees (whether white-collar or blue-collar, managers or workers, salarymen or part-timers) and their point of view. This perspective stresses the subjective experience of emotion as a reaction to normative control.

Emotion Management as a Critical Perspective

The concept of emotion management is treated in this book as a central mechanism of normative control and as a lens through which we can focus on the emotional lives of workers. As Dennis Mumby and Linda Putnam point out, "Companies incorporate Hochschild's notion of the 'managed heart' when they call on employees to exhibit forced niceness and to suppress anger. . . . Employee manuals urge clerks to express concern to customers, make their voices warm and friendly, and prevent the showing of impatience and frustration" (1992: 472). The same phenomenon can be found in Japan, although both the manuals and the employees' reactions to them are sometimes different. Nor is emotion management limited to the service industry, although its *display* is probably most blatant in that sector. Ubiquitous organizational practices such as socialization, promotion, teamwork

(in the office, on the shop floor, or on the production line), and decision-making procedures are also means of normative control through
which the interests of individual workers are welded to those of management.

In *The Managed Heart*, Arlie Hochschild coined the term "emotion
management" to describe the work of Delta Air Lines's flight
attendants. Emotion management, as defined by Hochschild, is a
transmutation of three basic elements of emotional life: emotion
work, feeling rules, and social exchange. These elements are part of
everyday emotional life, but employees of service companies are taught
to manage them in a special way. First, emotion work—the self-
management of one's emotions according to the situation—
is "no longer a private act but a public act, bought on the one hand
and sold on the other" (Hochschild 1983: 118). It is no longer the individual but the company as represented by the trainer, the manual,
and the management that decides the right emotion to display.
Second, feeling rules—social scripts that tell us what to feel and
how to express our feelings in various situations—cease to be unwrit-
ten, personal, and often vague formulations contingent on an individual's upbringing and character. Feeling rules are now spelled out publicly—in manuals, in training programs, and in the discourse
of supervisors at all levels. Third, social exchange is forced into narrow
channels. It is reduced from an improvised, real-time, on-the-spot,
face-to-face interaction to a carefully prescribed, pre-scripted and
stage-managed "show." Although emotions are most openly sold and
bought in the service industry, many other organizations also have
feeling rules.

In this book I use the words "feelings" and "emotion" interchange-
ably.[10] Emotion is a package of separate but interrelated components.

---

10. Sandelands (1988) and Rosenberg (1990) present feelings as more private sensations
that become emotions when enacted in social situations. This distinction draws on the
psychodynamic emphasis on feelings as inner states, for example, fear and anxiety (Hirschorn
1988). Sociologists, however, sometimes speak of feelings as emotional states and thus blur the
semantic distinction.

According to David Matsumoto's (1996) typology, emotion combines expression, motivation, and social glue (see also Hearn 1993: 146–47 for a complementary typology). Emotional expression consists of spoken and bodily, mainly facial, displays of emotion. Facial expressions of emotion are, according to research, universal. Matsumoto's (1996) study confirms that Japanese and Americans, for example, share the same basic vocabulary of facial expressions.

I concentrate here on the two other components of emotion: motivation and social structure. Emotion as motivation denotes the subjective experience of feelings. In order to understand motivation (why people do what they do), it is imperative to understand their emotions. For some psychologists, emotion is motivation (e.g., Tomkins 1962, 1963). The vast psychological literature on motivation in organizations can readily be subsumed under the ideological rubric of "devotion." Emotion as social glue stresses the intersubjective role of emotion in social relationships—how we perceive the emotions of others and how we manage our emotions accordingly.

Although emotion as motivation focuses on emotion as an individual resource, emotion as social structure emphasizes the cultural given-ness of emotion, the fact that various emotional scripts exist as "social facts" prior to the individual. One proponent of this view is Theodore Kemper (1978), who stresses the role of emotion as an invisible glue that binds the group together and cements social bonds. Emotion, however, can also be subversive. Emotion as motivation also includes experiences of fatigue, resentment, stress, and hostility. Emotions can therefore act not only as social glue but also as signals and mediators of social conflict.

The sociological study of emotion, unlike a psychological study, has the unique potential for emphasizing the roles of emotion as a structure for action and as a discursive element in the order of things. My focus in this book is hence on the institutional rather than the idiosyncratic, the discursive rather than the subjective, and the work group rather than the individual worker.

The Cultural Context of Emotion Management

A variety of factors affect the display of emotions by employees, such as sociocultural, organizational, occupational, work-group, and individual norms. These factors represent "ground rules," that is, rules for emotional display that are relatively stable. Organizational norms are significant in defining the degree of freedom (or "discretion") an employee has in displaying emotions. In addition, emotions are also the outcomes of the specific properties of the setting, the target person, and the employee's "real feelings" on the job during a particular emotional transaction. These factors represent "surface rules" that are potentially more dynamic and transient. The emotional transaction is a combined product of ground and surface rules. There can be considerable variation in displayed emotions between individual transactions, occupational roles, and organizational settings. Emotions displayed in a transaction may also vary as the interaction unfolds. Depending on feedback from the target person, the employee may maintain, abandon, or revise the emotions s/he initially displayed.[11]

Figure 2 summarizes the factors that determine variation in displayed emotions. It begins with ground rules that operate in regard to the (cultural and organizational) definition of role. Figure 2 suggests that the influences of the organizational culture and the surrounding culture follow independent paths. We see here the logic of the three-circle model (Fig. 1) as it applies to the emotional transaction. The interrelations among the three circles are dynamic, and their borders depend on the definition of the situation being studied. In some cases, there may be congruence between the ground rules of the organizational and the surrounding cultures. Ouchi (1981) regarded such a "cultural fit" as the source of strength and consistency he associated with "model Z" organizations. In other cases, the organizational and the surrounding cultures may be incompatible.

---

11. The model of the emotional transaction I develop here is based on the important psychological work of Anat Rafaeli and Robert Sutton (1989, 1987). Whereas they focus on the surface rules of the transaction, however, my work concentrates on the ground rules.

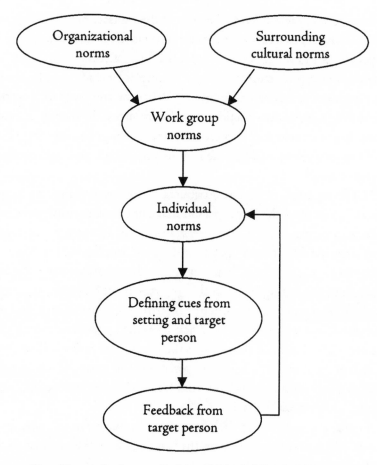

Fig. 2 The emotional transaction (adapted from Rafaeli & Sutton 1989: 17)

As we move to the everyday level of workplace culture, we encounter the work group and the individual, where both ground and surface
rules are at work. Work groups can provide guidance about which
emotions should and should not be displayed as well as serve as an
agent of socialization that influences the emotional behavior of members. Working in teams or participating in a quality control circle, for
example, can be stressful without proper socialization. This may explain the difference in attitudes toward work groups and quality control circles in Japan and the United States.

In addition, each individual brings to the transaction enduring personal attributes as well as the actual emotions felt in a certain situation. Psychologists have identified hundreds of such attributes that may influence emotional display. Major examples include gender, self-monitoring, and emotional stamina.[12] What the employee feels on the job during a certain transaction may also influence the display of emotions. Some people may express their true feelings because they cannot suppress them as demanded by organizational and occupational socialization.[13]

"Defining cues" represent attributes of the setting and the target person. Cues from the target person that can influence displayed emotions include gender, age, race, dress, and so on. Waiters, for example, may distinguish between "good" and "poor" tippers on the basis of their dress, a distinction that may affect the emotions they display. Cues from the setting are such things as temporal features (e.g., night or day), interactional (the amount of crowding), and spatial and atmospheric features. Finally, feedback from the target person may also influence the display of emotions as the transaction unfolds. This level is dynamic and involves mutual negotiations and symbolic interaction. The employee usually relies on such feedback to determine the "next round" of emotional behavior.

Figure 2 suggests that each level sets the stage for the next level down. My main focus here is on the ways in which the organizational and surrounding cultures interact to set the stage for the actual display of emotions within workplace cultures. In the case of Japan, a long tradition—in both academia and business—has viewed Japa-

---

12. For example, findings suggest that women are more likely than men to display warmth and liking during emotional transactions (S. A. Shields 1991, 1995). Snyder (1974) showed that a self-reported measure of individual differences in self-monitoring predicted the extent to which subjects could control expressive behavior. Finally, individuals may vary in their ability to express certain feelings over an extended period of time (as Hochschild found in regard to flight attendants, for example).

13. Even organizations with rigid display rules may allow members to display their true feelings. In fact, many front-line and other people-intensive jobs include structured "time-outs" (Van Maanen 1989) during which employees have an opportunity for "role release."

nese-style management as emanating from certain patterns of the surrounding culture. The trope of "Japan, Inc." and the emphasis on group consensus have promoted the particularistic view of Japanese-style management as culturally unique. The depiction of Japanese life as overly orchestrated has also spawned a conflict in interpretation. On the one hand, the Japanese "devotion" literature regards the Japanese as super-emotional. On the other hand, global opinion underpinned by the design paradigm views the Japanese as emotionless.[14] What is the solution to this contradiction? My answer is that the contradiction arises because we wrongly juxtapose the global and the local. It is an artificial paradox created by applying to Japanese life the Western split between public and private.

Culture, in Japan and elsewhere, is designed to manage emotions. This is the goal of the various norms and rules that govern individual life. As Matsumoto claims, "Although superficially the existence of these rules may lead some to suspect that the Japanese are relatively emotionless people, in fact, they are highly emotional people, and to discount the importance of emotion to them would be a travesty (one that, unfortunately, has occurred all too often)" (1996: 4).

Anthropology has centered on the Japanese "culture of shame" as the main emotional vehicle for fostering commitment to social values.[15] Japan as a "society of shame" illustrates the power of emotion as a social sanction and the profound impact social norms and feeling rules may exert on the subjective emotional experiences of individu-

---

14. The Japanese themselves have propagated and popularized the Western image of the "emotionless Japanese." For example, a typical women's college workbook for OLs confidently states that "since Japanese express emotions differently from foreigners, the latter often say that they don't know what Japanese are thinking because of their expression-less faces, as if they had Nō masks on" (cited in McVeigh 1997: 169).

15. On Japan as a "society of shame" see Benedict 1946, Sakuta 1967, Lebra 1976, Doi 1973, and Pelzel 1986. This list, bringing together both American and Japanese scholars, represents the "Great Tradition." Fewer studies have discussed "shame culture" in the context of Japanese workplace cultures. Early sources include Hagen 1965 and to some extent Cole 1971: 180–85. For interesting discussions of the ritual of the public apology (hansei), which is an important organizational practice of "shame culture," in anthropological studies, see Rohlen 1974 and, more recently, Roberts 1994 and Kondo 1990.

als.[16] It used to be quite fashionable in anthropology to distinguish between shame and guilt cultures (for a review, see Creighton 1990) on
the basis of which emotion, shame or guilt, was used as the primary
social sanction. In this dichotomy, Japan was characterized as a shame
culture. Shame is an outward orientation, a consciousness of others
and what they will think and feel. One can be shamed by one's family,
neighbors, friends, co-workers, and managers. The fact that the average Japanese white-collar worker takes only half the paid holidays to
which he is entitled has been explained, in this vein, as reflecting an
unwillingness to be seen as less committed to his job than his co-
workers. The sense of committing a wrong means losing face in relation to others. Shame represents an ethnocentric, relativist universe of
morality. This is in contrast to guilt cultures (such as, arguably, the
United States), which use individual guilt as a primary means of
maintaining social order.[17] In guilt cultures, one is expected to answer
to oneself and to control one's own behavior so that it conforms to the
behavior one expects from others. Guilt therefore draws a liberal line
between the private and the public. As an ideal type, guilt represents a
universalistic conception of morality, whose Western epitome is
Kant's categorical imperative.

Although the concept of "shame culture" has lost its scientific appeal, social psychologists in Japan now speak about the "interdependent view of self" and its related "experience of other-focused emo-

---

16. Other influences of the local might include religion, for example. As Mauro Guillen
(1994: 297) argues, "Confucianism or Buddhism generally endorsed the idea that there are in-
trinsic satisfactions to be derived from work"; hence the Japanese ethic of cultivating one's self
through work. Christianity, in contrast, is generally said to underscore the extrinsic rewards,
placing the emphasis on individual effort—elements that are more consistent with scientific
management.

17. Anthony Giddens (1991), in contrast, argues that it is shame, and not guilt, that characterizes the social organization of late modernity. This is because "shame bears directly on self-
identity. . . . It is essentially anxiety about the adequacy of the narrative by means of which the
individual sustains a coherent biography" (ibid., p. 65). This reverse picture illustrates that (1)
generalizations regarding "shame" or "guilt" cultures are essentialist and hence misconstrued
(Creighton 1990), and (2) grand theories do not merely express representations of reality but
also mirror their own theoretical lineage.

tions" (Ando 1994: 3) as opposed to American "ego-focused" emotions. This is, in fact, a generalization of the discourse on shame culture, since "shame" is also an other-focused emotion. Psychologists have extended the discussion of shame to encompass such emotions as *shi-tashimi* (the feeling of familiarity with someone), *oime* (indebtedness), *fureai* (connectedness), and, of course, *amae* (expectation of someone's indulgence and favor). The use of Japanese terms for these emotions seems to strengthen their sense of cultural uniqueness.

"Emotion management" can now be read in its cultural context. To American scholars inspired by Hochschild's work, emotion management has negative connotations. For Mumby and Putnam (1992: 472), "Emotional labor, similar to bounded rationality, alienates and fragments the individual." Hochschild (1983) speaks about "being phony" and about the alienation from a "false self." Rafaeli and Sutton (1989: 36–37) argue that "the shift to a service economy . . . means that an increasing number of employees hold jobs in which they are expected to follow carefully specified display rules about which emotions they should and should not display. The impact of such norms on employee well-being is . . . an aspect that executives should be concerned with, for both humanistic and financial reasons." Ferguson comments that "the flight attendant's smile is like her makeup; it is on her, not of her." Moreover, "like prostitutes, flight attendants often estrange themselves from their work as a defense against being swallowed by it, only to suffer from a sense of being false, mechanical, no longer a whole integrated self" (Ferguson 1984: 53–54).

These reactions of American sociologists to the commercialization of human feeling are framed within a decontextualized criticism of emotional (public/private) dissonance and the "false self." What sociologists often fail to acknowledge is that such criticism also hinges on a cultural context. American workers' reaction to emotion management can be read in the context of "guilt society." A double socialization is at work here. First, there is the local, surrounding socialization of respondents as members of an American culture, a culture that regards "being phony" as *a priori* immoral (hypocritical), something to feel guilty about, particularly when done as part of one's formal duty.[18]

Second, there is the professional socialization of sociologists. The stress on the commodification of human feelings in late capitalism is a legacy of Karl Marx's critical views. Marx saw labor as the form production takes when the worker is expropriated from his or her own means of production. The industrial worker no longer produces a whole thing but rather fragments of something; not something that he or she will personally use but a commodity to be sold elsewhere and by someone else (Marx 1967). Emotional labor, like physical labor, is another means of increasing surplus value. The only difference is that the service worker does not manufacture anything but sells "service," emotions and smiles included. Hochschild opens her book by quoting a section from *Das Kapital* entitled "The Working Day" and later tells the reader that "Marx . . . has told us the factory worker's story. I am interested in telling the flight attendant's story in order to promote a fuller appreciation of the costs of what she does" (1983: 17).

This approach to emotion is culture-specific. In the United States and the West, emotion has typically been viewed as "something natural rather than cultural, irrational rather than rational, chaotic rather than ordered, subjective rather than universal, physical rather than mental or intellectual, unintended and uncontrollable, and hence often dangerous" (Lutz 1990: 69). Charles Cooley (1922), a leading figure in the study of symbolic interaction, argued that emotions are a sign of the "I," the personal/private side of identity, rather than of the "me," the social/public aspect of identity. Furthermore, emotion was typically regarded as lower in status than other, "higher" faculties, particularly rational thought. This contrast obviously also has a gendered aspect, since women were typically regarded as "emotional" and men were characterized by (higher) "rational" dispositions. American organizational theory, which contrasts rationality with uncertainty and

---

18. The public outrage against President Bill Clinton over his affair with Monica Lewinsky can be read as an example of the American cultural conditioning against the hypocrisy underlying such expressions of "untrue" behavior.

largely ignores emotion, is thus also the product of a larger, Western cultural discourse.

In Japan, emotion has typically been viewed as part of culture (society, the "me") and not just nature (personality, the "I"). Emotion in Japan is part of culture (rather than nature) because Japanese culture depends in large measure "on the strict adherence by all members to display rules. . . . Many native Japanese believe that one cannot be considered a 'full-fledged' Japanese until one has mastered the art of managing one's emotions in all aspects of life" (Matsumoto 1996: 63).[19] Moreover, emotion has been regarded as equally significant to cognition. Finally, although gendered differences in the cultural construction and apportionment of emotion do exist in Japan, both men and women are equally regarded as emotional beings.

Feeling rules, as Hochschild notes, exist in every culture. Yet Japanese culture differs from American culture in the extent of its feeling rules. American society tolerates, and to a great extent fosters, a wide range of emotional behavior, even though it has its display rules. The Japanese allow less variety and are less tolerant of transgression of display rules. The resulting *appearance* of conformity in Japanese emotional display does not mean that individual variation or transgression does not exist. On the contrary, psychological studies suggest that the Japanese experience emotions with greater frequency and with more intensity than Europeans or Americans (Matsumoto et al. 1988; Scherer et al. 1988). Yet the Japanese, men and women alike, are generally socialized to separate their control of emotions in public places from their subjective emotional life. According to David Matsumoto's psychological study of the emotions of the Japanese, "They have learned to modify their emotional reactions so well, and from such an early age, that as adults their reaction patterns are automatic with little conscious effort" (Matsumoto 1996: 64). In other words, the Japanese are emotionally subjugated (or bounded). Emotion management,

---

19. It is no coincidence that Doi's *amae*, one of the most famous psychological constructs of "Japanese mentality," refers to codependence—a state of bounded emotionality.

in their case, is an internalized, rather than external, form of self-control. It is a cultural phenomenon that has become second nature.

The managing of one's emotions is further culturally constructed in Japan as a cultivation of the self rather than alienation and hypocrisy. This positive approach to bounded emotionality is reflected in the "relational self" or "social relativism" of the Japanese (see, e.g., Bachnik 1986; Doi 1973).[20] Kondo's (1990) study of the discourse of identity in a Japanese workplace begins with the claim that the Japanese self is not "the self" as Americans know it. According to Kondo, "Selves are multiple, fraught with tension and contradiction, and asserted in specific performative contexts. . . . Selves are embodied and constructed oppositionally and relationally. They are not referential symbols, the Transcendental signifier, but strategically deployed signifiers, stories which we narrate and perform for each other" (p. 307). This brings us back to the interplay of the public and the private.

In Western individualist societies, so the generalization goes, the "self" is by and large a fixed identity whose emotions reflect that identity's internal mental states. The internal is given prominence and accorded an aura of authenticity; in contrast, the formal prescriptions of external, "public life" are seen as less authentic.[21] Emotional expressions are, by that cultural definition, outward signals of more important inner, emotional states. Variation in emotional display is hence encouraged in American society because it implies that every person has a unique "inner" personality that needs to be expressed. As Jeff Hearn (1993: 144) comments, "There is, in talking of emotions, the obligation, experienced or perceived, to tell the truth about oneself, or at least to talk about 'the truth.'" Authentic behavior or a "true self" is maintained by matching the internal and the external, one's personality and one's behavior. This cultural expectation has yielded various

---

20. There is nothing *intrinsically* Japanese here; it is, rather, a particular configuration of a universal balance of detachment and involvement. Norbert Elias (1987) conceptualized this universal regulative mechanism as the *We-I-balance*.

21. On the often-repeated claim by anthropologists that the experience of wholeness, continuity, and autonomy that we normally associate with the "self" is a culture-bound, Western notion, see Ewing 1990.

norms such as "straight talk," the hallmark of the hero in the Westerns, John Wayne, for example.

To recapitulate, the "individualist self" is constructed by a culture that (1) clearly distinguishes, psychologically, between inside and outside and (2) idealizes the authentic expression of inner emotions. This is the prototype for the American "emotional self." Individualism, as a Western ideology, is based on the magnification of the boundary between the internal and the external. Emotion is defined in the West as something inside the individual (Lutz 1990: 73). It follows that emotion is a personal resource that individuals must self-exploit (according to Hochschild, women are expected to self-exploit emotion more than men). In the West, therefore, discourses on emotionality have come under the control of those experts whose professional gaze presumes to penetrate the inside of the person—namely the medical or quasi-medical professions (mainly psychiatry and psychology; see Foucault 1980). Furthermore, because emotion is constructed as relatively chaotic and irrational, its individual expression might challenge authority, and this legitimates the need for control. This is, for example, how the human relations school has typically regarded emotion at work.

The "collectivist self" associated with Japan is, in contrast, constructed by a culture that blurs the psychological distinction between inside and outside and always defines the self in relation to its social surroundings; inside and outside are, in contrast, distinguished at the social level (in-group and out-group). In addition, personal experience (inside) and personal display (outside) are considered separate domains, and they are not expected to correspond. This can lead non-Japanese to complain that the Japanese act according to double standards. For the Japanese, the cultural dialectics of the socially appropriate and the personally felt is captured by such pairs as *omote-ura* (front-back) and *tatemae-honne* (outside display–inside experience). Emotional behavior is governed to a great extent by feeling rules that constrain public display, and some emotions are social constructs generated outside the person, by social relationships or group membership. In Japan, discourses on emotionality have come under the control of those experts whose professional gaze covers the social surroundings of the person—such as educators, mentors, and managers.

Hochschild's sociology of emotions generalized on her American respondents' conceptualizations of, and reactions to, feeling rules and emotion management. She sometimes ignored the fact, however, that these conceptualizations and reactions were themselves part of a larger cultural system that extends beyond service culture, commercialization, and capitalism (in this sense I agree with some of Wouters' [1989] criticisms). When flight attendants (and Hochschild) worry about "true" and "false" selves in the culture-specific way they worry about them, it is not just because of the "commercialization of human life" and their work in the service sector; it is also because they are American.[22]

---

22. Loseke and Cahill 1986 describes a similar dilemma of "true" and "false" self in the context of social work students. Their helping role often necessitated that they mask their real feelings from clients, and yet they experienced this masking as fraudulent and as an indication that they were not *bona fide* social workers. This dilemma was experienced in a professional, not commercial, context. Even though the students knew that masking their real feelings was often in the interest of their clients, they still felt bad about it.

CHAPTER TWO

Emotional Genesis: Enterprise Unionism
in Ideology and Practice

Many books on the theory of increasing efficiency have already been published in Japan. . . . However, since almost all of them are no more than translations of works originally written in America, their relevance to the situation of Japan's workers is highly tenuous. . . . There are many [Japanese] factories which temporarily adopted scientific methods of management . . . but they have for the most part ended in failure. The reason for these failures lies in having brought in American-style practices which attach much importance to material things. . . . Japanese workers are more inclined to be moved by things spiritual.
                                                    —Uno Riemon 1921 (cited in Tsutsui 1995: 71)

Oh paternalism (*onjōshugi*)! Oh familialism (*kazokushugi*)! We hear about them all the time but when have they actually improved our lives? It's all just a swindle that the management—which is afraid of our resistance—keeps pulling to make us obedient and really squeeze us!
                                    —From a 1930 Japan National Railroad labor broadside (cited in Tsutsui 1995: 75)

Japanese-style management is often identified with practices that were first formed on the shop floor and applied to it. Toyotism, now usually mentioned as the Japanese antidote to Fordism, takes its name from the practices used at the large Japanese automobile manufacturer. Human relations, the American managerial technique for fostering devotion, was similarly conceived on the shop floor, as a consequence of the Hawthorne experiments.[1] It is therefore logical, from a histori-

---

1. The Hawthorne experiments were a series of observations conducted between 1927 and 1932 at the Hawthorne Works of the Western Electric Company in Chicago. Initially a study

cal standpoint, to start with the shop floor in the search for emotions at work. The focus of this chapter is the premises of Japanese-style management, which arose in the context of enterprise unionism for regular workers.

Industrial firms were the seedbed of practices that crystallized after World War II in the form currently known as the three pillars of Japanese-style management. Career wage laborers first appeared in Japan in shipyards, arsenals, machine factories, and steel mills. The term "career wage laborer" contains a covert contradiction, since a wage laborer can be a temporary worker. The "career" of a wage laborer straddles both membership motivation (staying put in one company) and market motivation (working for multiple companies). In industry these contradictions took shape at an early stage and led to the creation of such categories as *shain* (staff) and *kōin* (workers), permanent and temporary work. The industrial sector can therefore be seen, retrospectively, as a testing ground for Japan's mainstream managerial ideologies of normative control.

The Ideology of Managerial Paternalism

Paternalism, widely regarded as the overarching ideology of Japanese management, is currently associated with the enterprise unionism of postwar Japan. However, the ideological roots of paternalism predate the postwar formation of enterprise unionism and can be traced to industrializing Japan at the turn of the twentieth century.[2] Although some of the more culturalist explanations of Japanese labor relations trace managerial paternalism back to the Tokugawa era, there are historical reasons for doubting that paternalism was a continuation of

---

of the effect of lighting conditions on workers and their performance, it led to a recognition of the importance of informal organization, group affiliation, and feedback.

2. On prewar paternalism, see Gordon 1985; Marshall 1967; Fruin 1983. Hazama Hiroshi is one of the major proponents of this view in Japan; he asserts that contemporary Japanese-style management is based on feudalist notions of paternalism, which for him mean "the beautiful customs" of "groupism, feelings of dependency, and a high regard for harmony and cooperation" (Hazama & Kaminsky 1979: 104; see also Hanami 1979, 1981).

traditional cultural practices. In fact, managerial paternalism was an instrumental response to pressure for a Western-style "factory law" from both workers and bureaucrats. The capitalist managerial elite of the late Meiji era articulated a coherent ideology of paternalism to counter government pressure for factory legislation. Eventually, managers and bureaucrats came to defend paternalism as a progressive concept that "took the best of Japan's past and applied it to insure an economically and socially healthy future . . . as the special Japanese key to solving the labor problem" (Gordon 1985: 64–65).

Shōda Heigorō, director of the Mitsubishi Nagasaki shipyard, stated in 1898 that a factory law would be a "great evil" since it would sow the seeds of self-interest and lead workers to oppose managers.[3] In 1910, Shōda explained what he saw as the single, best, most efficient solution to labor-management relations: paternalism.

Since ancient times, Japan has possessed the beautiful custom of master-servant relations based firmly on a spirit of sacrifice and compassion, a custom not seen in the many other countries of the world. Even with the recent progress in transportation, the development of ideas about rights, the expansion of markets, and the growing scale of industrial society, this master-servant relationship persists securely. This relationship is not weak like that of the Western nations, but has its roots in our family system and will persist as long as that system exists. Because of this relationship, the employer loves the employee and the employee respects his master. Interdependent and helping each other, the two preserve industrial peace. . . . Today, there exist no evils and we feel no necessity [for a factory law]. We cannot agree to something that will destroy the beautiful custom of master-servant relations and wreak havoc on our industrial peace.

A half-century later, paternalistic ideologies still pervaded the legislative approach to labor relations in Japan. The emotional discourse of Japanese-style management reappeared in the cultural translation of

---

3. Andrew Gordon (1985: 66). Note that in the United States, whose labor law was later to travel to Japan during the postwar occupation, legislation assumed an adversarial relationship between workers and management, relationships that required a legally regulated collective bargaining.

the American labor law during the postwar occupation. The concept of unfair labor practices, which is at the heart of the Wagner Act in the United States, "made no sense in Japanese" (Brody 1993: 197; see also Gould 1984). Japan's Trade Union Act of 1949 reformulated the term as "improper" labor practices and framed it within patron-client relations.

Paternalism was used by managers and business leaders to fend off or weaken labor legislation as well as to reinforce policies of direct control and education in the factory. What did paternalism mean in practice? By the end of World War I, most industrial firms had implemented a number of benefits in addition to wages. This more substantive paternalism came in response to the rise of the labor movement; it was an attempt to satisfy workers' demands without recognizing independent labor (trade) unions. These benefits took three major forms: company welfare programs (health, recreational, and housing facilities, cafeteria and lunch subsidies, discount stores, and saving plans), company education programs, and permanent employment. In the 1920s, company welfare programs included subsidized rice, disability compensation and medical care, awards for long service, and a variety of mutual-aid organizations, savings plans, and pension funds.[4] Traditional values and cultural practices facilitated both management's choice of these policies and labor's acceptance.

---

4. A comparison between the early formation of Japanese welfare corporatism and the pioneering experiments of Ford with welfare plans shows that for all their differences, in both cases such practices emerged in response to labor problems. In 1914, when Henry Ford faced grave organizational problems, he founded a Sociological Department that employed 250 people. Aiming to correct a daily absentee rate that exceeded 10 percent and a yearly turnover rate of 370 percent, Ford designed a new program for loyalty and conformity. He decided to pay $5 a day to every "qualified" employee. The Ford Sociological Department assumed the role of determining who was qualified to receive this bonus. These "sociologists" visited homes and interviewed neighbors and priests to determine who conformed with the company's code of conduct, which stressed family and community values, thrift, and personal character. They used strict criteria for unsuitability: single young men, men who were divorced, those who did not spend their evenings "wisely," those who drank, or those who did not speak English. They also gave lessons in home management to workers, taught them how to shop, and how to preserve moral values (this description, taken from Shenhav 1999: chap. 9, is based on Marcus and Segal 1989: 236–38).

Company education programs provided formal vocational training and even general education for male workers. These early forms of the now-famous Japanese "in-house education" were instituted in the face of inadequate public vocational training, a labor shortage, and a high turnover rate.[5] Some of these training schools were tuition-free for children of company workers. In 1905 the Shibaura Engineering Works announced a new education program aimed mainly at foremen. The announcement illustrates the rhetoric of paternalism. The training program was instituted

in order to develop the skill and knowledge of our workers, to improve the quality of our products and the personalities of our workers, and to encourage educated and disciplined workers. . . . We believe that this action was undertaken out of devoted loyalty to our country and reverent affection for our workers. We thus expect that those who are chosen to attend this school will, with careful attention and mindful of the company's motivations, faithfully bear the above in mind and not falter for even one moment. (Gordon 1985: 61)

In contrast to the rosy view of paternalism and the "enterprise community" supposedly established in the interwar years, historical analyses such as Gordon (1985, 1998), Kume (1998), and Tsutsui (1998) show that labor-management relations in Japan were characterized by mutual distrust, antagonism, and weak commitment. Companies built stability on authoritarian control and the use of council-like organizations. In the 1950s and 1960s, firms introduced the "second" union that was to support the company line and resist the (first) trade union.[6] Managers spoke of their enterprises as communities or families, but before World War II blue-collar workers were not full members of these families. All companies had separate entrances for workers and managers, and the workers were subjected to body checks at the gate. "If the enterprise was a family," summarizes Gordon (1985: 254), "then

---

5. Yearly turnover rates of about 75 percent were the norm in most industries during World War I (Gordon 1985: 87).

6. For an excellent description of how a coalmining company formed a second union and broke up the first union during a 101-day strike, see Allen 1994: 166–69.

workers were servants using a separate entrance; if a community, workers were misfits liable to steal or cause trouble."

Paternalism and Workers' Quest for Dignity

In the discourse of Japanese-style management, the manager-employee relation reproduces traditional dyads such as the lord-vassal and the father-child. Even so, the emotionalism of Japanese-style management seems to have been articulated mainly through the voices of managers. What role did workers play in this dyad? How did workers receive managerial paternalism? So far, I have presented the workers as generally hostile to Japanese-style management. Many workers correctly perceived paternalism as a self-serving managerial ideology. Indeed, it was as a result of workers' struggles and labor-market problems that managers forged paternalistic welfare programs and seniority systems.

Another view regards workers as supportive of management paternalism. According to this view, Japanese-style management was made possible because Japanese workers seeking recognition and dignity appropriated the emotional discourse of paternalism to support their own interests. At the turn of the twentieth century, Japanese workers suffered from a stigma. Industrialization provided jobs but no status. Factory workers who "practiced new and little known skills in places full of dirt, noise and smell . . . were often new to the communities in which they lived . . . crowded together in slums with scavengers, pick-pockets, street entertainers, rickshaw men, carters, ditch cleaners, navvies, and the traditional outcast group, the *eta*" (T. Smith 1984: 591).

Strikes were "emotional" because they reflected workers' feelings of moral oppression. The Kure Naval shipyard strike in 1902 began, for example, when a new shipyard manager ordered workers to travel to and from work in their work clothes. The workers saw it as an "unfeeling measure which forced upon them the humiliation of walking through the streets in work clothes. . . . There were work-rule issues in the strike as well, but the worker manifesto in justifying the strike listed the clothing issue first" (T. Smith 1984: 595). Similar strikes were held not only by workers but also by engineers, whose status was low compared to that of management.[7] The engineers who shut down the Japan Railway Company's Tōhoku line in 1899 demanded equal treatment with "officials" (*yakuin*)—clerks and stationmasters. The engineers argued that they were entitled to honor and respect commensurate with their heavy responsibilities.

Workers depended on their company for status. Consequently, some of them bought into the managerial discourse of paternalism as a means of promoting their own interests. They appealed for self-definition by stressing their dependence on the employer. Labor disputes were articulated in petitions that appealed not to natural rights but to sympathy and a record of loyal service. The language of such petitions was "cannily honorific and full of implications of dependence and humility difficult to translate without parody" (T. Smith 1984: 596). It was also extremely emotional, as a section of a 1902 petition for higher wages at the Tokyo Arsenal reveals: "If out of extreme generosity and humanity you were graciously to adjust wage rates so as to restore our incomes [which had been reduced by inflation], that act of special favor would be a great good fortune to us. It would allay our worries and raise our spirit a hundredfold. . . . We pray for your consideration of this petition" (T. Smith 1984: 596).

Workers' quest for recognition, according to Thomas Smith, eventually found a concise articulation through the idiom of *jinkaku*, or character. In the 1910s, this Christian concept was widely adopted by workers despite an almost total lack of interest in Christianity. *Jinkaku* defined morality as an inner quality and could hence replace the external qualities of *hinkō* (refinement) and *hinsei* (breeding) that workers lacked. Uno Riemon's claim that "Japanese workers are more inclined to be moved by things spiritual" found expression in a 1914 letter, written by a worker: "I am only a poor worker looked down on

---

7. The low status of engineers is arguably also behind the dominance of emotionality in Japanese-style management. The antithesis of emotionality—the rational discourse of scientific management—was launched in the United States as a professional struggle to legitimate the knowledge claims of high-status civil engineers (see Shenhav 1999).

by society as rubbish. Yet I am a man who does not regard his life as his own. I am ready to give my life for my lord and country: like a train on a track, I will forever follow the way of righteousness (*seigi no michi*)" (quoted in T. Smith 1984: 607).

Paternalism and Scientific Management

The widespread articulation of the ideology of managerial paternalism in the 1910s and 1920s coincided with the introduction to Japan of Taylor's scientific management. How did these two protagonists of devotion and design, respectively, get along? According to Hazama's analysis, paternalism and Taylorism are antithetical, and scientific management never gained a foothold in Japan because of the culturally rooted emotionalism of the Japanese management system. Others, however, see paternalism and Taylorism as co-existing. In the first place, paternalism was most powerful (and most frequently used) as a rhetorical device rather than as a comprehensive managerial strategy. Because paternalism was a rhetorical facade, managers could appropriate Taylorism as a complementary, rather than a contradicting, praxis. Whereas paternalism prescribed no model of production management, scientific management paid little attention to welfare and cultural amenities. According to Tsutsui (1995, 1998), the two could hence join forces, paternalism as the *tatemae* (appearance) of managerial ideology and Taylorism as the *honne* (true reality) of the shop floor.

Scientific management was domesticated in Japan through the ideology of paternalism and the praxis of normative control. Tsutsui (1995: 71–72) illustrates this claim by quoting from the writing of Uno Riemon, one of the most dedicated theorists of *onjōshugi* in prewar Japan. The first epigraph to this chapter (p. 55) is representative of Uno's views. Although Uno denounced (what he perceived as) the materialistic premises of Taylorism, he admitted that scientific management (*gakuriteki kanrihō*) could very well "increase profits while elevating workers' income." Taylorism could thus complement paternalism, provided that it was used as part of the "warm treatment of labor." Moreover, Uno read spiritualism into scientific management, arguing that "importers of Taylorism misconstrue it as merely a scientific technique, a dry-as-dust intellectual framework. They are unable to grasp its true meaning, that the vitality of the system lies in its 'Mental Revolution'"[8] (quoted in Tsutsui 1995: 72; and in Hazama 1978: 186).

Tsutsui (1995: 72–75) further illustrates the interlocking of paternalism and Taylorism through the case of Suzuki Tsunesaburō and the Nikkō Electric Copper Smelting Company. Whereas Uno was a theorist, Suzuki was a manager, one of the early breed of Meiji managers, a graduate of Keiō University who had studied accounting at Harvard. In 1912 he was appointed head of the Nikkō smelter, a workplace with a history of labor problems. As head of the smelter, Suzuki's rhetoric was replete with paternalism. His essays (published under the revealing title *Labor Problems and Paternalism* [*Rōdō mondai to onjōshugi*], 1915) "dripped with praise for 'beautiful customs' and emotionalism, and were generous with scorn for Taylorism's cold and dehumanizing edge" (Tsutsui 1995: 73). Yet Suzuki's experience at Nikkō suggests a different story. Suzuki's factory, while promoting the usual welfare facilities of the time—such as rest areas and workplace beautification—was not the "warm," familial, cooperative, and group-oriented environment one would expect of a self-declared paternalistic plant.

Despite his criticism of Taylor, Suzuki adopted an incentive wage system at Nikkō and emphasized competition on the shop floor. In what might well be cast as the Japanese version of Taylor's infamous "Schmidt experiment," Suzuki is reputed to have gathered half of the haulers at the warehouse and offered to split the gains in productivity with them if they could double the amount they carried in one day. The group obliged, whereupon Suzuki fired the other haulers and distributed a portion of their wages to the more productive workers.

---

8. Taylor's "mental revolution" has received readings in addition to Uno's. Some organizational theorist-practitioners have argued that although Taylor concentrated on the physical aspects of the job, still he "did not neglect the human element, as is so often suggested, but stressed the individual and not the group side of man. . . . Taylor's synthesis came through his call for a 'mental revolution' which sought to fuse the interests of labor and management into a mutually rewarding whole" (Wren 1972: 146).

This pattern was repeated throughout the Nikkō plant (Tsutsui 1995: 75). Suzuki's success became legendary: within two years he had cut production costs by a third, halved the number of workers, and doubled the income of those who remained. Ironically, Nikkō became a model factory of paternalistic management and Suzuki one of the most celebrated proponents of paternalism in the 1910s and 1920s.

Suzuki's smelter was not an exception.[9] Kanebo, originally a textile company established more than 100 years ago during Japan's early modernization, was experiencing labor trouble at the turn of the twentieth century. As was common in the Japanese textile industry at that time, Kanebo had a high labor turnover rate (around 70 percent); women workers from rural areas worked on a short-term basis to assist their households and then returned home. Mutō Sanji, president of Kanebo, developed special management techniques to counter this situation. Muto introduced a company-wide welfare system, including health insurance, a "suggestion box" system, a house newsletter, and an honor system. These early practices were accompanied by an adaptation of Taylor's standard motion and efficiency measurements. Muto therefore created a "spiritualistic, family-style management that was coupled with the scientific management systems" (Fujimori and Ouchi 1996: 36).

On a national level, scientific management was promoted through an industrial research center (Sangyō nōritsu kenkyūjo), established in the early 1930s by Kyōchōkai (Cooperation society), a joint research organization of government and business. The center was headed by Ueno Yōichi, another person who, like Suzuki, exemplifies the adaptation of Taylorist rationalization into Japanese emotionalism. Ueno was a graduate of Tokyo University in psychology and had been working on applications of scientific management (on Ueno, see Saitō

---

9. Additional examples of the implementation of scientific management in prewar Japan include Sumitomo (Nakase 1993), Mitsubishi and Shibaura Manufacturing (Sasaki Satoshi 1992; Levine & Kawada 1980), and Japan National Railways (Daitō 1989). For more examples of how prewar managers implemented scientific management while mouthing paternalistic platitudes, see Okuda 1985: 349–61.

1984; and Greenwood & Ross 1982). As a psychologist, Ueno is said to have cast Taylorism in a "human relations" rather than an "engineering" mode (Kinzley 1991: 103).

The Japan National Railways, famous for its cult of familialism, was also among the most systematic users of scientific management methods in prewar Japan. Tsutsui (1995: 75) cites the following 1930 labor broadside as an excellent illustration of workers' recognition of management hypocrisy:

Brothers at the Ōmiya works!
How are your wretched lives these days?
It's intolerable that we can be driven 'til we drop by motion study, made to work for nothing by rate-cutting and threatened with being fired if we complain.
Oh paternalism (onjōshugi)! Oh familialism (kazokushugi)! We hear about them all the time but when have they actually improved our lives? It's all just a swindle that the management—which is afraid of our resistance—keeps pulling to make us obedient and really squeeze us!
Down with motion study! Down with rate cutting!

Paternalism, therefore, was used to construct a rhetorical facade of emotional benevolence. As an ideology, paternalism was presented as Japan's cultural solution to labor-management adversity; it made labor laws unnecessary and even potentially dangerous. Some workers bought into this ideology and used it to gain an occupational status that was tied to their company rather than to an abstract, democratic notion of natural rights. This historical background is important in defying culturalist stereotypes. Japanese-style management, however, was not design in the guise of devotion. It may not have been devotion, but neither was it all design.

Paternalism in Postwar Workplace Culture

Several American studies of Japan's industrial relations made after World War II were instrumental in propagating the image of paternalism. John Bennet and Ishino Iwao (1963) suggest that Americans in

the Supreme Command for the Allied Powers (the central Tokyo bureaucracy of the Occupation, headed by General Douglas MacArthur)
had difficulty determining who had responsibility in Japanese organizations. Paternalism, and its generalized pattern of *oyabun-kobun*,
served to explain and interpret the "unique" Japanese to their occupi-
ers.[10] According to this conception, the *oyabun* (the boss, also "parent")
assumes obligations toward his subordinate *kobun* (worker, also
"child"); in turn, the subordinate is loyal and dutiful to his superior. In
workplace culture, the labor boss and the foreman are prominent instances of the *oyabun* role.

The "labor boss system" is a method of recruitment in which the
oyabun is a labor recruiter, a "straw boss," and sometimes a teacher of
occupational skills. This system had several characteristics that Occupation analysts regarded as undemocratic, such as the prevention of
collective bargaining and the legal exercise of civil rights and the boss's
confiscation of a percentage of the worker's pay. After the Labor
Standards Law and the Employment Security Law were promulgated
in 1947, a new system of public employment replaced the labor bosses.
A decade later, labor bosses had officially disappeared from Japanese
factories (see Cole 1971). Consequently, blue-collar workers have
gradually abandoned the term *oyabun-kobun*, which was not in the
spirit of postwar democratization and unionization.

The labor boss system persists, however, in industries with large
numbers of unskilled workers and no permanent labor force. Labor
bosses play a major role in contemporary day-laborer communities in
Tokyo, such as construction workers who get their jobs off the street.
Gathering places for casual laborers (*yoseba*) provide a cheap workforce for Tokyo's construction firms, allowing big companies (such as
Kajima-kensetsu, Kumagai-gumi, or Shimizu-kensetsu) to reduce
costs by keeping many workers off their payrolls. The *yoseba*, which

---

10. Bennet and Ishino worked for the Supreme Command for the Allied Powers at the
time of their research, as part of the Public Opinion and Sociological Research Division, Civil
Information and Education Section.

typically have an unemployment rate of 50 percent, are to a large extent controlled by labor bosses, who operate as labor brokers and subsubcontractors (see Fowler 1996; Imagawa 1987).

Under the labor boss, the work group (*kumi*) is a close-knit social unit. Formal initiation rites are still sometimes used by *oyabun* to promote group solidarity. The formal initiation ceremony used to include two parts. In the first part, an "oath taking" in front of witnesses symbolized the initiation of the new recruit, who sometimes received a new given name. The second part included the traditional exchange of *sake* cups. These rites have gradually been abandoned by modern-day, foreman-led work groups in Japanese industries, who might mark the "initiation" of a new member by a night at the *karaoke* bar. Similar rites for similar purposes nevertheless persist in groups in which the *oyabun-kobun* structure is strictly maintained as part of the organizational legacy, such as the *yakuza* (organized crime syndicates). The traditional rites of initiation and termination persist in such groups as long as "job security" is provided by the group leader on a personal basis. In such primary groups, recruits are "born" into the group, and the employer gives the members' wages to the boss, who distributes them. As work groups on the shop floor became more bureaucratically organized, they abandoned such formalized *oyakata* practices.

Nevertheless, Japanese work groups still exhibit a far greater sense of solidarity and cooperation between workers and the group leader than do comparable groups in the United States. For example, many Japanese workers view group relationships as based on democratic consultation; the American image of the "arbitrary foreman" is almost unknown. Japanese workers generally regard foremen as co-workers and not management representatives. Support for this generalization comes both from ethnographic studies conducted on the shop floor (e.g., Cole 1971: 186–88) and from large-scale comparative attitude surveys. Interestingly, "democratic consultation" exists side by side with paternalism. Foremen might, for example, counsel group members about personal matters. For recruits from distant prefectures, the foreman is a particularly important figure who serves *in loco parentis*.[11]

Foremen played an interesting part in the formation of the "second," company-based unions in the postwar period. Supervisors had a key role in building a union dedicated to cooperation with the company. Management expected line supervisors to nurture workers' "enterprise consciousness." In the 1960s, most group leaders served as both local union officers and supervisors, and in this dual role they were an important node in labor-management relations. This dual role was later manifested in the supervisors' involvement in quality control. During the 1960s, supervisors were encouraged by engineering staffs to organize "self-inspection" teams that monitored quality, for example, in the steel industry (Gordon 1998: 168). These teams later evolved into quality control circles.

Paternalism was an organizational package of ideologies and practices that was enacted in workplace culture within such dyads as the management-union or the foreman-worker. The workers in this context are all regular employees, unionized, and overwhelmingly male. As a dyadic practice, paternalism evidently requires the cooperation of employees. Indeed, both company-based unions and regular workers (not to mention management) have a vested interest in paternalism.

For regular white- and blue-collar employees, the obvious benefits of paternalism include permanent employment and various welfare plans. Western observers of this Japanese organizational culture often question its value for the company and argue that a worker with guaranteed tenure has less motivation to work hard. Some observers argue, however, that even with tenure, worker motivation is maintained through periodical appraisals that determine promotion and through

---

11. The line supervisor is an important substitute parent, but not the only one. Personnel managers, for example, may pay money (often out of their pocket) to help workers out with funerals and weddings. Indeed, most personnel staff members, except the head, are unionized and take the workers' side in negotiations with the accounting department over wages and bonuses. This is quite in contrast to the strong identification of the personnel department in the United States with management (see also Cole 1971: 177).

performance-linked pay systems. This argument is indeed relevant to the reality of the Japanese seniority system.

From the perspective of emotion management, regular workers should also be seen as participants in a particular cultural performance. It is precisely because they anticipate permanent employment that they want to make a good future for themselves. Because much of the worker's social life revolves around the company, he naturally wants to make the best of it, which for Japanese workers means being accepted and respected, not just being promoted or better paid. Furthermore, the culturally accepted view that it is desirable to spend one's entire career in one company also promotes worker investment in a long-term relationship.

To sum up, economic and culturalist explanations of the relatively high motivation of the regular Japanese worker are complementary. Paternalism, as an emotionally laden culturalist explanation, is complemented rather than opposed by an economic explanation that highlights the long-range cost-benefit calculations attributed to the Japanese worker.[12] In a similar manner, paternalism is both a culturally conditioned choice and an instrument of management. Perhaps it is this unique marriage of economic and culturalist reasoning that has made Japanese-style management so prominent.

The next question is why and how Japanese unions, particularly the militant postwar unions, were "tamed" by management. This question has received different answers from many scholars. Following the typology suggested in the preceding chapter, these answers can be divided into three categories: devotion, design, and defiance. According to Kawanishi Hirosuke (1992: 128–32), the first paradigm for the study of the enterprise union focuses on cultural explanations that see the *ie* (traditional Japanese household) as the foundation of the company. Hazama Hiroshi (1964) is presented as the most serious (academically speaking) proponent of this approach (subsumed here under devotion). Even though Hazama did not write specifically about the formation of enterprise unions, his research implies that pa-

---

12. Interview with Koike Kazuo, June 3, 2000.

ternalist management (Japanese-style management) could facilitate
the emergence of a strong employee sense of identity with the firm;
this would promote company unionism and discourage trade (class-
based) unionism. For Kawanishi, this approach is the "mainstream" in
Japan, despite (or maybe because of) its "non-academic orientation."
Kawanishi calls the second paradigm the "labor economy" view. This
is the "internal labor markets" approach of scholars such as Ōkōchi
Kazuo (1972), who emphasized the "migrant wage laborer," and Shirai
Taishirō (1979), Taira Kōji (1977), and Koike Kazuo (1988), who
pointed to more universal aspects of the labor market in capitalist societies. This approach can be subsumed under the design rubric. Finally, a third paradigm (defiance) is presented under the title "power
relations in labor-management relations." This approach is valuable,
in Kawanishi's eyes, as a "micro-political" perspective that can explain
how or why the enterprise union was established at a given firm.

Enterprise Unionism Today: Alternative Forms, Same Emotions?

The stylized model of the Japanese management system is a package
deal of lifetime employment, the seniority system, and enterprise
unionism. This combination led to a strategic internalization of human resources. Since firms could count on a relatively long-term
commitment from employees, they could safely invest in human
capital formation, "in-house education," recruitment of new graduates,
and promotion from within. In reality, however, this strategy was limited only to the core or regular employees within large firms. These
core employees were protected by a legal framework and by their enterprise union. Such strong protection was never extended to
contingent employees. The demarcation between the two was much
clearer in Japan than in other countries, including the United States.

In the past decade, both Japan and the United States have experienced an increase in contingent employees. This term encompasses
various categories such as part-time workers, casual workers, and

workers dispatched by temporary employment agencies. The common theme that unites the individuals in these diverse categories is that they have no expectations of long-term employment, receive little or no fringe benefits, are excluded from the enterprise union, and occupy a position secondary to the regular employees. Estimates of the number of contingent workers vary since there is no accepted definition of the category. Susan Houseman (1997) estimates that 31 percent of the U.S. labor force were non-regular in 1997. Non-regular workers accounted in 1997 for about 23 percent of the labor force in Japan (Japan Institute of Labor 2000). Part-timers, the largest category among non-regular workers (13.7 percent), consisted mainly of housewives working in three industries: retail, food, and services. The increase in the numbers of contingent workers is therefore part of the process of post-industrialization or the turn from secondary to tertiary industries. As companies combine the use of regular and non-regular workers to reduce personnel costs and handle specialized tasks, the hiring of more contingent workers is likely to increase.

The growth in contingent employees may bring a change in the social contract in the workplace. As more and more such employees join the labor market, sometimes taking the place of regular workers, the periphery threatens the dominance of the core. For example, Japanese human resource management systems have relied heavily on the workplace morale and the commitment of employees to the firm. As measured in many attitude surveys,[13] it was quantitative proof of the emotional element of Japanese-style management. Can we predict the impact of the increased use of contingent employees on the emotions of regular employees?

A survey conducted in 1998 by the Joint Labor-Management Commission at the Japan Productivity Center for Socio-economic Development (1999; see also Morishima & Feuille 2000) analyzed that

---

13. Ham (1991) found that commitment levels were generally lower among part-time workers than among regular employees. Lincoln and Kalleberg (1990) showed that the morale and commitment of regular Japanese employees were higher than those of regular American employees.

impact. The survey identified three categories of companies on the basis of their human resource strategy: flexible, traditional, and separation employers. Firms in the flexible employer category were hiring contingent and mid-career employees to staff regular positions. A surprising finding was that such firms constituted the largest proportion (almost 40 percent) in the sample. Firms in the traditional employers category (about 36 percent of the sample) maintain strong internal labor markets. They emphasize the traditional practices of Japanese-style management, keep the number of contingent workers to a minimum, and separate the work allocated to these two groups. The third category of separation employers (about 24 percent) uses regular employees to fill core positions but is increasing the proportion of contingent workers, who are assigned to separate types of work.

The survey found that regular workers in firms classified as traditional employers have the most negative attitudes toward the increased use of contingent workers. In firms that emphasize the internalization of human resources, the increase in contingent workers is undermining the morale and the trust of regular employees. They apparently are not buying management's argument that the increased use of such workers will create a "buffer" area that will protect their employment. Rather, they interpret the increase as a threat to the traditional relations of trust and benevolent paternalism. This negative interpretation is particularly strong among regular employees in firms that traditionally kept their use of non-regular workers to a minimum.

It is a little difficult to differentiate fully between traditional and separation employers. Separation is, after all, the traditional style of Japanese firms. The basic difference between traditional and separation employers is that traditional employers are increasing (or at least maintaining) the proportion of regular employees and separation employers are increasing the proportion of contingent workers. For the employees of traditional firms, the presence of contingent workers in the workforce is a violation of the "psychological contract."[14] In tradi-

---

14. Personal communication with Professor Morishima Motohiro, July 17, 2000.

tional firms, the increased use of contingents is a major change; in contrast, the "separation" employers have a history of hiring contingents. As all organizational analysts will affirm, workers are generally suspicious of change.

In separation firms that are increasing the proportion of contingent workers but still distinguish the two types of workers, the increase in contingent workers does not violate the psychological contract of the protected core workers. In these firms, no significant relationships were observed between the increased use of contingent workers and the attitudes of regular employees. The small but protected core of regular workers remains part of the internal labor market apart from contingent workers. Their morale and their trust in the firm are consequently unaffected by the increased use of contingent workers. Finally, in firms employing the flexible strategy, the relationships between the increased use of contingent workers and the attitudes of regular employees were negative, but not significantly so. Perhaps in these firms, regular employees already had lower expectations.

The remainder of the chapter discusses two contemporary alternatives, at least in theory if not in practice, to enterprise unionism. The first is represented by the National Union of General Workers (NUGW), a Japanese union mainly for non-regular workers that cuts across company lines. NUGW illustrates an alternative, American-style unionization existing alongside (and in conflict with) traditional Japanese company-based unions. The second alternative is co-partnership management, a German-inspired managerial philosophy that does away with unionization.

The National Union of General Workers

Despite the declines in membership that unions in Japan have been experiencing, traditional labor movements seldom target contingent workers. More than half of the unions sampled by Salmon et al. (2000), for example, reported no attempt to enroll women, temporary,

74 Emotional Genesis

fixed-term or agency workers, which have been among the fastest-growing employment sectors in Japan.[15]

The NUGW was organized at the Fifth Annual Congress of the General Council of Trade Unions of Japan (Sōhyō) in 1954. From its start, the NUGW has concentrated on small and minor enterprises, since many of the workers in such firms are not organized. Its membership rose from 40,000 in 1955 to 140,000 in 1978, but it then underwent a gradual decline, which coincided with the general trend in union membership. In 1988 the NUGW joined the unified union confederation Rengō but later broke from it. In 1999, the NUGW had about 50,000 registered members organized in some 1,500 branches (in comparison, Rengō currently has about 7.5 million members). Most of the branches are in small firms, 70 percent of which have fewer than 100 employees. Sixty-five percent of the members are male, and 35 percent are female. Not surprisingly, the NUGW organizing strategy is particularly attractive to workers in volatile, small businesses characterized by unstable employment.[16]

The NUGW has a unique style of action in Japanese terms. In 1981, the union opened a telephone consultation system to help part-time workers in distress. In 1984 it opened another line to respond to questions and recommend job opportunities. The emphasis is on individual workers rather than workers as a group. There is a onetime consultation charge of ¥1,500 (about $14) for these services, and the union expects that many of those who contact the service will become members.

In addition to consulting and representing workers, the NUGW also operates a mutual aid society whose activities include gifts of

15. An exception is Zensen, a mainstream union, which has been trying to organize part-time workers (Kuwahara 2000).

16. The NUGW is also the parent organization of two interesting small unions, the Managers Union and Network Union Tokyo. The former concentrates on organizing middle managers who were laid off because of restructurings, downsizings, or bankruptcies. Since 1993, membership dues have automatically been deducted from these ex-managers' postal savings accounts and remitted to the union. In 1995, the union had more than 300 members. The Network Union Tokyo focuses on rank-and-file workers, organized mostly through consultation services over the telephone ("special hot lines") and the Internet.

money for weddings and funerals, loans for housing, credit sales, life insurance, pension plans, and so on. For a monthly membership fee of ¥300 (about $3), the society guarantees services from "wedding to funeral." According to the society's brochure for 2000, it is natural for an organized worker to "have a consciousness of being a member of the working class" and thus "to think of his colleagues' joy and sorrow." The unorganized, non-regular worker is therefore encouraged to become organized in order to develop this consciousness. Workers are advised to let the mutual aid society help them take their future in their hands. In 1999 the NUGW opened a homepage for its "cyber union"; general workers can now register online and receive help and advice. The cyber union was declared "a return to the origins of the labor movement with the help of modern communication." Interestingly, the rhetoric presented the cyber union as "open," "common," and "free." This contrasts with the "closed," "insider" society of regular employees and enterprise unionism, as seen from the NUGW point of view.

The NUGW is interesting because it is exceptional. In Japan, where over 90 percent of the labor unions consist of enterprise-based unions and their industrial federations (Japan Institute of Labor 2000: 41), a general union is something of an anomaly. NUGW is a union designed for the unorganized, non-regular worker who does not belong to the firm-as-family. As an outsider, however, the NUGW actually emphasizes the system. From the point-of-view of the NUGW, Japanese-style management (paternalistic management, the firm-as-family) is very real. The emotional discourse of Japanese-style management is for the NUGW not a rhetorical facade but the wall between "them" (regulars) and "us" (non-regulars).

What sort of emotions does this situation of otherness breed? The NUGW's discourse lacks all the characteristic elements of Japanese-style management, such as trust, love of the company, benevolent paternalism, or group harmony. These elements have been appropriated completely by Japanese-style management for its management-labor dyad. In contrast, the NUGW describes itself in rational, civil-rights terms, rather than through emotions. Instead of "trust," the NUGW invokes "mutual aid." Loyalty to the company is replaced by class consciousness. The NUGW is very American, almost Marxist-oriented. I am not implying that the enterprise-based union lacks rationality and pragmatism or never opposes management. However, the way in which the two types of unions present themselves is quite different.

The NUGW also has its share of emotions. Feelings verging on desolation and despair were vividly expressed by NUGW representatives in a session held at the annual congress of the International Industrial Relations Association (co-organized by the Japan Institute of Labor) in May 2000. Kusajima Manao, a representative of the Tokyo branch, lamented that the situation of NUGW members is tough, with no prospects for bargaining. Employers do not approach the NUGW directly. When union representatives seek to talk with employers, the latter become unavailable. "If we let management know we're coming in advance, they put us off. But when we come without advance notice, they say they don't have time." The gradual decrease in NUGW membership was explained as part of the general decrease in unionization rates (from 35 percent in 1975 to about 20 percent in 1999; see Japan Institute of Labor 2000). This decrease is usually explained as a result of the increase in the number of unorganized, contingent workers. Yet it is precisely these workers that the NUGW targets. No one in the NUGW had an explanation for this conundrum.

The NUGW finds much of its inspiration in American labor union activity. In the United States, the unionization rate has also declined: from 39 percent in 1954 to 10 percent today. Unions associated with the American Federation of Labor (AFL) currently have about thirteen million members, including over five million women (Clawson & Clawson 1999). A strategy of union enlargement (Wever 1998) has been an important feature of recent organizing activity in the United States. Much of this has been directed at female and minority ethnic workers in relatively low-paid service industries. Contingent workers who face lower wages, job insecurity, and few if any benefits are helped by the labor union as well as by independent labor agencies. Usually an industry union is involved, as, for example, in the construction industry, where contingent work is common. Another interesting example is the high-tech industry, where temporary workers are also common. Nonprofit agencies and labor councils for temporary workers are now common in the Silicon Valley. In the summer of 1997, teamsters shut down the UPS parcel-delivery service over the issue of part-time work and won thousands of full-time jobs for part-timers. These stories were told in the NUGW session of the International Industrial Relations Association congress by an invited guest speaker from the United States. Meant to inspire, the stories nevertheless also threw into relief the relative disadvantage of the NUGW.

Co-partnership Management

During World War II and in the 1950s, German companies practiced a system of cooperation among directors, managers, and workers called "co-partnership management." The two general financial features of co-partnership management were profit sharing and co-ownership of company assets. The social aspects of the concept included the cultivation of human relations, communication, and co-determination (the involvement of workers in company decision making). Japanese companies became interested in the idea of co-partnership management in the late 1950s. In Japan, as in Germany, it is predominantly medium-sized companies that have implemented a version of co-partnership management. This is probably because in large companies the union is too strong, and in small businesses there is usually no need for the formalities of management-labor partnership. The Japanese version of co-partnership has highlighted the social aspects of the concept while downplaying the original financial features. Great importance is attached to a formal signing of a co-partnership contract between the company and employees, the issuing of a co-partnership certificate to every employee, and the formation of a co-partnership committee.[17]

---

17. The description of German co-partnership management is based on Gaugler 2000. The analysis of the three examples is based on Toyama 2000, Ogawa 2000, and Abe 2000,

Ibaraki mokuzai sōgōichiba, a wholesale retailer of timber from Ibaragi prefecture, was established in 1955 and currently employs 46 regular employees and two part-timers. The workers are not unionized. Shareholders include the directors (30 percent), employees (8 percent), retired employees (8 percent), and customers and others (54 percent). In 1968 the company instituted "co-partnership management." Starting in 1977, it began sending employees to the Japan Institute for Co-Partnership (established in 1964) for training. In an article entitled "Running a Company and Human Beings," published in the magazine of the Japanese Personality Psychology Research Association (1994, 1: 12), company president Ōsuga Hatsuzō explains that before the initiation of co-partnership management in 1968, the company suffered from feelings of deep distrust, conflict and competition among factions, and confusion among employees. In 1962, seven years after the firm was established, the discovery of a vast amount of unaccounted expenditures by some employees caused serious unrest. The directors concluded that distrust had caused an extreme deterioration of employee morale and had led to the peculation. Some of the loss was covered by a cash payment from the directors; the employees involved received only an admonition.

The directors decided to enhance the confidence of employees by implementing the method of "employee counseling" (started in the United States in the 1940s by the human relations school). Co-partnership management was integrated, in 1964, with counseling. According to the president, the company's new attitude of valuing human dignity made employees feel confident, and they started to express capabilities that had been suppressed. On May 17, 1968, the management and employees of Ibaraki mokuzai sōgōichiba signed a Declaration of Co-partnership. At the core of the declaration were four statements:

Dialogue together (two-way communication)

---

supplemented by discussions with the presenters and by materials published by Nikkeiren on co-partnership management in Japan.

Notice together (empathy and responsiveness)
Decide together (co-decision and responsibility)
Act together (motivated and enlightened activities)

The Ibaraki mokuzai sōgōichiba story, as told by the president, represents an emotional epiphany. A period of distrust, seen as the root of all evil, eventually culminated in a "vast amount of unaccounted expenditures by some employees." In other words, the problem of the company was a case of bad emotions at work. The logical solution, or denouement, is hence also emotional, namely, regaining the trust of employees. This was achieved, first, through the benevolent responsibility expressed by the directors (who made up the unaccounted expenditures out of their own pockets) and then through the implementation of the trust-building practices of employee counseling and, later, co-partnership management. The story shows that trust and mutual responsibility are not necessarily bound to the discourse of enterprise unionism. Rather, they can be appropriated just as well by a management that seeks to establish normative control of its employees while keeping labor unions out.

Addressing the philosophy of work that characterizes Ibaraki mokuzai, Managing Director Toyama Takeshi characterized the organization as "an important place for the people to live until death" (2000: 9). Furthermore, "the purpose of business is not simply to achieve a profit, but it is to be found in its very existence as a community of persons . . . where members establish their identity in maintaining harmony with the whole" (2000: 9–10). All the rhetorical baggage of enterprise unionism is here, with one difference: there is no union. Bonuses and profit sharing are treated as part of the employee's salary. No bonuses have been paid since 1990, and in 1998, employees' salaries were reduced by 10 percent because of the general economic stagnation. This was also done "on the basis of understanding and the trust of employees."

The emotional discourse of "co-partnership management" covers several examples of seeming exploitation. For example, in the "employee deposit system," money "voluntarily" deposited by employees

becomes an interest-earning company's asset that is "enormously important for the liquidity of the company and cannot be ignored" (Toyama 2000: 13). Despite much talk about co-ownership, the employees' share is limited to 15 percent. Furthermore, only employees with
more than five years of seniority are allowed to be shareholders. Finally, employees are not guaranteed lifetime employment, and any
form of organization outside the co-partnership arrangement is discouraged. In the words of Managing Director Toyama, "We want
workers to be usable for the company but at the same time we want to
guarantee their stability."

Mitsuwa Corporation is a Tokyo-based producer, retailer, and ca-
terer of noodle and rice products. The firm is an example of the diver-
sification of the labor market; it has 305 regular employees, 247 semi-
regular employees, 201 fixed-term employees, 81 contractors, 38 casual
employees, and 15 contract employees (for a total of 887, as of March 1,
2000). It is a medium-scale company with five divisions, two factories,
and about 100 stores in Japan, some of them in an independent chain
run by employees. In 1976, Mitsuwa introduced co-partnership management. Ogawa Masamoto, chairman of the company, explained that
the shift to co-partnership management came about when he realized
that the "apprentice system" in the shop was "wrong in terms of human relations."

The process was not without problems. As the company grew and
many general employees joined it, they misunderstood the concept of
co-partnership management, "taking only the comfortable side of it
(respect of human beings) without being responsible and accountable"
(Ogawa 2000: 6). In the words of the chairman, "everyone became
buddies and thought they could participate anyway." In an attempt to
correct this, management opened the "Mitsuwa Academy" to teach
employees the ways of co-partnership management. According to the
chairman, the academy is a kind of an "ethics center" (see Kondo 1990)
in which workers undergo self-development in the traditional merchant spirit (*shōnindō*). This ethics of work implies that self-
development can take place only within the framework of organiza-

tional development and that "meaningful work" means a "meaningful life." The academy provides training in "speaking together (two-way communication), feeling together (co-responsiveness), deciding together (co-decision), and taking responsibility together (co-responsibility)" (Ogawa 2000: 8). Interestingly, one of the rules of co-partnership developed in the company is "self-training," which stresses that all partners (i.e., employees) should endeavor to build character and to achieve self-development and self-discipline so that they will become "attractive members of the company" (Ogawa 2000: 9). Self-training is evidently a hallmark of normative control, an institutionalized form of self-inspection.

Mitsuwa, like Ibaraki mokuzai, uses the co-ownership principle to capitalize on workers' money to a certain extent; 70 percent of bonuses, for example, are retained in the company as employee "deposits." If the company's capital increases, workers can convert this money into stocks and become shareholders. To further encourage trust-based relationships on the shop floor, the company emphasizes autonomous group activity at all levels. The "tyranny of the team ideology" (Sinclair 1992) is in full swing here. The company motivates its employees with performance bonuses, measured by each employee's achievement of company-set targets.

The last example, the Shinano Pollution Laboratory, is a small-scale high-tech company established in 1972. In 2000, it had 39 employees (25 males, 14 females), including two workers from a temporary agency. The company assesses water, air, and noise pollution as well as offensive odors in the workplace. In 1996, the company began introducing co-partnership management. Once again, the motto for this project was emotional: "creating an environment within the company where mutual trust prevails among all stakeholders" (Abe 2000). Ongoing supplementary changes in management include a system for information sharing, fair distribution of gains, and co-determination. Yet like Mitsuwa and Ibaraki mokuzai, Shinano employs a predominantly emotional discourse to sell co-partnership management and downplays the fact that this is the only option offered employees.

Both trade unionism and enterprise unionism are forbidden. In fact, co-partnership replaces enterprise unionism by establishing an independent "locale" for labor-management relations within the company. This probably explains the support that co-partnership management has received from Nikkeiren (the National Federation of Employers). Japanese employers have found in co-partnership management a way of paying lip service to emotionalism without having to bargain with a union.[18]

As these alternative forms of labor-management relations demonstrate, industrial relations in Japan are becoming less homogeneous, but the emotional discourse of the once-prominent Japanese-style management still serves as a template or a reference point. I now turn from managerial systems and ideologies to the implementation of organizational practices within small groups and circles on the shop floor.

---

18. Co-partnership management is similar in principle to Japanese-style management and enterprise unionism. Their emotional discourses reflect and emphasize that similarity. Co-partnership management was also tried by a much larger and more traditional Japanese company, Kanebo. Kanebo managers have historically promoted the company union. After the war, as the textile industry underwent a series of recessions, Kanebo did not lay off employees and remained loyal to its motto of "humanitarian love and justice" (Fujimori & Ouchi 1996: 37). In the 1970s, a form of co-partnership management was added to the existing labor-management arrangement. The dissolution of Kanebo's enterprise union into a form of co-partnership management shows that large Japanese companies, with their strong enterprise union, in fact resemble employee-managed firms. Enterprise unions are not necessarily the representatives of employee interests, because the activities of employee-managed firms usually supersede the functions of labor unions. When employees and managers share core areas of management, labor unions with a confrontational attitude lose their reason for existence or are forced to change (see also Kuwahara 2000).

CHAPTER THREE
Normative Control in Blue-Collar Workplace Cultures

I. QUALITY CIRCLES AS A MECHANISM
OF NORMATIVE CONTROL

The concept of quality control circles (QCCs) has an interesting genealogy. QCCs are thought to promote workers' participation in company decision making, and managers have sold them to workers, unions, and the public as the most democratic form of personnel management. In reality, however, the true justification for QCCs has been their potential for increasing productivity and morale and reducing costs, grievances, and resistance to change. Employee participation is to be encouraged, and its outcomes implemented, only as long as they promote the goals of the company.

Japanese companies began organizing shop-floor workers into QCCs in the 1960s. By the late 1970s, some 50 percent of Japanese firms with more than 30 employees were practicing small-group activities. QCCs were the most popular form of these (Cole 1985). In 1994, according to Kumazawa Makoto (1996: 87), 162 enterprises in the steel industry reported a total of 19,000 circles, with 113,000 participants. Although workers' participation in small-group activities might seem to be a human relations practice, the design of QCCs owes much to statistical research. Their development is therefore an interesting illustration of the recurrent interlocking of design and devotion in the workplace.[1] QCCs illustrate the blurring not only of the rational and the emotional but also of the global and the local. Quality control was a major theme in the management seminars conducted by the American Occupation Forces for top Japanese businessmen in 1949–50. Local proponents of quality control included the American-inspired Japan Productivity Center, the Japanese Union of Civil Engineers, and the Japan Federation of Employers' Associations (Nikkeiren).[2]

To become a small-group activity, total quality control had to be extended from the specialized professional staff to both management and the production line, from statisticians and engineers upward to executives, across to middle managers, and downward to shop-floor supervisors and workers. This process began in the late 1950s and early 1960s and entailed a redefinition of methodology as well as a strategy for promoting total quality control. Inspired by the writings of Armand Feigenbaum, who probably coined the term "total quality control" (see Feigenbaum 1961), Japanese managers again utilized emotionalist rhetoric to argue that quality control required the cooperation and understanding of all members of the organization.

As had the advocates of paternalism, the proponents of total quality control mouthed feeling rules (cooperation and participation in the promotion of the "quality spirit") while implementing Taylorist prem-

---

1. Rather than using small groups for straightforward work-study, Japanese employers often relied on them to introduce Taylorism (Warner 1994: 519). Such small-group activity was already apparent in the prewar years, for example, in the Japanese National Railways, and can be regarded as a precursor of QCCs.

2. In Japan, quality control is widely associated with W. Edward Deming, the American statistician and management consultant. Deming began teaching and working with the Japanese Union of Civil Engineers in 1950, but only in the 1980s was his role "discovered" by the American media. He was hailed as "the American who single-handedly taught the Japanese all they know about quality," "the Commodore Perry of Management," and the "mascot" and "talisman" of the Japanese quality control movement (Tsutsui 1995: 262). Although Deming's lectures certainly stimulated a broad interest in quality control at a crucial time, quality control would not have conquered Japan without the involvement of the Japanese Union of Civil Engineers. For an inside account, see Ishikawa 1985.

ises (the appropriation of craft knowledge) and rational modes of operation (statistical research design). Moreover, as small-group activities, QCCs were mechanisms (rather than merely ideologies) of normative control. Workers were expected to join in QCCs not because they were paid to do so (on the contrary, in Japan QCCs meet before or after one's work shift) but because they should "participate." The circle concept was an unprovocative means of injecting quality control thought into workplace culture.

As long as the quality control movement remained the province of experts, it encountered "American-style" resistance and antagonism from workers. Experienced workers resisted what they regarded as the coerced imposition of complex and esoteric knowledge unrelated to their work. The Japanese solution was to decentralize the quality control movement by training foremen in quality control techniques and then sending them to the shop floor to spread the word and organize circle meetings. "Quality control" was transformed into "quality circles" and centralized Taylorism (design) was domesticated into Japanese-style management (devotion). The choice of "circles" as the primary mechanism for this transformation was not coincidental. In the 1950s and the 1960s workers developed a workplace recreation culture of "circles" (*sākuru*)—clubs for such leisure activities as singing, music appreciation, movies, reading, and sports. These circles, although outside direct union jurisdiction because they are defined as voluntary small-group activities, were union-supported. By enlisting the union's support for total quality control and using circles for bottom-up implementation, management took advantage of an existing structure of workplace culture and modified it for its new purposes.[3]

A QCC typically meets one hour a week and consists of a small group of production or clerical workers. Workers are taught elementary statistical techniques and are guided by their leaders (usually foremen or line supervisors) in selecting and solving job-related quality problems and improving methods of production. As mechanisms of normative control, QCCs promote personal responsibility, evalua-

---

3. See Gordon 1998: chap. 8.

tion of workers, and education of foremen. These three goals of QCCs are founded, respectively, on three processes of indirect managerial control: normalization, surveillance, and selection.

In the introduction to the translation of Kamata Satoshi's account of Toyota's assembly line, Ronald Dore (in Kamata 1982: xv–xvi) describes a "show and tell" presentation by M., a subforeman and the leader of his QCC at Toyota. This account captures the normative control inherent in QCC activity.

M. was a team chief and a leader of a group of nine workers, one of 44 into which the 370 employees of the power department were divided. He had been leading the group for five years. The group was known as the Hotto-manzu (Hot Man's) group. Its basic spirit was to emphasize harmony and cooperation. The four pillars of the house of improvement were cooperation, initiative, harmony, and work satisfaction. They held meetings twice a month, but things did not go very well in the initial stage, which M. called the "groping in disorderly darkness period." A lot did not come to the meetings. There was a tendency for a few to monopolize the discussion. Too much depended on the leader. Too many had the attitude: "Tell me what to do and I'll do it."

M. decided that some stimulus was needed. He proposed that they should set themselves the objective of winning a prize for group achievements. There was opposition on the grounds that this was not a production department. M. convinced them that even in the boiler house improvements were possible. They actually did get a prize for a project to improve the efficiency of an electric furnace. But there were still too many reluctant passengers, people who thought they were just being too obedient to orders from above. Here M. decided that new methods were necessary. He got engineers to come to advise on technical matters. At one stage he declared a three-month moratorium on meetings so that they could start again with fresh enthusiasm.

He rated the contributions of his group members under various headings: speaking, reporting back, doing the summary work for reporting, cooperativeness, attendance, contribution to solving problems, etc. He studied the personalities of the members of his group to see how they could be better integrated into a harmonious team. He introduced the habit of shouting "good morning" the first thing on entering the shop in a firm, loud, positive, and enthusiastic voice until even the misanthropes were forced to respond. And so it went on. Later he started meetings at 7:30 A.M. instead of after work (in the workers' own time, though from 1980 onward the firm began to offer overtime pay for two or three hours of meetings a month). They taught themselves the various quality analysis techniques of Pareto diagrams, histograms, graphs, critical path analysis, etc.

M.'s story, as recorded by Dore, is similar to other such narratives.[4] As a presentation, M.'s tale is an epiphany. It proceeds from a problem through intermediary stages to a happy ending. In M.'s depiction, the initial problem was a lack of cooperation from group members. Following their transformation, the members of the group cooperated, responded, and wholeheartedly committed themselves to their work. What occurred in between was normative control. Since neither remuneration nor physical coercion were available as incentives, the only feasible means for resolving the problem were normative.

M. began his presentation by reporting that the basic spirit of the group was "to emphasize harmony and cooperation." These are the traditional catchphrases of managerial paternalism. The QCC, however, provided practical means for implementing these slogans that went beyond the familiar ideology. M. took advantage of the normative power of QCC. His tactics, it should be stressed, were not idiosyncratic but typical and even standard. He motivated the group and instilled spirit in the meetings by establishing an objective: winning the efficiency prize. Later, since some members were still unresponsive, M. instigated a discourse of evaluation. He rated the members of his group under such headings as speaking, reporting back, helping in preparing reports, cooperating, attending meetings, and contributing to problem solving.

The goal of such evaluation went beyond individual appraisal. Rather, it strove to generate a new normative order of responsibility. This is what Michel Foucault termed a "discourse of normalization":

---

4. See Kumazawa 1996: 87–125 for a wealth of reports on QCCs that can be used for comparison.

motivating people to act in a particular manner by constructing a taken-for-granted notion of "normalcy" that is then used to judge deviance and to sanction its punishment. Responsibility, as defined by M., became the benchmark of normalcy. Personality tests administered by psychologists feature prominently in the modern discourse of normalization; M. adopted this strategy in "studying the personalities of the members of his group to see how they could be better integrated into a harmonious team."

Among M.'s other normative prescriptions was introducing the "habit of shouting 'good morning' the first thing on entering the shop in a firm, loud, positive, and enthusiastic voice until even the misanthropes were forced to respond." Forced to respond, I should add, so as not to differ from those who do the "normal" thing (although such a greeting if performed in other workplaces and in other languages might be seen as quite abnormal).

The QCCs benefited companies in another way. They turned out to be excellent leadership-training schools. Through QCCs, companies educated their managerial reserve on the line, the subforemen, efficiently and at practically no cost. In M.'s case, management demonstrated its appreciation of the educational function of QCCs; his presentation was part of the ceremony marking the awarding of a commendation to M. at his department's "show and tell" session (Kamata 1982: xiv).

QCCs as Norm-Processors

How do QCCs succeed in instilling compliance without resorting to overt coercion? How do they generate cooperation that comes from inner compulsion bred from submission to the norms and targets that the organization has set? Normative control is a large part of the answer to that riddle. Other aspects of the answer are macro-organizational factors such as the involvement of interest groups, labor market dynamics, and union orientation, which we will consider when we compare experiences with QCCs in Japan and the United States.

Responsibility and Normalization

Spontaneous and voluntary in theory, circles were in fact management-controlled devices for instilling a sense of responsibility toward the company. Most important, workers perceived nonparticipation or even halfhearted participation in QCCs as potentially damaging to their merit ratings and chances for promotion. This threat, implied or direct, is behind the impressive participation rates of 80 percent or more. QCCs were designed to create an environment in which employees would naturally align individual interests with corporate goals. As circle activities flooded the shop floor with official expectations of responsibility, each worker was supposed to embrace management norms and self-police his or her own performance.[5]

Worker Evaluation and Foreman Education

QCCs were used as tools for personnel management, for example, in cultivating "intra-group" competition among shop-floor workers. From the late 1960, firms increasingly used QCC participation as a basis for worker evaluation, creating what Watanabe Osamu (1987; cited in Tsutsui 1995: 326) called a "competitive order" for spurring "spontaneous obedience" in the workplace. Kamata (1982: 71), in his Toyota diary, recounts how "the company always fills up the work breaks with speeches and orders. Once in my workshop, the general foreman spent ten minutes encouraging us to submit Good Idea Suggestions. He left 30 blank sheets with the foremen to be filled with the good ideas. That's two sheets for each worker in the group."

The program of Good Idea Suggestions operates at several levels of normative control. First, it is a mechanism for inducing participation and responsibility. The basic criterion for showing responsibility is

---

5. See Tsutsui 1995: 320–21; 1998. Cole (1992: 296) similarly observed that "management sought to make participation a responsibility, an obligation, of each employee. Participation was not seen as providing an opportunity for employees to express their individual talents or self-actualize, California-style."

filling in and submitting the suggestion sheets, regardless of the quality of their content. This aspect is significant since it creates a mutual framework of "normalcy"—everybody can and should participate. Second, workers are told that management will examine their ideas, a notion that arguably creates the impression that the quality of the suggestions, and hence of the workers making the suggestions, is being evaluated. Third, the program includes a mechanism of surveillance. As Kamata recounts, the number of Good Idea Suggestions submitted by each worker is announced on a large sheet of paper posted on the locker-room wall.

The Toyota suggestion system was introduced in 1951 in imitation of a practice in Ford's Baton Rouge plant. In Toyota's system, a quota is set for each worker, and the results are posted in the shop. Workers who make few suggestions are given warnings. A small prize is awarded—a coupon worth ¥250 at the co-op store. Once a month a ceremony is held on the shop floor. The section manager in charge hands out the rewards to the workers in envelopes that have "Good Thinking, Good Products" printed on them. This is typical of the total quality control "philosophy," which relies heavily on show-and-tell presentations, posters, signboards, and prizes. All these rituals serve not only as vehicles for the total quality control gospel in the workplace but also as subtle mechanisms of surveillance.

In the 1980s, some circles began videotaping their members at work. The members of the group would analyze the films as a group to find ways of simplifying and speeding up production. The circle thus turned each worker on the assembly line into an efficiency engineer. Surveillance was stronger than ever as workers were turned into inspectors watching over themselves. QCCs succeeded in instituting a norm of self-policing for the sake of quality control.

Finally, QCCs were designed from the start as a means of educating foremen, improving their management skills, and co-opting them into the managerial hierarchy. In the early days, QCC was referred to as FQC ("foremen quality control"; Tsutsui 1995: 319). By putting front-line supervisors in charge of circle activities, managers and engineers were continuing the prewar trend of "in-house education" for foremen (see also Gordon 1985). According to Tsutsui (1995: 322), foremen were taught basic human relations methods as a means of strengthening their supervisory authority over QCCs.

Small-Group Activities in American Manufacturing

Mechanisms for employee participation were sold to management, and subsequently advocated by management, not as a natural part of social life at work but always as part of a discourse of normative control. In the United States, the importance of the small group in industry as a repository of norms had to be "discovered" through an experiment and presented as scientifically proved to management before the first company-wide human relations intervention could take place. To illustrate this intriguing cultural difference between the United States and Japan, I turn to one of the formative moments of the human relations movement, the well-known Hawthorne experiments. Beginning with tests involving illumination in 1924 and continuing through such stages as the relay assembly test room, the bank wiring room, interviewing, and counseling, the Hawthorne experiments gradually developed from a study of the effects of specific work conditions on productivity to an attempt to gain a broader understanding of the motives and behavior of people at work. My focus here is on the bank wiring room phase of the Hawthorne experiments, which started in November 1931. The experiment was designed, following the earlier assembly test room studies at Hawthorne, to obtain exact information about social groups within the company.

For about six months, before the depression ended the experiment, the researchers (among them industrial psychologists Elton Mayo and Fritz Roethlisberger and anthropologist W. Lloyd Warner) observed a group of fourteen male operators working under constant conditions. According to Loren Baritz (1960: 92–95), the major discovery of the research was that it was the small group, not management, which determined the level of production. It was on this basis that the Hawthorne researchers (and human relations experts after them) argued the importance of the "small group" to management. In the case of the wiring room group, it was found that by adjusting reports of their daily production, the wiremen controlled the amount of their work and prevented management from imposing production quotas. The group itself decided how much work was to be done, and no effort by management could overcome the informal sanctions of the group (for the complete report, see Roethlisberger and Dickson 1939).

By convincing management that small groups can be the seedbeds of "restriction,"[6] the human relations school introduced the manipulation and control of such groups as a necessary tool for management. The inevitable groupings of workers must be controlled by management through the techniques offered by human relations. To be sure, even before the bank wiring room experiment, there had been discussions of informal groups within American industry. "Team systems" were already used to increase production, and psychologists were writing on the importance of "we-feeling" in the modern factory as early as the 1920s.[7] When QCCs appeared 30 years later, they were yet another example of turning the ubiquitous informal groupings of workers into formal "circles" that think along "constructive" lines.

Loren Baritz (1960: 99) cites the following poem as perhaps the best expression of the sentiments that impelled workers to regulate their production despite incentive plans and bonuses. This poem, entitled "Harmony?," was written in the late 1920s by a worker and hung

---

6. "Restriction" is management's term for workers' bottom-up regulation of output. The term goes back to Taylor, who wrote in 1911 that "the workmen together have carefully planned just how fast each job should be done, and they had set a pace for each machine throughout the shop, which was limited to about one third of a good day's work" (cited in Baritz 1960: 98) Scientific management was to remove the control and determination of rates of production from the hands of the workers and place it in the hands of management. A related term, equally threatening to management, was "soldiering." Psychologists recycled issues already defined by the rationalization movement and offered normative control as a new solution to old problems.

7. See, e.g., Benge 1920; Pruette & Fryer 1918.

on the bulletin board of an industrial shop. It is not only an expression of emotions at work but also evidence of the feeling rules imposed by the workplace.

HARMONY?

I am working with the feeling
That the company is stealing
Fifty pennies from my pocket every day;
But for every single pennie
They will lose ten times as many
By the speed that I'm producing, I dare say.
For it makes me so disgusted
That my speed shall be adjusted
So that nevermore my brow will drip with sweat;
When they're in an awful hurry
Someone else can rush and worry
Till an increase in my wages do I get.
No malicious thoughts I harbor
For the butcher or the barber
Who get eighty cents an hour from the start.
Nearly three years I've been working
Like a fool, but now I'm shirking—
When I get what's fair, I'll always do my part.
Someone else can run their races
Till I'm on an equal basis
With the ones who learned the trade by mining coal.
Though I can do the work, it's funny
New men can get the money
And I cannot get the same to save my soul.

The researchers at Hawthorne concluded that the regulation of output by the wiring room group was "irrational" and hence emotional. This labeling served two purposes. First, it placed the diagnosis of the situation within the accepted discourse of management and organizational theory. The group *was* "irrational" from the point of view of managerial rationality. Second, by labeling the behavior "irrational," the researchers placed the solution outside the rational discourse of incentives or work design.[8] The remedy to the problem lay within normative control, namely, the discourse of human relations.

Elton Mayo (1945: 115) phrased these concerns in the emotional rhetoric that would come to characterize human relations in the United States. According to Mayo, "restriction" revealed the workers' sense of exasperation and "personal futility." What the workers needed most was "improved understanding." To Mayo, restriction of output meant that workers did not trust management. It was a defensive mechanism to counter the superior power, especially arbitrarily exercised power, of management. As a result of the Hawthorne studies, Mayo concluded that workers increase or decrease their efforts in proportion to their trust in their management.

The Hawthorne experiments began with the so-called illumination studies. In a series of tests, a group of female workers ("the girls") in a relay assembly test room had to work under varying levels of illumination (and later, rest breaks and so on). To the surprise of the researchers, the women increased their production irrespective of the changes. According to Mayo, the relay assemblers were oriented toward management's goals because the researchers confided in them and even asked them for suggestions. The women's participation in policy making gave them a sense of trust and confidence. It became important to them that the experiment "turn out right." The wiremen, on the other hand, were left alone by the researchers. This was the crucial difference. They were allowed to maintain the informal group they had developed before the study began. Consequently, there was no participation in decision making, no confidence, and no trust. The result was

---

8. The argument that the rational design of work does not remedy the "irrational" behavior of workers but instead strengthens it among some workers is an old one and was voiced by some followers of rationalization. P. J. Conlon, vice-president of the International Association of Machinists, testified before the Commission on Industrial Relations that "we believe that scientific management builds up in the industrial world the principle of sabotage, syndicalism, passive resistance. . . . We did not hear of any of these things until we heard of scientific management and new methods of production" (cited in Davis 1983: 95). It was arguably the coerced and often arbitrary introduction of "speed-ups" on the part of management that engendered "slowdowns," "soldiering," and even "sabotage" on the part of workers.

"irrational" behavior in the form of restriction. Interestingly enough, this conclusion was reached through a negative process. The importance of trust was discovered in its absence. This observation is not trivial, since the Japanese experience with trust as part of labor-management relations followed a different, some would say opposite, course.

The discovery that trust built on participation could be the remedy to restriction was behind the first company-wide human relations intervention. This intervention took the form of interviewing, later to be labeled "counseling." The interviewing program at Western Electric in Chicago (the company that sponsored the Hawthorne experiments) was originally designed to determine ways of improving supervision in the company.[9] To the surprise of management, the interviewers could not keep the workers on the preselected subjects. Employees wanted to talk about what they thought was important. The researchers decided to experiment with undirected interviews. After this change, several workers commented on the "improvement" in working conditions, although nothing had in fact changed. According to Baritz's (1960: 102) account, "One of the researchers said that nondirective interviewing provided several advantages: a feeling of confidence on the part of the employees was stimulated, many employees experienced an 'emotional release,' and others gained a 'feeling of recognition.'"

The sense of emotional catharsis released by the more open interviews was seen as a trust-building device. Workers seemed to be happier following the opportunity to blow off steam. Furthermore, this "happiness" did not cost management much. In 1936 this discovery was made the basis of an active (and later, permanent) program entitled "personnel counseling." Counseling, as the management of Western Electric defined it, was to be a method of helping workers feel and think in such a way that they would be happier with their jobs. Of no less importance was its manipulative use as a means of normative control. Jeane Wilensky, who was employed as a personnel counselor at

---

9. On this counseling program, see Dickson 1945; Levinson 1961; and Murphy 1988; for critical analyses, see Rose 1988; and Hollway 1991.

Hawthorne from 1947 to 1950, wrote that "Western Electric . . . has not only entered the worker's social life, his financial life, and his intellectual life, but now, through personnel counseling, his most intimate thoughts, deeds, and desires may be laid bare to a representative of the company" (Wilensky & Wilensky 1951: 266).

The company always pointed out that the counseling process was voluntary. Workers were supposed to initiate counseling sessions and to repeat them because, after all, it makes them "happier." From 1936 to 1955, employees initiated nearly 120,000, or about 22 percent, of the interviews conducted at Western Electric. However, over 73 percent, nearly 400,000, were initiated by the counselors with the consent of the worker, and 3 percent were initiated by the worker's supervisor (Baritz 1960: 104).

In 1949, the United Auto Workers' (UAW) monthly magazine, *Ammunition*, published an article entitled "Deep Therapy on the Assembly Line" about Mayo, the Hawthorne results, and the whole human relations approach.

The Prophet is Elton Mayo. . . . The Holy Place is the Hawthorne Plant of the Western Electric Company (the wholly owned subsidiary of one of the nation's largest monopolies, the AT&T). . . . For nine years about every kind of experiment a very bright Harvard professor could think of was tried on the women [at Hawthorne]. Everything you do to white mice was done to them, except their spines and skulls were not split so the fluid could be analyzed. . . .

What did make them produce and produce and produce and produce with ever-increasing speed was the expression of interest in their personal problems by the supervisor; interviews by psychiatrically trained social workers and (later on) the way they were paired off with friendly or unfriendly co-workers.

Now obviously this is the greatest discovery since J. P. Morgan learned that you can increase profits by organizing a monopoly, suppressing competition, raising prices and reducing production. (cited in Baritz 1960: 114–15)

This article is revealing in several ways. The hostility of American labor toward the introduction of human relations attests to the active role of trade unions in the United States in resisting normative control. (This role will become clearer below when we compare these attitudes to the much more uncritical disposition of Japanese company unions.) Furthermore, despite all its negativism, the union's stance discloses a real conflict over who is to set the norms on the shop floor. Management has presented participation, counseling, and trust building (and later, quality circles) as neutral attempts to benefit the worker and democratize the workplace. There is some truth in these claims, and their actual value must be tested against the existing alternatives. However, these claims are not the whole truth. Such mechanisms of trust building were historically conceived, in the United States, as devices to combat worker restriction of production, and their articulation and development were aspects of an increasingly more sophisticated discourse of normative control.

In contrast, small-group activities were promoted in Japan as a "natural" corollary of the emotionalist discourse of managerial paternalism as well as of Japanese socialization in task-oriented teamwork. The company-as-family has not emerged as a root metaphor in the American discourse of trust building and human relations. Although the normative control of a company's workforce as a whole did arise at an early stage in industrialization (at Ford Motors, for example), it was implemented in a rather coerced manner and was gradually abandoned. This crucial difference between Japan and the United States also had implications for more specific practices of human relations within the plant. Although personnel counseling was the American solution to the problems resulting from informal groupings of workers, QCCs were institutionalized in Japan as an extension of the company-as-family discourse.

At the risk of overgeneralization, it could be argued that American managers and their social scientists perceived the social group with mixed feelings.[10] The social group, as the Hawthorne experiments

---

10. American labor studies have paid much attention to the phenomenon of shop-floor resistance by informal small groups, especially to piece-rate systems. See, e.g., Nelson Lichtenstein 1980 and Daniel Nelson 1982.

showed, was the informal cell for resistance. Informal groups harbored their own norms and feelings and were easy targets for hostile union influence. They posed a threat to management. The American solution, by and large, was to break up the group by caring for the individual. When it was understood that small groups such as the Hawthorne wiring room group were strong enough to thwart management, the Hawthorne researchers, in their counseling program, reverted to an individual approach to the problems of the factory.

In contrast, for Japanese management and workers groups were an accepted part of social life. Groups were the natural agents of socialization and control. The natural corollaries of these normative premises were to formalize social groups and to appropriate their social role by determining their activities, schedules, and goals. QCCs can be seen as the realization of this managerial scheme. Conversely, there was no recourse to "individualized" personnel counseling.

My claim can be illustrated further by turning to one of the founding fathers of American human relations, Elton Mayo. Mayo (1931, 1941) wrote extensively on the "destruction of all standards of living" resulting from the maladjustments of modernization through industrialization. According to Baritz (1960: 110), Mayo "pictured a happy preindustrial America, arguing that individual isolation, rootlessness, the 'lonely crowd,' were caused by industrialism." His ideal was a romanticized agrarian society of individual farmers. In this "simple and good preindustrial America," the individual lived a "full communal life and knew that his services were a necessary social function."

Mayo's commitment to an agrarian Golden Age can be located in an American tradition fathered by Jefferson and supported by the historian Frederick Jackson Turner. For Mayo, the factory—being an artificial assembly removed from nature, the land, and the forests—had to be devoid of virtue, loyalty, and the agrarian sense of community.[11]

---

11. Continuing the Mayoist legacy of "devotion" from a different perspective, William Ouchi bases his Theory Z on identical historical lamentations for a paradise lost: "In American life, intimacy has traditionally been found in the family, the club, the neighborhood, the

Social groupings in industrial society were potentially hostile to management because of the rupture between industrial society and the individual. For Mayo, the typical institutions of industrial society promoted conflict instead of cooperation.[12] Social ties and groupings within the factory therefore had to be re-created, and the necessary means of social cooperation regained. This approach contrasts with Japanese management's ready appropriation of social groups as taken-for-granted vehicles for participation.

Another implicit assumption of Mayo is drawn from the mainstream American managerial discourse of rational design. Generally speaking, this assumption claims that workers act from emotions and particularistic feelings, whereas management responds to logic. This is the mind/body = management/labor paradigm of scientific management. Mayo seldom referred to unions. His view of the worker emerged from his prototype of the modern individual in an atomized industrial society. The "worker" for Mayo and his followers, and also for American managers, was ideally an unorganized, nonunionized worker: an individual.

For all their cultural value, teamwork and groupism would not have persisted in Japanese firms had they not served a managerial purpose. Furthermore, Japanese managers are aware of work groups' potential for restriction. The broad autonomy given to work groups in fact increases the likelihood that an individual work group might develop interests and objectives in conflict with those of the rest of the firm. To align the goals of each work group with those of the rest of the firm,

---

lifelong friendship, and the church. Yet all of these traditional sources of intimacy, or primary contact with others, are threatened by our present form of industrial life" (1981: 8–9).

12. I focus on Elton Mayo as the protagonist of the human relations school, which became one of the pillars of the American managerial discourse. From an opposite ideological direction, labor relations scholars could easily confirm Mayo's contention that "labor-management relations are a classic form of conflict" (Kerr 1964: 169). Unlike Mayo and the human relations school, Clark Kerr and the school of industrial relations did not see irrationality or ill-will at the core of this conflict. From the point of view of labor relations, the conflict is inevitable, since "if management and labor are to retain their institutional identities, they must disagree and must act on the disagreement. Conflict is essential to survival" (Kerr 1964: 170).

managers have developed a practice called *satei*, or personnel appraisal. *Satei* is a personal assessment made by the worker's foreman and supervisor. It influences remuneration by determining the rate of promotion and the level of monthly pay, and it is applied to both blue- and white-collar workers. The supervisor assesses not only objective performance (i.e., production quotas) but also such work-related attitudes as eagerness, personableness, and team spirit (Endō 1994).

As a practice of control through rewards, *satei* reinforces the highly praised normative values of "teamwork," "groupism," and "harmony." The *satei* system makes it difficult to refuse overtime work, since doing so may lower one's evaluation. Groups and teams in Japanese firms operate with the minimum number of workers needed, and other group members would have to work harder to compensate for an absent member. This is often regarded as a source of normative pressure. In addition, however, workers also know that refusing to do overtime or going on a vacation is likely to be assessed as a poor team attitude. For the same reason, it is difficult for workers to refuse voluntary activities outside work hours such as QCC meetings and events to foster friendship among team members. Through *satei*, obedience is measured and remunerated, just as Taylor preached in his system of scientific management. Western scholars have often praised Japanese-style management as "post-Fordist" and hence more favorable for workers (see, e.g., Florida and Kenney 1991). The experience of working in teams itself engenders—according to both Western and Japanese descriptions of the devotion school—trust, loyalty, and commitment. Japanese lean production is therefore sold as a more humane, communal system. Practices such as *satei* expose a different reality behind the ideological facade.

QCCs in Japan and the United States

The point of the following comparison of QCCs in Japan and the United States is to show that managerial systems of normative control, and workers' reactions to them, are not conditioned on some vague "cultural" mentality; rather, they develop within historical situations

Table 3
Attitudes Toward QCCs in the United States and Japan

Managerial ideology	Interest groups	Worker orientation	Union orientation
United States			
Human relations; suspicious disposition toward group activity	Weak involvement; quality control associations more concerned with capital and technology	Market motivation; unwillingness to share ideas	Often hostile, suspicious, and uninterested; QCCs perceived as threat to craft knowledge and unionism
Japan			
Paternalism; positive utilization of the small group	Strong involvement; quality control professionals committed to creating a thorough quality control agenda	Membership motivation; sense of belonging	Cooperation with management as part of emphasis on job security

and industrial relations. The spread of QCCs in Japan and the United States can now be considered against the backdrop of these countries' different managerial ideologies. According to Robert Cole (1985), QCCs re-entered the U.S. automobile industry in the late 1970s and early 1980s as a result of Japanese competition. American managers were led to believe that they failed to mobilize human resources. Yet QCCs were introduced in the American automobile and electronics industries in a different way. This comparison will also serve as background for discussing the "Japanization" of the U.S. auto industry, particularly in the joint-venture plants of the late 1980s and 1990s. The various factors affecting the institutionalization of QCCs in the United States and Japan are summarized in Table 3 and discussed separately below.

Managerial Ideology

When faced with the labor-supply problems of the late 1960s, Japanese managers readily turned to QCCs as a means to arouse in workers a sense of loyalty and an internalization of company values—goals that were traditionally defined within paternalism. American managers working in the tradition of direct (Fordist/Taylorist) control, in contrast, have been suspicious of informal groups as sites of shopfloor resistance.[13] The American discourse of contractualism, exemplified in U.S. labor legislation, has generated (and has been fueled by) a pattern of industrial relations that tends toward "mutual suspicion, weak ties, and fear of opportunism" (Jacoby 1993: 239; see also Selznick 1969).[14] American companies that have incorporated group activities often justify it as means of further inculcation in company values.[15] The participation fad that once swept American industry was described by sociologists as "vicious" and seen by managers and outside observers as a way of getting rid of individuality.[16]

This tendency resurfaced in Japanese transplants in North America in which, despite (or because of) the stress on teamwork in Japanese-style management, American managers were afraid that

---

13. Managerial suspicion of "the floor" exists in various sectors, not just in industry. Benson (1983, 1986), for example, argues that bosses in American department stores see the sales floor as the turf of the clerks, with its own elaborate rules and social system that are distinct from and often in conflict with the store's formal structure. The informal work group is therefore potentially in need of suppression, but managers usually also rely on the "clerical sisterhood" to maintain good order.

14. In comparative surveys of Japanese and U.S. workers, the Japanese often expressed positive attitudes toward values that coincided with managerial paternalism, such as close supervisor-subordinate ties. These attitudes were seldom echoed by Americans, who preferred a more contractual, instrumental connection to the company (Whitehill & Takezawa 1968; Takezawa & Whitehill 1981).

15. Cessna Aircraft, for example, advised that "the group leader's job is to mold the human weaknesses of his men and women in the proper direction" (Baritz 1960: 187).

16. William White, then an assistant managing editor of *Fortune*, wrote of the participation movement that "now one no longer needs be ashamed of going along with the herd; indeed, with the aid of the new jargon he can be articulately proud of the fact. He is not just conforming, he is using 'group skills.' He is maintaining 'equilibrium.' He is 'participating'" (cited in Baritz 1960: 188).

team members together might look upon managers as the "out group." . . . [We] run a risk in nurturing work teams in that the solidarity developed between team members could be used against management and management efforts toward goal achievement. If the work team norms and goals should become incongruent [with the company philosophy], individual workers have been equipped with a powerful weapon to support counterproductive behavior and attitudes. (Besser 1996: 72–73)

Interest Groups

In contrast to the strong involvement of the Japanese Union of Civil Engineers in promoting total quality control in Japan, there was no similar participation by an American interest group. The status of the American Society of Quality Control, for example, which might have played the role the Japanese Union of Civil Engineers did, was not high, and the society failed to provide leadership for the movement (Cole 1985: 571). Likewise, the American Productivity Center, established in 1977, "saw the path to productivity improvement in traditional approaches like enhancing availability of capital, technology investment, and taxation policy. . . . These associations were more at home lobbying in Washington than in the factories and offices of America" (Cole 1985: 571).

Worker Orientation

Worker orientation is the flip side of managerial ideology and to some extent a reflection of union orientation. For QCCs to succeed, workers arguably need to have confidence in the fairness of the overall distribution of the proceeds and to feel sure that the extra income generated by their individual efforts will be fairly shared. In other words, workers must have trust that management is *not* merely and cynically trying to appropriate their craft knowledge through QCCs. This argument thematizes "emotion" in a similar manner to the place of "emotion" within managerial discourse. That is, I am not necessarily talking about the subjective experience of *trust* among workers. Rather, I am referring to a shop-floor *discourse* of trust, a "feeling rule" that promotes trust.

Once that trust is there, workers may find that looking for ways of doing the job better can make their lives more interesting.

Such a disposition toward trust has arguably emerged for some workers in the context of Japanese-style management. Employment security, workplace unionism, the seniority system, and company welfare programs are designed to promote such trust and a sense of membership motivation. Equally important, once the feeling rule of trust is established on the shop floor, participation in QCCs becomes a legitimate measure of "membership motivation." A worker's willingness to offer his or her ideas for free depends in part on a sense of "belonging" to the firm. The ability of the firm to mobilize such feelings is what Dore (in Kamata 1982: xxviii) terms "membership motivation." The opposite is "market motivation," namely, being propelled by one's career prospects and traveling for new job offers and better individual terms. Market motivation is what presumably characterizes the American labor market and what promotes its practices of headhunting and job switching.[17]

Union Orientation

In the United States, unions in the 1960s and 1970s were suspicious of QCCs and viewed small-group activities as a management scheme to get more productivity from workers.[18] Another concern was that these approaches would result in speed-ups and reduce manpower requirements. Finally, small-group activities, as a means of fostering loyalty to the company, were seen as a threat to unionization. This orientation reflects American unions' emphasis on the control of job boundaries (Perlman 1968; Cole 1985). This emphasis was shaped by

---

17. Job switching has recently entered Japan, particularly in financial management and engineering, where employees are being lured from lifetime jobs by hefty pay offers. The phenomenon has received a lot of attention from the popular media (e.g., Kawashima 1988a, b).

18. However, the union's position on small-group activities could change, as illustrated by the UAW's acceptance of the team concept and arrangements in GM and Ford plants in the 1980s, which paved the way for the "Japanization" of the American car industry.

the history of struggle between craft unions and management to control the production process (Stone 1975).

To these factors, we can now add the element of emotion. Work groups breed strong emotions and require a specific set of feeling rules. Working in teams or participating in a QCC can be stressful without proper socialization. Emotion is not on Cole's list because of his rationalist, macro-organizational, structuralist orientation. Yet emotion is crucial in accounting for the difference in attitudes toward the work group and QCCs in Japan and the United States.

Quality circles are an established fact of life in Japanese factories, offices, and service companies. They are much less popular in the United States. QCCs in America have relatively short life expectancies (Leonard 1983) and are perceived unfavorably by supervisors (Klein 1984) and as exploitative by workers (Lawler & Mohrman 1985). It is not uncommon to hear complaints that people are "tyrannized" by a team ideology based on the use of work groups as a key to effective performance (Sinclair 1992). Participation in work groups is often a source of stress rather then satisfaction (Rothchild & Whitt 1986). Some American observers in the 1980s even criticized QCCs as the "neo-Tayloristic method of this period," since they "do not attempt to increase the decision-making power of workers and appear to provide another means of appropriating worker knowledge and putting it under management's control" (Bramel & Friend 1987: 249).

The stereotypical American attitude to the work group reflects the American preference for rationalism over emotionalism. Work groups are "emotional" and therefore potentially "dangerous." The short-lived practice of group dynamics in American organizations (e.g., T-Groups, growth groups, and sensitivity training) resulted in a backlash. The emotional side of such groups has stereotypically been regarded by both managers and workers as disruptive rather than productive, and its expression has been discouraged. Groups expressing emotion have typically been treated as escaping work.

II. TRANSPLANT CULTURES IN THE

U.S. AUTO INDUSTRY

GM . . . has developed a new production method . . . correcting the great flaw in the assembly line concept that tends to exclude the creative and managerial skills of people who work on the line. . . . There are no longer workers and bosses in the plant, just "associates" and "advisors."

—From a GM advertisement in
Business Week, 27 April 1987, 127
(cited in Parker 1993: 249)

[During the huddle at the end of the morning team meeting], each Associate extended his or her left arm into the center of the circle, hands clenched into fists. The team leader then called on one member to deliver an inspirational message to the team. The usual message was, "Let's have a safe and productive day." . . . For the most part, it was embarrassing to be called upon and the jokes [told by a few team members on such occasions] were a way for us to insert some control over the process.

—Laurie Graham, on working on
the line at the Subaru-Isuzu
U.S. transplant (1995: 69–70)

Toyotist methods of "lean production" have become increasingly global. In this section, I trace the export of Toyotism to Japanese subsidiaries in the United States. These transplants emphasize the practice of such Japanese-style practices as just-in-time deliveries, teamwork, total quality control, and QCCs, but downplay the ideological notion of paternalism. This was arguably done by the management of these transplants in order to facilitate the smooth transfer of Japanese know-how to a new host culture. The transplants therefore offer an intriguing case study of the interplay of the global (Japanese-style management) and the local (American practices and attitudes).

I begin with a concise overview of Toyotism in Japan, as a backdrop for comparison. I use for this purpose Kamata's account of his participant observation of Toyota as a seasonal worker on an assembly line. Two caveats should be noted: first, Kamata was hired as a seasonal worker, and his account describes the life of a temporary worker, not of a regular worker. Second, Kamata's account is evidently personally biased. Nevertheless, his narrative is the best discussion of the actual practices of Toyotism.

The Toyota Prototype: Life in an Auto Factory

Kamata Satoshi, a Japanese free-lance journalist, worked for six months in 1972–73 at Toyota as a temporary worker. This was about ten years before the opening of the first transplants in North America. His account, *Japan in the Passing Lane*, was translated into English and published in 1982. It is still an important ethnographic source (indeed, one of the only sources) about factory life from the worker's point of view.

As one of many temporary workers hired for six months, Kamata left his family far behind him to work at Toyota. His new surroundings proved to be a total institution composed of the plant, dormitories, and nearby Toyota City. Kamata describes the dormitory as a prison camp, with a guardhouse and gates. There are five men to a room. Visitors, whether families or friends, cannot enter the dormitory freely; they must have permission. For shopping one has to travel to Toyota City. "You get up in the morning, walk to the plant, work, come back, take a bath, eat, and go to bed. That's what 'life' at Toyota is all about" (32).[19]

The system of company dormitories developed at the turn of the twentieth century, partly as an instrumental protection against labor mobility. Later, it became a major element in paternalism. Living in company dormitories often brought about a reliance on company-sponsored leisure activities, which were controlled by the company and filled with educational lectures designed to instill appropriate values of loyalty and responsibility. Worker acceptance of this "paternalistic," company-controlled leisure is seen by Arthur Whitehill and Takezawa Shinichi (1968) as basic to understanding the high motivation of Japanese blue-collar workers.

---

19. Similar descriptions exist for other company towns in Japan. The most extreme cases were perhaps the coal mines. Apart from coercive control enforced in the mine, the company often controlled the miners' place of residence. Shops, entertainment areas, religious festivals, schools, and banks were all controlled by the mine (see Allen 1994).

Toyota, like many other Japanese companies, has always fostered its "family" image. In a Toyota-approved publication, writer Kusaya-nagi Daizō wrote of life at Toyota:

The rice is cooked instantly in a vacuum cooker. After eating the rice, the workers go to work in the plant. And when they have finished work, they go back to their dormitories, which are well equipped with modern facilities and have cost the company $200 million. . . . Toyota Motor Company is try-ing to create human beings, too. I was fascinated and much impressed by this "Great Country Town" after the complete tour of the company. (Cited in Kamata 1982: 32)

Kamata was antagonized by this description. Although it is true, Ka-mata writes, it is not the whole truth. What the objective observer should have written is:

The rice served here is bad for the digestion because it's cooked too fast. The workers eat the rice in a hurry, go to the plant in a hurry, and work in a hurry in order to keep up with the "famous" assembly line. After they are fi-nally released, they have no choice other than to go back to the dormitories, which have facilities that are advertised by the Public Relations Department to have cost the company $200 million. There, former Self-Defense Forces men now working for Toyota keep a close eye on everyone's private lives.

The "instant" Toyota rice that is cooked too fast serves as a cultural signifier of the failure to re-create the family in the plant. This failure, argues Kamata in the remainder of his book, is not necessarily deter-mined by the artificial and military-like environment of the plant. For Kamata, the crucial reason is emotional. Toyota fails to be a "family" because, despite its self-presentation in public, it does not really care for the worker. The company worries about its production quotas, not about its workers. Time ("do everything in a hurry"), space, and emotions are appropriated and controlled for speedy production.

Another discrepancy, according to Kamata, between ideology and practice in the "Toyota family" is the relationship between the com-pany and its suppliers. This aspect of Japanese industrial organization also plays an important part in the "family" discourse of the *keiretsu*.

The *keiretsu* is a business group modeled on the prewar family-owned industrial conglomerates, or *zaibatsu*—literally "financial lineages" or "financial families." This business group consists of an extensive network of organizational relationships. In the automobile industry, the just-in-time, or *kanban*, system requires a close relationship between the manufacturer and its suppliers. Since supplies are needed "just in time," in relatively small portions and within a flexible schedule, suppliers must work with manufacturers on a long-term basis. In the case of Nissan, for example, the just-in-time or "lean" production system has created a multitier organizational structure. In 1995, 38 of Nissan's first-tier parts suppliers were Nissan's *keiretsu* members, and 118 were nonmembers. Second-tier suppliers were responsible for stamping and tool making. Of these, 2,000 were *keiretsu* members and 3,000 were nonmembers. A third tier consisted of about 7,000 to 10,000 contractors, almost half of them cottage industries, most of them operated by a few family members (Shimizu 1995: 85).

According to Kamata, "The Toyota method of production appears to the outside world as the systematization of 'the relationship of a community bound together by a common fate.' But truthfully, it's nothing more than the absolute determination to make all movement of goods and people in and out of these plants subordinated to Toyota's will" (1982: 200). The "relationship of a community bound together by a common fate" is a quotation from Ōno Taiichi's (1978) well-known book on the Toyota method of production. It fits exactly the definition of normative control as a form of "bounded emotionality." Within each *keiretsu*, the main firm is called the *oya-gaisha* (father company). The business family, headed by the father company, imposes a common fate, trust, and "goodwill" (Ronald Dore's term). This public image, argues Kamata, also has its "dark side," a backstage reality of a master and his subordinates, a market structure held together by normative control.[20]

---

20. A similar view of the abusive relationships between the core manufacturer (a car maker) and its suppliers is vividly described in Shimizu Ikkō's industry novel, *Keiretsu*, translated by Tamae Prindle (see Shimizu 1995).

Kamata's description is divided between *tatemae*, the public, declarative level of the company, and *honne*, the private, subjective level of the workers. Neither level, it should be pointed out, has representational or even moral precedence; the private level is no more "real" than the public, or vice versa. Both levels are real; both construct the social reality in the plant. An important part of *tatemae* is found in company manuals. For example, a manual entitled "Safety in General Operations" says: "1. Go to bed early, get up early, and be cheerful. 2. Be properly and neatly dressed. 3. Try to get acquainted with your surroundings quickly. 4. Pay attention to your safety and security, and follow instructions and regulations." Cheerfulness, a normative requirement imposed by management, is ubiquitous in company manuals in Japan.

In contrast to this declarative demand for cheerfulness, Kamata describes the private, subjective alienation experienced by himself and other workers. His overall experience of the workplace is dominated by military-like regimentation. The dormitories are prison camps. The Toyota uniform worn by all workers carries stripes of rank. Workers are assigned a serial number. Even after the first shock of arrival fades away, alienation remains a dominant theme. Working the conveyor belt is physically demanding, numbing, and monotonous. An additional source of alienation is Toyota's speed-ups, which increase production quotas in a way that causes accidents.[21]

Kamata's account is a temporary worker's account. Are temporary workers alienated because they have no share in enterprise unionism and Japanese-style management—since they lack employment security, union support, and prospects for promotion? Kamata rejects this possibility and argues that the life of regular Toyota workers was even

---

21. The difficult experience of Toyota's temporary workers as described by Kamata should be read in its historical context. As Ronald Dore notes in his introduction to Kamata's account, Kamata worked at Toyota in 1972, during the last year of the pre-oil-crisis growth period. Wages had been rising, and Toyota, competing with Nissan, had to get maximum production. Hence the speed-ups that Kamata describes. In this period there was also a shortage of labor, which made Toyota resort to high levels of overtime as well as to more temporary workers.

worse. However, this observation should be taken as reflecting his overall ideological disposition.

Management by Stress

The sophistication of Toyotism owes much to a combination of direct and indirect measures of control. Toyotism combines the rational as well as the normative, production as well as paternalism. The point is that the just-in-time / total quality control regime, known around the world as a rational scheme for production, also has significant normative corollaries. Just-in-time and total quality control are complementary philosophies or, rather, toolboxes of techniques. Just-in-time essentially means matching the production process with market demand by controlling supplies and production in an integrated way. Total quality control, in a similar manner, aims to build quality into the production process, rather than dealing with problems after the quota has been produced. Furthermore, the small inventories of stocks at the interfaces between just-in-time production processes starkly expose quality problems.

The notion of just-in-time and total quality control as complementary components in the normative order of Toyotism has been studied by Graham Sewell and Barry Wilkinson (1992). They define this order as constituted by two major disciplinary elements: visibility and peer pressure through teamwork. One of the striking features of a just-in-time / total quality control factory is the ease with which an outside observer can understand the production process and flows of materials. Flow is simplified: the shop floor has been organized around products rather than specialist functions. The result is a factory layout that offers better visibility. Such visibility facilitates better surveillance of inventory and work flow. This means that the responsibility for quality can be pinpointed more easily. The higher visibility of the labor process also means less room for workers to create "idle" time or to "hide" work. Productivity, aided by such high visibility, can now be measured against daily—or even more frequent—targets, rather than the monthly ones. Mike Parker (1993) calls this "management by stress." Unlike the occasional time-and-motion studies so beloved of scientific managers, the productivity and quality performance of individuals and teams in just-in-time / total quality control plants are constantly monitored through hourly progress charts.

At an assembly shop in Great Britain owned by a Japanese manufacturer of electronic consumer goods, a final electronic test on the completed product "instantly identified any defects and traced it to the individual operator responsible. This would result in the normative sanction of an identifying or 'black' mark being placed above the operator's station" (Sewell & Wilkinson 1992: 280). Any worker who accumulated four black marks was taken off the line for an interview with the team leader. Visibility, magnified by electronic technology, produced "responsibility," narrowly defined in the context of faults. This is what Sewell and Wilkinson term the "electronic panopticon": a superstructure of control in which a disembodied (electronic) eye sees and records all details of the labor process (see also Zuboff 1988). Whereas Taylorism stressed solitary confinement (related to the specialized functions of craft), just-in-time / total quality control provides a more developed "open prison." A similar "neighbor-watch system" at a Nissan plant in Great Britain enables managers to trace faults "down the line" to specific work teams and individuals (Garrahan & Stewart 1989, 1992). In Japan, Toyota has installed photoelectric cells in some stations that check for failures to complete all operations in the allotted time. Other checking devices, according to Mike Parker (1993: 269), include "floor mat sensors that are triggered if an operator moves too far from the assigned position."

Sewell and Wilkinson also argue that in just-in-time / total quality control, teamwork has become a means of exercising discipline over workers. This is in line with my view of QCCs as mechanisms of normative control. However, the QCC is just one activity of the team, and it takes place off the assembly line. The "real" production is done by work teams on the assembly line. The work team, and not the individual, is the basic productive unit of the just-in-time / total quality control regime. Production quotas and quality targets are set for the team as a whole. The work team thus inevitably becomes a site for self-discipline. Collective responsibility drives members to cover for an absent worker; usually no replacements are sent from a central labor resource. This places a great obligation on team members to be present at all times. The team leader or team members also confront any worker who is not pulling his weight.

Dick Nanto (1982: 8; cited in Dohse et al. 1985) makes similar observations on the strength of team pressures under just-in-time / total quality control:

Japanese automakers often point out that any worker who finds anything defective in the product has the right and the obligation to shut down the whole line. Shutting down the assembly line, however, does not necessarily reduce the number of cars the team is required to finish that day. The peer pressure is tremendous, therefore, for each individual in the group to achieve 100 percent quality control and efficiency. . . . If one person slacks off or does not show up for work, it places a burden on others.

Although teamwork seems to be a delegation of authority from management to employees, in fact it increases the power of the delegating agency. Responsibility for the deployment of team members on the line, for example, is usually delegated to the team, but the teams must marshal their available human resources to achieve production targets set from above. Production managers can further experiment with changing the team's location and/or number of members and compare it to the team's analysis reports in order to speed up production. On a more general level, peer pressure can be seen to increase the power of the delegating agency (management) by discouraging class conflict and encouraging individual peer competition and conflict (Garrahan & Stewart 1992: xi).[22]

Visibility and peer pressure are put to work within the broader normative order of management by stress (MBS). When everyone can

---

22. Garrahan and Stewart (1992) are very critical of Nissan, charging the company with exploiting British employees as well as abusing the British government's willingness to provide subsidies. The authors argue that Nissan's indoctrination of employees "has been so effective that they do not know how miserable they are" (cited in Besser 1996: 24).

see who is responsible, peer pressure can be brought to bear on those who fail to respond to the demands of the system. The just-in-time / total quality control regime uses stress, rather than coercion or remuneration, as its prime mechanism for coordinating the system. When a single work station is in trouble because it has run out of inventory, parts are defective, or a cord is pulled, this becomes instantly apparent. The crisis generates pressure to solve the problem and catch up. The whole just-in-time / total quality control regime is designed to maximize that crisis, to constantly push the system to the edge of crisis, in order to define the system's cost-effective "point of equilibrium." Just-in-time/total quality control causes management to be happy about red lights (halted production), not green lights. Red lights indicate that the system is pressured. "All green" signals inefficiency (Parker 1993: 262). When a department works with no problems, management will trim its resources until the "red light" is flashing again.

Just-in-Time / Total Quality Control as a Normative Order in "Japanized" Auto Plants

The "Japanization" of the U.S. car industry, as represented by several transplants, is now a well-known phenomenon. "By the end of the 1980s, the new consensus was that superior Japanese productivity arose not so much from lower wages or extensive robotics, but from what seemed the willing consent of the work force" (Parker 1993: 254). The "Japanization" gospel was therefore sold in the United States as a package deal—not only production technology but also (and no less important) people strategies. Contrary to its reception in the United Kingdom, where the process accumulated negative connotations, in the United States "Japanization" has been accepted largely with equanimity. For example, the UAW has remained in favor of the new work systems proposed within "Japanization." The "lean production system" of the Japanese was "in the end" based on "the dynamic work team that emerges at the heart of the lean factory" (Womack et al.

1990: 99). Furthermore, in efficient work teams, tasks are rotated, and workers can fill in for each other. This meant the "reskilling" of workers, an imperative that was backed by the view that late twentieth-century industry must replace earlier forms of Fordist mass production and division of labor with flexible specialization in small-batch production (Piore and Sabel 1984).

Deployment of these new forms of work organization took place in transplants such as the New United Motors Manufacturing, Inc. (NUMMI) plant in Fremont, California, a joint venture of GM and Toyota, which started production in 1984. Other transplants included Honda in Ohio (opened in 1982), Nissan in Tennessee (1983), Mazda in Michigan (1987), Subaru-Isuzu in Indiana (1988), and a Chrysler-Mitsubishi joint venture in Illinois (1988). NUMMI, however, was the most successful: in 1986, it required a total of 21.2 labor hours per vehicle as compared with about 37 at other GM plants producing similar cars.[23] The UAW, which cooperated with management initiatives in GM and Ford plants, also saw NUMMI as a success story.

Mike Parker (1993) opens his astute description of the "team concept" that emerged with Japanization with a quote from GM's 1987 advertising campaign. GM declared that it had developed a "new production method" by rejecting the principles of Taylor and Ford. GM was correcting "the great flaw in the assembly line concept that tends to exclude the creative and managerial skills of people who work on the line" (Parker 1993: 249). Citing an example from GM's Fort Wayne, Indiana, assembly plant, another advertisement asserted that there are no longer workers and bosses in the plant, just "associates" and "advisors" (*Business Week*, 27 April 1987, 127; and 4 May 1987, 115; cited in Parker 1993: 249).

Parker's sardonic exposition anticipates his analysis of the "team concept" as an ingredient in the new management by stress. In his view, MBS represents a new packaging that has given the assembly

---

23. GM, *D-150 Labor Performance Report—Passenger Assembly*, week ending 5/11/86, #36; cited in Parker 1993: 259.

line and traditional scientific management methods a new lease on life. Worker empowerment and participatory management schemes were in this view cynically sold to labor in order to camouflage an intensification, not an abandonment, of classical Taylorism. MBS was not invented in the American transplants. Rather, it was imported from Japan as an original component of the just-in-time / total quality control regime. Imai Masaaki, president of the Kaizen Institute of America, described in the institute's newsletter how Ōno Taiichi, Toyota's founding practitioner of *kaizen*,[24] gave his department managers only 90 percent of the manpower, space, and equipment needed for straight-time production. Each manager was then expected to implement *kaizen* until the department could meet its production targets without overtime. "As soon as a no-overtime equilibrium was met," notes Imai with approval, "Mr. Ōno would come in and would again remove 10 percent of the resources. His way of managing came to be known as the OH! NO! system."[25]

There is a straight line running from Taylor's infamous "Schmidt experiment" through Suzuki Tsunesaburō's reputed labor competition at the Nikkō Electric Copper Smelting Company to Ōno's MBS *kaizen*. Alongside the more carefully designed shop-floor regime, the Japanization trend also represents an intensified form of normative control. To be sure, American manufacturers such as GM and Ford have been experimenting at least from the 1970s with a variety of organizational reforms to address the "labor problem" (as seen by management). Such attempts at QCCs and employee involvement schemes were costly, and the results were ambiguous. The just-in-time / total quality control regime, with its discourse of control, consent, and commitment, therefore also meant a Japanization of the workforce in a normative sense.

---

24. *Kaizen* is the concept, developed within total quality control, of continuous improvement.

25. Imai Masaaki, *Kaizen Communiqué* 2, no. 3 (Winter, 1988-89); published by the Kaizen Institute of America, Camarillo, Calif.; cited in Babson 1993: 8–9.

Just-in-Time/Total Quality Control
and Workers' Emotions in Japan
and the United States

How have Japanese and American workers responded to the "new paternalism" of just-in-time / total quality control? How have they reacted to the normative control of QCCs and teamwork? In this section, I move from "emotion" as it is put to work in managerial discourse to "emotion" as a theme of workers' culture.

On the surface, the transplants—car assembly factories staffed by American workers in the United States according to Japanese management schemes—seem like a worker's paradise. They were certainly hailed as such by the UAW (see Parker 1993: 259–61). Ruth Milkman argued in 1988 that NUMMI was

the ultimate in capitalist efficiency—based, paradoxically, on giving workers what socialism alone once promised: real participation in managerial decision-making. . . . By embracing the team concept, management validates the left's traditional call for increasing workers' control and dignity and respect on the job. It's not easy to face the prospect that such a basic transformation can occur on the factory floor while leaving capitalist property relations intact, but that's what NUMMI is all about. (Milkman 1988; cited in Parker 1993: 26)

Were NUMMI and the other transplants Trojan horses that sold Japanese-born paternalism and mutual trust to American labor while keeping "capitalist property relations intact"? This question provides the theme for a discussion of several recent studies of the transplants, notably such books as Joseph Fucini and Suzy Fucini's *Working for the Japanese: Inside Mazda's American Auto Plant* (1990), Ruth Milkman's *Japan's California Factories* (1991), Laurie Graham's *On the Line at Subaru-Isuzu* (1995), Terry Besser's *Team Toyota* (1996), and James Rinehart et al.'s (1997) account of Canadian Automobile Manufacturing, Inc. The similarities among the major U.S. transplants are summarized in Table 4.

Table 4

Japanese Practices in American Transplants, 1990

Trans-plant	Loca-tion and SOP*	Work teams	No. of job classi-fica-tions	QCCs	Annual avg. wages (US$)	Union
Honda	Ohio 1982	Yes	3	Modified	33,685	No
Nissan	Tennes-see 1983	Yes	4	Modified	32,579	No
NUMMI (GM + Toyota)	Calif-ornia 1984	Yes	4	Modified	36,013	Yes
Toyota	Ken-tucky 1986	Yes	3	Modified	29,598	No
Mazda	Michi-gan 1987	Yes	2	Modified	32,970	Yes
Subaru-Isuzu	Indiana 1988	Yes	3	Modified	28,995	No
Big Three U.S.	—	No	90	No	36,089	Yes

*Start of production.
SOURCE: Adapted from Florida & Kenney 1991: 385.

Transplants, which are either wholly owned by a Japanese company or represent a joint venture with one, appear to have several key managerial elements in common. All transplants follow the Japanese pattern of work teams, with responsibility for production and rotation of workers among the tasks assigned the team.[26] All transplants utilize

---

26. Although Table 4 provides a general view of Japanese practices in the transplants, it should be further tested against the actual implementation of these practices in each transplant. For example, a transplant might utilize work teams with a declarative ideology of workers' participation in decision making, even though in practice management assigns the team leader. Or, a transplant may implement rotation with the avowed purpose of reducing repeti-

a small number of job classifications, which is a key characteristic of the Japanese model. This contrasts sharply with traditional U.S. division of labor, in which trade unions view a variety of job classifications as the basis for wage increases. All transplants harness workers' intelligence through some form of suggestion system and quality circles. The major modification is that all transplants pay their workers for participating in quality circles. The actual level of *kaizen* achieved in transplant QCCs is, however, around 50 percent of the Japanese levels. Richard Florida and Martin Kenney (1991: 388) cite in this context a transplant manager who claimed that "education and effort are required to remove American barriers to worker initiative." From the perspective of emotion at work, it is not that American workers generally lack voluntary initiative; rather, the transplants' selection, socialization, and group activities fail to achieve normative control.

As in Japan, transplants pay relatively high wages, though somewhat less than the average paid by the "Big Three" automakers. Yet with overtime, the average worker in a transplant earns over $50,000 annually (Florida & Kenney 1991: 389). Transplants pay uniform wages for each class of workers, with raises at regular intervals. Bonuses, on the other hand, are not common and tend to be relatively small, across-the-board wage supplements. Transplants have countered the potential challenge from American trade unions by either choosing to avoid unionization (and locating in rural, "greenfield places" for that purpose) or reaching independent agreements with their respective union locals. This system of decentralized plant-specific "locals" resembles Japan's enterprise unions (see Taira 1961; Koike 1988). Most transplants have also re-created Japan's segmented or "dual" labor market with nonunionized, temporary workers working side-by-side with regular employees or "associates."

---

tive motion injuries, but in fact many team workers are denied rotation because of injuries. I attempt such local analysis in the ensuing section. Florida and Kenney therefore mistakenly interpret the appearance of isomorphism in Table 4 as a basis for claiming that the transplants have "effectively recreated the basic Japanese system" (1991: 394).

The Fucinis are critical of the Japanese model and report on adaptation problems by Mazda workers at Flat Rock, Michigan. They found that the initial high hopes of the workers broke down in the face of shop-floor reality. Although managerial rhetoric stressed "an emphasis on pulling together like a family" (Fucini and Fucini 1990: 71), the just-in-time work pace and the collapse of the team system proved otherwise. Steve Babson reported similar disillusionment. Based on a plant-wide union survey of 2,380 (out of total 2,800) workers at Mazda, he found a general attitude of disappointment and hostility. For example, only one out of seven Mazda workers said they could consistently count on their supervisor ("unit leader") to implement the company philosophy of participatory management. Many commented that the supervisor "play[ed] favorites" or adhered to the company philosophy "only when it suited him" (Babson 1993: 6).

In contrast to the philosophy of empowerment as represented, for example, by controlling one's work, each Mazda worker had to follow a programmed "work sheet," in which the job cycle was described in minute detail, including specific tasks, their sequence, and the number of seconds allotted to each. In practice, team members could not alter the programmed work sheets without approval of the supervisor. Contrary to the declared philosophy of "continuous improvement," workers or their teams were not permitted to initiate change unilaterally. Rather, a structured process controlled by supervisors and plant engineers screened proposals from QCCs and implemented those deemed consistent with production goals.

Mazda workers reacted by negotiating for change through their union, the UAW. The presence of the UAW made possible changes in management policies, for example, the election of the team leader by team members (Babson 1993). Milkman's 1991 analysis of the Linden GM plant similarly portrays a technologically advanced installation that led to skill polarization, not re-skilling, and to little "humanizing" of work. Rather, "jobs . . . continue to involve extremely repetitive, machine-paced, unskilled work." David Robertson and his colleagues, who studied Canadian Automobile Manufacturing, a joint venture between GM and Suzuki in Ontario, argue that most workers (who were unionized) found the team concept essentially *meaningless*, since it implied neither equality of members nor partnership with management. A socialization for teamwork as well as for *tatemae* was perhaps missing here. As many as 70 percent of the respondents be-lieved that working in teams was simply a way of getting them to work harder (Robertson et al. 1993: 75). The growing disenchantment at Canadian Automobile Manufacturing culminated in a five-week strike in 1992, after workers demanded (and received) the right to elect team leaders (since rescinded; see Rinehart et al. 1995).

NUMMI workers were described, in contrast, as more motivated and satisfied than they had been at their previous GM jobs (Adler 1993; Milkman 1988). Paul Adler's explanation was the delegation of responsibility to workers, or in his words: "What the NUMMI ex-periment shows is that hierarchy and standardization . . . can build on a logic of learning, a logic that motivates people and taps their poten-tial contribution to continuous improvement" (cited in Graham 1995: 10). An alternative explanation is provided by Lowell Turner (1991), who stresses that the formative experience of NUMMI workers was unemployment due to the closing of GM's Fremont plant. NUMMI was located in the former GM plant. Many of NUMMI's "associates" were former GM workers, who were probably grateful to regain their jobs. The debate over the reception of the Japanese model therefore cannot be resolved by the conflicting experiences of workers in the dif-ferent transplants. It seems safe to say that when real cooperation be-tween management and labor (whether unionized or not) took place, there were prospects for creating governance structures that increased workers' motivation. When, in contrast, workers found that there was no partnership and working conditions were imposed from above, their reactions were hostile and resentful. This is illustrated in the fol-lowing ethnographies of workers at Subaru-Isuzu Automotive and Toyota.

Life at the Transplant

Laurie Graham has provided a detailed ethnography of Subaru-Isuzu Automotive, a nonunion transplant in Indiana, based on a long-term, covert participant observation study. Her general conclusion regarding the "Japanese model debate" is that "the Japanese model . . . is grounded in Fordism but steps well beyond Fordist principles with its focus on controlling workers' culture" (1995: 3). This is in line with the argument presented in this book. According to Graham, Subaru-Isuzu Automotive's normative control begins with pre-selection practices.

Pre-selection, a relatively long and competitive process, involves a Japanese-like stress on interpersonal skills. There was no direct mention of emotional skills, only the requirement to "work in a team." Many workers who passed the screening admitted to Graham (in her capacity as a coworker) that they had manipulated the system, lying on questionnaires and pretending to be team oriented in order to get through the selection process (1995: 19). American workers thus proved their capacity for surface acting in response to the (rather primitive) emotion management of pre-selection. As part of the screening, applicants were separated into teams of four. The team's exercise was to build a series of circuit boards in one hour. Teams were informed that everything they said would be written down by the observers and assigned a numerical ranking; participants had to score at a certain level in order to pass this selection.

The team was then given money to buy parts from an observer. The mission was to assemble and sell enough circuit boards to make a profit. Before they could be sold, circuits had to pass a stringent inspection. "The atmosphere in the room during the exercise was very tense," recounts Graham (1995: 23–24):

Such intensity quickly separated out those of us who were able to function effectively under pressure. I observed two teammates as they worked furiously toward the stated goal of the exercise. They narrowly focused all of their attention on production in an effort to make a profit. Because they were working so hard, they were saying very little so there would be no information on which to base a score. I tried to keep in mind that it was our interactions that the observers were scoring and not the number of circuit boards the team would actually assemble.

Graham stresses that most applicants realized the company's expectations and played along, "participating in the charade." Many workers readily acknowledged their willingness to lie and trick the company. This approach is similar to the public acknowledgment of submission to the group by Japanese workers. This social skill is often attached to the Japanese socialization that distinguishes *tatemae* from *honne*, appearance from feelings. Subaru-Isuzu Automotive workers, despite their lack of a Japanese socialization, revealed no inner conflict to their undercover researcher. They knowingly "played the game," manipulating the system to benefit themselves, feeling one thing and doing another. Graham's account is illuminating in collapsing the stereotypes through which we differentiate self (American) from other (Japanese). At the end the day, it might very well be that most of us are playing the same game. But then again, perhaps it should come as no surprise that a transplant—built on a Japanese normative order—should encourage such games. However, although the demonstrated ability of American trainees to play along may have improved their chances of being hired, it also meant that the company could not count on teamwork from them.

Training for Teamwork

The "game" of socializing continued through orientation and training, where it became more and more serious. As Randy Hodson and Teresa Sullivan (1992) also found, socialization was the most important factor in the orientation and training experience. Each day during this three-week period, trainees were assigned "socialization time" between 8:30 and 9:00 A.M. This time, in American style, had no prearranged activities; rather, it led to class members smoking or drinking coffee outside the training center. It was an arranged opportunity for informal group activity. A more formalized procedure of behavior training, comparable to the socialization/training in the service sector, took place within the training sessions that followed the orientation. Several three- and four-hour sessions of a video-driven program called "Interaction" presented the trainees with three key principles:

Maintain or enhance the other person's self-esteem.
Listen and respond with empathy.
Ask for help in solving a problem. (Graham 1995: 47)

The program also included a list of "interaction guidelines," described as especially useful when "kaizening" (the Japanese term was anglicized in this manner):

Describe what you want to talk about.
Gather and review the details.
Explore alternatives.
Agree on actions to be taken.
Agree to a follow-up time. (Graham 1995: 47)

These directives were repeated over and over in what Graham found to be a condescending manner. Two class members mentioned during the presentation that "the techniques should come in handy when trying to get our children to do things they don't want to." The program's underlying message was that as associates (Subaru-Isuzu talk for "workers"), trainees must be willing to conform when confronted with the requirement for change. The message was presented through videotaped vignettes of a young and savvy worker who came up with an idea for improvement and used the key principles and interaction guidelines on an older, disgruntled worker, who finally was won over to the new way of doing things.

A two-and-a-half-hour class entitled "Cross-Cultural Training" was meant to prepare the trainees to work under Japanese trainers ("advisers"). "The instructors," described Graham with disenchantment (1995: 48–49),

showed the class a map of Japan and pointed out how because it was made up of islands, the country was very conservation minded. They listed some common stereotypes that Americans often held about the Japanese and then stereotypes that the Japanese often had concerning Americans. There was no discussion of any of these perspectives. . . . We were told not to talk pidgin or broken English to the Japanese trainers because it would not help them learn to speak the language. . . . To drive home the egalitarian nature of the Japanese model . . . we were informed that the president and VPs of the company as well as all clerical workers and middle management had their desks in the same room. . . . The class concluded with our learning some Japanese vowel and consonant sounds and then we wrote our names using the characters representing those sounds.

Terry Besser's 1996 study of Toyota's Camry transplant in Kentucky also reveals a managerial emphasis on teamwork. The central elements in the socialization for teamwork in this plant included hiring of inexperienced applicants, screening and training (called "assimilation training"), task allocation to work teams, equal pay and job rotation among team members, and official encouragement of a warm relationship between team members supported by small team size (4–5 members), stability of teams, and company money made available to teams for social events such as picnics, Christmas parties, trips to baseball games, birthday parties, and group pizza lunches (Besser 1996: 67, 159). However, unlike Graham, Besser does not provide an ethnography of the selection trials and the training rituals. His study, which was completely overt and authorized by management, was based instead on interviews with a sample of employees. The interviews and manuals show that managerial rhetoric was infused with the team concept, which applied equally to the workers (members of a work team), the company (the "company team" representing the company-as-family), and the global corporation ("Team Toyota").

One focus of socialization was the initiation of team leaders. Team leaders, elected by the team members, had to attend "prepromotion classes," where they were further familiarized with the Toyota philosophy. They received a trip to Japan to "fire them up" to implement that philosophy (Besser 1996: 70). Besser does not describe the actual contents of these initiation practices or reactions to them. His conclusion is that "the team leader is seen as a benevolent lead worker, a respected member of the team. Combine this with the low team-leader to team-member ratio and we have the formula for close, unobtrusive observation and monitoring of team members" (p. 71). Clearly the prospect of being promoted to a team leader was used by the company to foster membership motivation. Overall, the plant's workers and team leaders are described by Besser as "true believers" in the Toyota philosophy and in the superiority of teamwork over individual work.

Domesticating Japanese-Style Management

From a sociological perspective, the question whether the transplant was successful in domesticating the Japanese management system boils down to two interrelated queries. First, did American shop-floor practices come to correspond to Japanese managerial ideology and shop-floor practices? Second, was the message sent by management correctly interpreted and put into practice by the workers? The first question focuses on the top-down institutional transplantation of Japanese-style management; the second stresses a bottom-up cultural reading.

Many studies conducted in the transplants found a marked disjunction between ideology and practice. In the Subaru-Isuzu Automotive plant, for example, the selection of team leaders, a practice meant to institute the ideal of teamwork, was often hampered by manipulation. During training sessions, the ideology of the "Japanese model" was presented in an exaggerated form that served to reinforce stereotypes. Idealized emotional themes such as mutual trust, commitment, consent, and pride in one's work were inscribed in "interaction guidelines" and in the manuals ("Associate Handbooks"), but they never necessarily became part of shop-floor reality. Once production was under way, for example, the morning team meeting— presented by management as a bottom-up communications channel— lasted only five minutes, and workers complained that their suggestions were seldom acted on. For example, workers' requests to rotate jobs were simply ignored. One group of workers who needed to devise a method to prevent injuries decided what they needed and made the redesigned tool without involving the team or group leader. The reason was that going through the regular kaizening procedure would have taken months (Graham 1995: 82). Another serious discrepancy was that despite all its rhetoric of concern for worker safety, management ignored the increasing number of hand and wrist injuries on the shop floor and took no preventive measures, from the workers' point of view.

Hand and wrist injuries due to stressful and repetitive motion ("carpal tunnel syndrome") also occurred at the Toyota Camry plant in Kentucky. Workers who sought medical help were put "on restriction" by management, which meant that they were restricted to their station and were unable to transfer. This created, as Besser (1996: 127) explains, a potent disincentive to admitting an injury like carpal tunnel. Workers have to weigh the pain and possibility of permanent damage against the stigma of being a "sissy" and the likelihood of getting transferred to a less injurious job (Besser 1996: 137). Surprisingly, in Besser's account, the frequent injuries, the seeming inability of management to find and correct the causes, and the coercive practice of "on restriction" did not provoke resentment or hostility against management.

"None of my informants," concludes Besser, "indicated that team members used strategies that could be construed as contrary to organizational goal achievements or hostile to TMM [Toyota Motor Manufacturing]. Some told me of team members with 'bad attitudes,' but even these workers were not actively destructive. Instead, a bad attitude is manifested in refusal to participate in cleanup operations, group discussions, company, group, or team social functions, or quality circles" (1996: 144). Besser's study arguably lacks Graham's perspective of participant observation. His status as a management-approved researcher no doubt provided him with invaluable access, but it also labeled him in workers' eyes. When interviewed by a researcher who is (even vaguely) connected with management, workers and managers are inevitably aware of the public implications of their comments and often assume a defensive stance toward the company.

In fact, the different interpretations of Terry Besser and Laurie Graham undoubtedly owe much to their different methodologies.

Another gap between ideology and practice is described by Mike Parker. "Pulling the cord" at NUMMI stops the line; the presence of this cord is touted by management as a hallmark of the reskilling of responsible workers, workers committed to quality who can be trusted with a practical means of resisting arbitrary speed-ups. During the training period, argues Parker (1993: 268–69), "the cord" seems to work for everyone.

It helped workers get help when problems came up, and it helped keep quality high. . . . However, once the job was well defined and most of the bugs worked out, the cord became oppressive. As the line speeds up and the whole system becomes stressed, workers found it became harder and harder to keep up. Once the standardized work . . . had been in operation for a while, management assumed any problem was the fault of the workers, who had the burden of proof to show otherwise. . . . Such pressure translates into an extreme reluctance to pull the cord.

At Subaru-Isuzu Automotive, a similar discrepancy existed in regard to the cord as a symbol of workers' authority (Graham 1995: 78–79). Each station had two cords, yellow and red. Despite what they were told in orientation and training sessions, workers were allowed only to pull the yellow cord; this was a signal to the team leader to get to the troubled station within a few seconds. Pulling the red cord stopped the line immediately, but only team leaders were authorized to do so.

The case studies also reveal a gap between the organizational message and its reading by workers. Although the encoding of the message represents the global influence of Japanization, its decoding reflects both shop-floor culture (which can be different from managerial ideology) and the local surrounding culture (where socialization may differ from the behavioral training at the plant). Most of the studies found that the paternalist practices of Japanese-style management often triggered resentment among the American workers, who viewed them as condescending. Similarly, the morning exercises were embarrassing for many and regarded as "juvenile" (Graham 1995: 69). Graham describes cynical reactions by workers ("Do we get slapped on the wrist for being late for exercises?" p. 68) that led to defiant actions ("The team leader left Terry in charge today so no one exercised this morning, except Reese; he did it because he said it makes him feel better. The rest of us sat at the picnic table drinking coffee watching him"; p. 69).

At the end of the morning team meeting, members performed a daily ritual of huddling in a manner similar to that of a sports team before a game (see the quotation on p. 106). Again, the reaction to this ritual was often cynical. "The jokes [told by a few team members on such occasions] were a way for us to insert some control over the process" (Graham 1995: 70). After the message, all team members brought their right arms around into the circle with everyone's hands meeting in the center clenched into fists. While doing this, members shouted "Yosh!" and then broke up and went to work. "It was our understanding that *yosh* was a cheer meaning something similar to 'Let's go!'" (1995: 70).[27]

Subaru-Isuzu Automotive declared that its corporate culture was being built on mutual trust between management and workers. Workers were asked to involve themselves in the company enthusiastically, in a spiritual manner, in the same way that they would take part in voluntary community activities. A typical emotional reference is found in the description of the company philosophy in the company handbook. Note how this reference domesticates the Japanese management system within an all-American cultural context: "The spirit

---

27. The American film *Gung Ho* offers a nice illustration of workers' life in a transplant, including the huddling and *yosh!* shouts. Released in 1986, the film (directed by Ron Howard) preceded the opening of Subaru-Isuzu Automotive and coincided with the first wave of transplants. In the film, a Japanese management team takes over a small town U.S. factory and inflicts its philosophies on the Americans. The result is disaster, until the Japanese succumb to the American business practices (i.e., the workers take control of production), and finally everyone works together. Interestingly, the term "gung ho" was adopted from a slogan used by the Chinese in their resistance against Japanese aggression during World War II. The U.S. Marines, under General E. Carlson, adopted the phrase as a slogan, and it spread throughout the Allied armed forces. This adoption is in evidence in the title of a 1943 war melodrama entitled *Gung Ho!* in which the Marines raid the Japanese-held Makin Island.

of SIA [Subaru-Isuzu Automotive] is Enthusiastic Involvement. Participation and involvement are traditional in American society. Many of us demonstrate this spirit in volunteer activities ranging from Little League baseball and civic groups to church picnics. Why not show the same spirit in our business activities?" (Graham 1995: 95). Most workers, according to Graham (1995: 96), were skeptical of this.

The transplants used normative control—an arguably weaker, American-type normative control—but emotion management existed only in embryonic form. Emotion work takes place when emotion is "no longer a private act but a public act" (Hochschild 1983: 118). Through training for teamwork, the company made it clear that it was no longer the individual but the trainer and the manual who decided on the right emotional display. However, emotions were scripted in a rather general and often superficial manner. The emphasis in Subaru-Isuzu Automotive was on display (of mutual respect, enthusiasm, being pleasant and considerate) and hence resulted in a surface play or "charade" (Graham's term). There was no complementary ideology of cultivating oneself through work and no formalization of feeling rules or manuals for emotion management.

Emotional Numbness and Emotional Resistance

In contrast to the transplants, Japanese plants show (not surprisingly perhaps) a relatively stronger match between ideology and practice as well as between encoding (message) and decoding (interpretation). As far as the objective work conditions were concerned, Laurie Graham found many similarities between Subaru-Isuzu Automotive and Toyota as described by Kamata: "Workers at Subaru-Isuzu Automotive experienced many similar difficulties, such as unannounced overtime, speedups, and exploitation of temporary workers" (1995: 11). From a subjective point of view, however, Subaru-Isuzu Automotive workers (who were nonunionized, like Kamata's temporary co-workers) reacted quite differently. The striking difference between Graham's and Kamata's accounts is in their descriptions of shop-floor resistance.

Table 5
Forms of Subversion Among Subaru-Isuzu Automotive Workers

Individual	Team	Collective
	Passive	
Remaining silent in morning team meetings; after SOP,* refusing to participate in morning exercise or company meetings	After SOP, team members remaining silent during morning team meetings	Jokes and humor, making light of company's rituals and philosophy; refusing to work unscheduled overtime; leaving a moving line early because of overtime
	Active	
Anonymous letters to the company as part of firm's program of "rumor control"	Complaining about speed-ups to group leader; if no changes occur, team members walking out without locking up tools or cleaning up; later, even stopping the assembly line	Plant-wide organized agitation

*Start of production.
SOURCE: Based on Graham 1995.

Graham describes a shop-floor reality that stands in stark contrast to the training ideals. According to her respondents, the plant was not filled with team spirit. There was a power struggle between the trainers for the car division and the trainers for the truck division. Team leaders were appointed (and replaced) by management and not by workers. Workers' suggestions were seldom implemented. Resentment increased considerably after production began, when the work became hectic, with abundant overwork and group activities that took time from working on the line. Consequently, workers reacted with various forms of subversion (see Table 5).

Kamata encountered only a single, minor form of subversion (jokes) in Toyota, compared to the variety described in Table 5, and indeed, he and his co-workers seemed to have internalized Toyota's normative prescriptions. For example, Kamata felt guilt for leaving the assembly line: "I had diarrhea today and had to go to the toilet twice while I was on the line. It must have been the painkiller, combined with the terrible canteen food, sheer exhaustion, and the mental pressure of following the line. Still, I hated to light the lamp and call the team chief. Even though it feels wonderful to leave the line just for a few minutes, I feel strangely guilty when I do" (1982: 83).

In other instances, Kamata retained a critical voice in the face of what he regarded as (without actually calling it) normative control or even subjugation. For example, Toyota has a feeling rule that requires injured workers to apologize.

The accident had happened when . . . the man had been operating two machines at once, and his hand got caught in one of them. Obviously, the accident was caused by the pressure to work faster. . . . The general foreman said that he would give the man proper indemnity because he cheerfully apologized to the section manager instead of making complaints. At Toyota, the victim has to apologize! (1982: 110)[28]

In another entry, Kamata (1982: 80) describes how workers' complaints following a speed-up that resulted in forced overtime culminate in jokes. Notice also the subtle play on the theme of responsibility:

During the break, everybody sits on the bench, exhausted.
"Do you think they'll take responsibility if my wife runs away?" 23-year-old Shimoyama says, not quite joking. . . . By now everyone is listening and commenting. "Last night I fell asleep in the bathtub and my wife woke me up," Fukuyama says. . . .
"If someone died on the line, would they realize how bad it's getting?"
"One wouldn't be enough."
"How about everybody on the line?"
"The other shift would have to die, too."
"Still not enough."

---

28. The apology described by Kamata is reminiscent of the public apology (hansei) described by Glenda Roberts (1994) in the context of blue-collar women workers. Kamata, however, does not describe it as a practice; rather, he mentions it as a single case.

Somehow, complaints about bad working conditions always turn into jokes.

Nobody listens to our complaints, so it's easier to joke.

In a stark contrast to Graham's and other Western accounts of emotional resistance to the "Japanese" model,[29] Kamata describes a kind of emotional numbness. When management scheduled meetings ten minutes before the beginning of the shift, he remarks, "It's not fair, but no one protests" (1982: 34). When management announced a speed-up, "it was infuriating. But no matter how angry we get, we go back to the line, and once the line starts, there is no time to complain. Our anger is always stillborn" (1982: 56). Overall, Kamata does not seem particularly intrigued by the consent of his co-workers. "Eventually, young workers full of potential are deadened by the monotonous work. . . . Rationalization of production changes even their personalities by making them overstrain a tiny fraction of their abilities. Ultimately, it's a kind of lobotomy." Such emotional lobotomy generates a "very passive personality" (1982: 151).[30]

In a broader context, the emotional lobotomy that Kamata mentions can be understood as the price of social controls that reward loyal employees and punish uncommitted workers in a Japanese auto plant. Normative control does not stand alone; it is always combined with remunerative and coercive control. An autoworker's annual income in Japan has two components: a seniority-defined base wage (a little more than half of annual income), and a part contingent on the performance of the individual worker, his (rarely her) work group,

---

29. A variety of incidents of individual discontent, blame and competition among workers, and collective grievances can be found in Delbridge's (1998) study of the workplace experience of lean production and the Japanese model in American and British transplants.

30. One can arguably link Kamata's "emotional lobotomy" with the recent phenomenon of *karōshi*. *Karōshi* (literally, "crash"), or death from overwork, is supposed to result from fatigue due to long hours of physical work and/or excessive stress. The usual killers are cerebral hemorrhage or heart failure. The long hours consist of more working hours (2,168 hours in Japan in 1986, world's record and 200 more than in the United States) along with more overwork (35 hours a month, twice the international average) and more off-work group activities (National Defense Counsel for Victims of Karōshi 1990).

and the company. Bonuses, profit sharing, and merit pay all subordinate the worker to company goals.[31]

"Emotional lobotomy" is a symptom of obedience rather than of voluntary commitment. Why, then, did the American transplants fail to generate obedience? Generally speaking, the transplants failed in implementing both normative and remunerative controls. Instead of transplanting the strong organizational culture of the original Japanese management system, the transplants mouthed one thing and practiced another. American workers reacted with emotional resistance to the gaps between company ideology and shop-floor practice, between declared meanings and their subversive interpretation. This triggered the failure of normative control. Moreover, many of the controls that obligate worker commitment in Japan could not be transferred to North America. As Babson (1993: 21) argues, company housing and other "corporate welfare" programs have little appeal in the United States, and the Japanese variant of enterprise unionism violates the American labor law. In terms of remuneration, the acceptable range of contingent pay (bonuses, incentives, merit) in the United States still falls well short of Japanese norms. No Japanese firm in the U.S. auto industry has, according to a survey conducted by Endō Koshi (1994), introduced *satei* (personal appraisal or merit rating). Japanese managers are reluctant to introduce merit ratings even in nonunionized transplants such as Nissan's plant in Tennessee for fear that this will anger workers and encourage unionization.

III. THE GENDERED SIDE OF
PATERNALISM: BLUE-COLLAR WOMEN

Blue-collar women have been working in light manufacturing industries in Japan since the infamous days of the spinning mills at the turn of the century. In 1985, 25 percent of Japanese women workers were

---

31. For the Japanese pay system, see Higuchi 1997; and Inagami Takeshi, "Japanese Workplace Industrial Relations," in Japan Institute of Labor, *Japanese Industrial Relations Series*, 14 (Tokyo, 1985).

employed in the manufacturing sector (Japan Institute of Labor 2000). This figure represents a shift in the locus of work from domestic piecework (*naishoku*) to work outside the home. Following the oil shock of 1973–74, many manufacturers reduced labor costs by hiring more *pāto* (part-time) workers, usually housewives (Shinotsuka 1982). A *pāto* is a nonregular employee on a short-term contract who is paid hourly wages; she has few benefits and is not allowed to join the union. Japanese employment security largely excludes women, who have been and still are a buffer protecting the stable jobs extended to male workers in large firms.

The paternalist ideology of management, or *onjōshugi*, has special consequences for women workers. The obvious implications are that female employees, especially young women, are to be "looked after" by their parents/managers. This approach has led to various forms of emotional behavior usually grouped under the concept of *oya gawari* or *in loco parentis* (described in Kondo 1990 and Lo 1990, for example). In the family-owned and family-managed small confectionery factory in Tokyo described by Kondo (1990), *in loco parentis* was pursued adamantly. Such a small company is a "family firm" in actual practice.

Kondo (1990: 178–80) lists several paternalistic practices. The owners' involvement with their employees began with the recruitment process. The owner (and household head), Mr. Satō, took special care to recruit new employees from the local prefecture. Prospective employees were often recommended by Mr. Satō's village friends, and he kept himself up to date about their family situation. A ceremonial dinner introduced new employees to the company. Living arrangements were also a company matter. Workers usually took their meals in the company lunchroom, and the food was often made by the owner's wife. The company also served as surrogate family in its involvement with important personal events in their employees' lives, such as birthdays, the birth of children, marriages, and deaths. The Satōs kept a list of people's birthdays and when the day arrived, Mr. Satō would ceremoniously present a gift. Like many bosses (see Rohlen 1974), the Satōs acted as go-betweens in most of their employees' marriages. When an employee bereft of close relatives (a childless widow, for example) died, Mr. Satō assumed the considerable expense of giving the late employee both a funeral and a proper cremation. Other familial company practices included arranging and financing the employees' annual trip (*shain ryokō*).

In loco parentis attitudes were also present in the Nagoya typewriter factory of Brother Industries described by Jeannie Lo, a much larger workplace than Kondo's confectionery. For example, the social life in the company dormitories represented "a home away from home" for many of the women employees who lived too far away to commute to work. Lo's ethnography of dormitory life shows how parental control was transferred from the family to the company. Employees in the personnel division assured Lo that "with the dormitory structure that we have, the parents of the girls need not worry. They are well taken care of. There is no way that they can get into trouble" (1990: 51). The women received housing, meals, and bathing facilities and in return were expected to behave like "obedient company daughters" (1990: 101–2). They had to do their own housekeeping and observe strict curfews and rules on morality and general tidiness.[32] Residents also took classes in the skills needed by housewives and often talked about marriage. They saw marriage as a way out of the dormitory and the workplace. For its part, management made it clear that female employees were expected to marry and to leave the company.[33] This expectation

---

32. The dormitories for male workers at Brother Industries had automatic washing machines, dryers, and janitorial service, whereas the women were expected to do all these chores themselves (Lo 1990: 57).

33. Managerial expectations regarding impending marriage of female workers were articulated, for example, through recruitment ads. Lo (1990: 65–66) cites a Brother recruitment pamphlet that portrayed the "manner in which you [the prospective employee] will ascend the steps of youth"—moving from graduation at age 18 to work and marriage preparations (bridal training classes, dates) until "stepping off the pedestal" and leaving the company to get married. The Brother company song, entitled "Song of Youth" ("Seishun no uta"), similarly conveys a paternalistic view of Brother's female employees as young and full of energy, "blooming white roses" who need to be molded into responsible adults. Brother presented itself not only as a workplace but also as a "finishing school."

is also a central theme in regard to "office ladies," the female office workers described in Chapter 4.

Another important ethnography is Glenda Roberts's (1994) *Staying on the Line*, a description of female blue-collar workers in a textile factory she dubbed Azumi. Most of these female workers were regular employees, with an average of ten years of service in the factory. Women constituted about 90 percent of the factory's workforce. The percentage of blue-collar female workers, however, had dwindled from 35 percent of the company's overall female workforce in 1974 to 9 percent in 1985. In contrast, the percent of saleswomen had grown from 35.6 percent in 1974 to 54 percent in 1985. Yet saleswomen, in contrast to blue-collar workers, were young, single women with an average of five years of service, hired straight out of high school and expected to quit at marriage (1994: 10–11). Blue-collar workers therefore referred to themselves as "the survivors." Roberts's book is about their struggle to "stay on the line" in spite of personal and family difficulties and cultural expectations.

The world of Azumi's blue-collar workers was gendered in several respects. First, the organizational culture reflected the gender of its members. An important cultural aspect was instilled in the rank-order of worker classification. The lowest supervisory rank in the factory was called *shisutā*, "sister." According to Roberts (1994: 13), "Management assigned the term *shisutā* to these work facilitators in the 1960s when there were many young recruits who needed a little extra 'sisterly' supervision and advice." The *shisutā* was not, despite a family resemblance, the equal of the male *senpai* (the senior employee who looks after the junior employees, facilitating on-the-job training). Sisters cannot affect the promotion of their female charges or bargain with the group leader.

The "sister" is an example of the two-pronged use of the family metaphor when it comes to blue-collar female workers. On the one hand, management continues to use the family metaphor, derived from the paternalistic ideology of *onjōshugi*. Supervisors are therefore called "sisters." On the other hand, female workers cannot really and fully be subjected to the family metaphor, since they are emotionally bound, in Japanese eyes, first and foremost to their natal or their husband's household. The "sisters" therefore lack real authority. Another example of the use of the family metaphor by management was encountered by Glenda Roberts following her transfer to another plant of the company, where new methods of inspection and packaging had to be learned. To stress this point, the male *kachō* (section chief) told the transferred employees they were like *oyome* (brides) who had to learn the ways of a new home (1994: 15).

The family metaphor illustrates the gendered nature of the Japanese workplace. Although the firm-as-family binds both male and female workers, in practice only men are equal members of that family. A woman's "real family" is, in contrast, at home. Women's first emotional obligation is not to the company but to their family, in their capacity as good wives and wise mothers.

Women Workers and the Culture
of Ryōsai kenbo

The main cultural construct that binds women to the home is the well-known dictum of *ryōsai kenbo* (good wife, wise mother). It is a major theme in the emotional discourse of female workers in Japan. The *ryōsai kenbo* model encourages women to work until marriage and then quit to raise a family. Women re-enter the labor force, if at all, after their children are grown. The resulting pattern of female employment is known as the "M-curve," the "M" consisting of two peaks of labor force participation rate: one of Japanese women in their mid-twenties (in 1990, 75.1 percent), and the other, slightly lower peak (71.7 percent) at ages 45 to 49 (see Fig. 3). The "M" is still largely in evidence, although the "trough" of the M is filling in somewhat because of the rise in age at marriage and at first birth, the smaller number of births per woman, and the postponement of exiting the workforce until the first birth. Roberts's co-workers were either in the trough of the

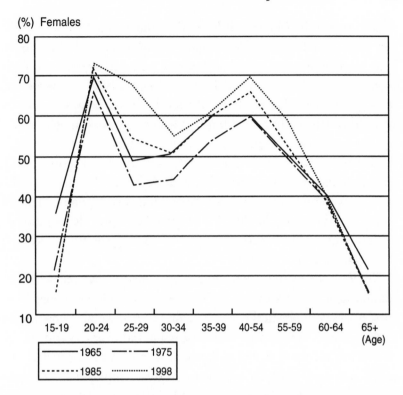

Fig. 3   Labor force participation rates for Japanese women (Japan Institute of Labor 2000: 16)

M or at the second peak and trying not to slip down the slope. They were married, with children, but continued to work in order to maintain a certain living standard.

Ryōsai kenbo is the Japanese version of the late nineteenth-century Western cult of female domesticity, adopted and made popular by the Meiji reformers. In the prewar era this ideology was aimed largely at middle-class women who did not work. Unlike the American-bred ideology, which grounded its rationale for domesticity and self-sacrifice in romantic love, *ryōsai kenbo* was based on the concept of the traditional household (*ie*). Women were to remain in the household as managers and educators (Uno 1988). This expectation was inculcated through the Ministry of Education, the national school system, and women's education (Sievers 1983; in Japanese, see Fukaya 1977). The ideological stress on *ryōsai kenbo* is ironic in light of women's prominent role in the industrialization of Japan. Since the 1870s, the same government that promoted the ideal of *ryōsai kenbo* was encouraging (through the Interior Ministry) women to work in light industry. Between 1894 and 1912, women formed an average of 60 percent of the industrial work force (Sievers 1983: 55; see also Tsurumi 1984). The discrepancy between *ryōsai kenbo* ideology and the practice of female labor should not surprise us. Japan's industrialization was fueled by female labor, and the doctrine of *ryōsai kenbo* provided a rationale for low wages and minimally acceptable working conditions (Kondo 1990: 272; see also Uno 1992).

The ideal of *ryōsai kenbo*, nurtured by a society that enables men's commitment to work by making women responsible for domestic affairs, places very practical constraints on married women who opt for a career. First, women are considered temporary workers and are expected to quit upon marriage. Second, women are relegated to the lower status of *pāto*. To qualify for regular employment, the *pāto* worker has to undergo a trial period (usually six months) during which no holidays or days off can be taken. This is a major problem for anyone who is also expected to be the only caretaker of children and in-laws, particularly when these are sick or ailing.

There is an apparent contradiction for working-class women in the "good wife, wise mother" ideology. Although this ideology was originally aimed at middle-class women who did not have to work, it nevertheless framed the social positioning of women workers within the factory. This gender ideology was used, for example, to justify the existence of discrimination in promotion. Managers knew that many of their blue-collar women workers were unable to quit work to fulfill the ideal of "good wife, wise mother," and yet they regarded them as a "secondary labor force." Although promotion was presented as being available to both sexes, only 3 percent of all female employees held positions of rank. Those who made it to managerial grades were often single or divorced "career women." This is still not unusual in Japanese companies, even after the implementation of an Equal Employment Opportunity Act in 1986 (National Institute of Employment and Vocational Research 1988).

That promotion is reserved for men is evident in company recruitment policy. When Glenda Roberts (1994: 32) asked a manager of the personnel department what sort of young woman the company sought for factory employment, he said they "took girls from mediocre schools who did not like school and were not high achievers. This type of girl would presumably be more suited to the tedium of the factory. They all entered as F (*futsū*, ordinary) group workers, and the management did not expect or desire them to go beyond the group, as they did male workers." Whereas women workers and office ladies who became skillful at their work could move up to the better-paying G group (*gijutsu*, skilled), few of them ever made the transition to the K group (*kikaku kaihatsu*, planning and development), which was required for any supervisory position above group leader. The existence of only two job categories for nonmanagerial work illustrates the relatively loose job/pay structure applied to the bulk of blue-collar workers in Japan. To be eligible for the K group, one had to be recommended by management to take an examination. Similarly, a variety of job assignments (following job rotation) was a prerequisite for promotion. The typical woman's inability to accept a job transfer is cited by managers as the reason why women are not considered for promotion.

The "New Life" Movement

Management attempts to control a worker's emotions by managing his or her family life. Indeed, the ideology of good wife, wise mother can be seen as part of the control of workers' emotions. In Japan's "worker society," women are relegated to the home and empowered there to act as domestic managers, thus supporting the organizational commitment and devotion of their husbands, the salarymen. In 1953 managers at the Japanese steel company Nippon kōkan initiated the "New

Life" campaign to train employees' wives to be supportive and professional homemakers. In 1955, the Japanese government supported a similarly titled national campaign. Women were taught how to run efficient and rational homes, in order to allow their men to realize the same ideals at work.

The case of Nippon kōkan is instructive. In 1952, just before the start of its New Life campaign for progressive homemakers, Nippon kōkan was a man's workplace. Only 6 percent of its workforce were women workers, and they worked mostly in offices. Nippon kōkan manager Orii Hyūga (1973: 113; cited in Gordon 1998: 75) wrote in his diary that "our goal was to elevate the housewives and establish the foundation for a bright, cheerful home, a bright society, and beyond that, a bright, cheerful workplace." Toshiba and Hitachi later joined Nippon kōkan's initiative. They advocated birth control—discouraging abortion and promoting contraception—and addressed such matters as nutrition, shopping and cooking, child rearing, and the productive use of leisure time. An official in the welfare section of the company was responsible for the New Life activities and oversaw hundreds of small groups of workers' wives and counseling centers located in each city district. By 1963, 63 percent of Nippon kōkan's 27,000 employee households were organized into New Life groups that met monthly to discuss various domestic issues and joined in excursions to the theater or the movies.

The New Life movement was full of emotional rhetoric that fit neatly into the traditional language of Japanese-style management. A Toshiba labor manager wrote in 1957 that it was a form of service to employees, a manifestation of "goodwill and caring that would naturally generate trust and intimacy" (cited in Gordon 1998: 76). Unions were aware of the managerial interest behind the seductive campaign. Although openly giving their blessing to the campaign, many workplace unions launched competing efforts to build and control the wives' groups. In the 1950s, the union at Nippon kōkan's Tsurumi Mill organized a housewives' discussion society, whose groups became active supporters of the union.

The attempt to rationalize family life and homemaking is not unique to Japan. In the United States during the 1920s there was an upsurge of similar welfare policies. American welfare capitalists, just like postwar Japanese managers, sought to reform the home in order to boost the efficiency of the workplace. As an article in the American journal *Industrial Management* put it in 1917:

It is not to be wondered that a man who has slept for six or seven hours in a room with ten others, only turning out of bed in the morning in time for a night-shift man to take his place between the same sheets, does not go to his work fresh, happy and cheerful. And after working hours he has no place to go except the saloon, and nothing to do but drink. It is not likely that his health will be so good or his efficiency so great as that of the man who sleeps in healthy surroundings and has a comfortable home. (Leslie Allen, "The Problem of Industrial Housing," vol. 54, p. 397; cited in Tone 1997: 90).

Many progressive reforms were premised on faith in the interconnection of domestic space and personal character. Model homes were the seedbed of model workers. This justified the inspection of workers' dwellings and family behavior under the auspices of moral reform. The best example was Ford Motor Company's famous five-dollar day, which started in 1914. This wage was actually a "profit-sharing payment" that workers earned only if they complied with rules of conduct at work and at home. Company investigators working in the "sociology department" at Ford Motors interviewed family members and scrutinized employees' home conditions. Poor sanitation, overcrowding, and improper behavior (such as drinking, smoking, and living with a woman to whom one was not married) were grounds for disqualification.[34]

Not all Japanese company unions embraced the New Life movement. Some were hostile or cool at first. But Japanese unions were surely less hostile than their American counterparts. American trade unions were not supporters of welfare capitalism. Although American Federation of Labor (AFL) leaders supported welfare work in princi-

---

34. On American welfare capitalism, see Tone 1997; Meyer 1981; and Brandes 1976.

ple, they often rejected it in practice on the grounds that employers used it to smother workers' independence. An interesting rhetoric of gendered emotionality framed the AFL's position. Union leaders spoke of beleaguered manhood, associating welfare work with dependency and emasculation. The AFL's official journal, the *American Federationist*, expressed in many editorials its determination to "stand for a policy that will develop real men . . . who pulsate with the discontent that makes men divine" ("Contented Cows," 1923, 30: 761–62; cited in Tone 1997: 186). Manly American unionists did not support what they saw as a paternalistic feudalism characterized by employer dominance and employee submission. AFL leaders urged workers to enjoy the practical fruits of welfare reforms while remaining wary of paternalist entrapment. From the perspective of the more extreme labor left in the United States, welfare was bad, part of a capitalist trick to confuse workers' loyalties and dissolve class solidarity.

American workers, especially men who were socialized in the "manly" culture of self-reliance, often found the idea of welfare capitalism repugnant. Workers did not want a female welfare worker—the icon of dependency—to prop them up. We see here a demonstration of the impact of the surrounding culture, through its values and norms, on the acceptance of organizational culture by workers. In Japan, the "worker society" embraced the New Life Movement; in the United States, both male and female workers often resisted efforts to modify working-class behavior by imposing employers' values. When company representatives tried to survey workers' homes, they were often barred from entering by resentful employees. Workers similarly resisted hygiene examinations and often refused to adopt and cooperate with suggestions made by the company nurse who visited their home.

In comparison to the United States, Japan's sustained and extensive experience with company welfare programs is noteworthy. The impact of the surrounding culture on the acceptance of the New Life Movement by workers is illustrated by the use of small groups, or circles, to mobilize and educate housewives. In the United States, welfare capitalists sent company representatives and officials to examine workers' homes in a coercive manner. In Japan, workers and their families participated in these activities, which were organized in small groups. Home reform was presented and accepted not merely as a duty but as a privilege that workers' wives were empowered to implement for their families. In Japan, workers and their wives became self-supervisors of the home reform, whereas in the United States workers and their wives were subjects of this reform. In Japan, the union joined the New Life activity and organized its own groups and association as a counterweight to the management campaign. The kitchen redesign problems tackled by the small groups of workers' wives in the 1950s were a prelude for the assembly-line redesign problems discussed in the 1960s by QCCs (see also Gordon 1997). The underlying common denominator was the successful mobilization of workers, through small group activities, in the collective pursuit of productivity and rationalization.

Mutual Trust and Public Apologies

Industrial order in the textile factories was largely based on normative, rather than remunerative or coercive, control. This policy was first termed by the management of the textile factory studied by Roberts as *sōgo shinrai,* or mutual trust, at the time of unionization in 1962. Under the policy of mutual trust, clock punching was abandoned. In return, the union declared that its members would never go on strike. One of the pillars of mutual trust was that the company set the standard of production, and those who failed to meet it were "resented" by management as well as by their group, in part because co-workers had to take up the slack. This practice of the work team as a site for self-discipline has also become one of the pillars of the "lean production" regime. Furthermore, in the textile factory the minimum standard was not linked to basic monthly pay, and those who failed to meet the target were not penalized. The system of control was therefore truly normative. "Every day we were required to chart how many pieces we had completed in how much time; this record was posted for all to see. Each morning the *kakarichō* (subsection chief) would announce the names of those who had met their targets from the previous day and would honor them with a '*gokurōsan deshita!*' (Thank you for your effort)" (see Roberts 1994: 46).

Mutual trust notwithstanding, tardiness and absenteeism were considered major problems. The *hansei* (practically speaking, a public apology; more generally, self-reflection) was the normative sanction devised to prompt worker diligence. The *hansei* included self-reflection on one's mistakes and what one planned to do to prevent it from happening again. Such *hansei*, for example, had to be made for all absences (Roberts 1994: 46, 74). If an employee was sick or for any other reason had taken the previous day off, he or she had to offer the group an apology at the morning ceremony. The most common was, "I'm sorry for having caused you trouble by selfishly taking the day off yesterday when all of you were so busy" (Roberts 1994: 74). According to Roberts, everyone thought the practice was too harsh. The humiliation of repeated *hansei* was seen as being an effective equivalent to firing.

The public apology provides an illuminating illustration of the interplay of public and private, or more aptly *tatemae-honne*, in the Japanese workplace. Were the workers sincere in their apology, or was it a matter of *tatemae*, wherein—and no less important—the worker reaffirms indebtedness to her company and co-workers? In Roberts's (1994: 75) words, "[Was it] more an expression of solidarity with the group than culpability in taking a day off?" Like many normative workplace practices in Japan, the public apology is an extension of school life. Public apologies were once quite common in Japanese schools as a means of making children reflect on their bad behavior (see also White 1987: 32). The practice has fallen from favor in postwar education, although some teachers still use it (Roberts 1994: 182n1). It is also used by the new religions and sports teams.

Hiroshi Wagatsuma and A. Rossett (1986) argue that the public apology reflects shame rather than guilt. In other words, the apology is made in public whatever one's feelings of guilt. Workplace apologies demonstrate not so much a feeling of culpability (that is irrelevant) but the public acknowledgment of submission and willingness to co-operate in the future. In contrast to the situation in Western culture, *honne* and *tatemae* need not be congruent for the apology to be "genuine." The internal state of mind of the person who tenders the apology is less important than the act itself.

CHAPTER FOUR

Office Rules: The World of the Salaryman and the Office Lady

Emphasizing trust and possessing an enterprising spirit, we will advance scientific administration. With mutual respect and affection, we will work with diligence, employed in maintaining systematic order.
> —From the principles of a Japanese bank (cited in Rohlen 1974: 36)

Other people are our mirrors.
> —A central aphorism of ethical training for Japanese employees as well as of Japanese moral education in general

Self Improvement: Reading the in-house journal is preferable to a newspaper or magazine. Nobody reads these things as a rule, so being seen to do so will ingratiate you horribly with the bosses. . . . Always make sure you're doing the right thing at the right time when the boss walks by.
> —Advice from a British personnel trainer, Judi James (1997: 160–61)

White-Collar Work in (Western) Sociological Perspective

White-collar workers were the subject of lively sociological discussion in the 1920s and 1930s, especially in Europe. The status of white-collar workers attracted attention from both neo-Weberians and neo-Marxists, who fiercely debated whether they were a "new class" or a *Mittelstand* of bureaucrats or proletarians in false collars (see Crozier 1965: 21–32 for an overview).[1] The sociological interest in white-collar

---

1. Marx devoted little attention to clerks, functionaries, managers, and the like. He distinguished the senior officers of capitalism (engineers, managers) from the junior officers (fore-

work waned following World War II, just at the point when the number of office workers began to multiply rapidly.

In *White Collar: The American Middle Classes*, C. Wright Mills (1951) adopted the German arguments concerning "the proletarization of the middle classes and the natural rapprochement between manual and nonmanual workers, both equally victims of capitalism" (Crozier 1965: 27).[2] Mills emphasizes the spiritual alienation of office workers resulting from the rationalization of methods (which simplifies and devaluates tasks) and the forces that exert pressure on them. Michel Crozier, in *The World of the Office Worker*, argues that white-collar alienation is more subjective than objective. Alienation is the sign of the profound contradiction that office workers experience in their situation as both exploited workers and collaborators who share in directorial power over laborers. In a thoughtful declaration that preceded the surge of sociological interest in emotion management two decades later, Crozier (1965: 28) remarked that "the individual is always necessarily limited by his place in the social structure; the commercial smile of the small independent shopkeeper is at least as alienated as that of the salesgirl. To understand the real import of the smile, there is no way of escaping the study of subjectivity."

Crozier's opening remark is almost Japanese in its acceptance of the dominance of social positioning. His ensuing assertion regarding the alienated smile, however, instantly brings the discussion back to

---

men, supervisors, superintendents, clerks) and emphasized the role ambiguity of the latter, who were both exploited and at the same time charged with maintaining the exploitation of others.

2. The "natural rapprochement between manual and nonmanual workers" brings to mind Thomas Smith's study of Japanese manual workers' emotional quest for dignity. The comparison is illuminating. According to Crozier, many of his white-collar respondents claimed that blue-collar employees were "persons with no self-respect" (1965: 148), "less well brought-up" (p. 168), and "have no dignity . . . do not try to improve themselves. . . . Out of the factory, into the bar" (p. 170). Similar perceptions of blue-collar workers, according to Smith, were prevalent at the turn of the twentieth century in Japan. Japanese blue-collar workers bought into the managerial ideology of paternalism in part because it enabled them to achieve a status of dignity. In Japan of the 1950s and the 1960s, manual workers were no longer looked down on. In France, however, office workers still carefully distinguished themselves from manual laborers, according to Crozier (1965).

Western and particularly Marxist definitions. The Marxist notion of alienation is based on and reinforces the Western distinction between private life (which embodies real feelings) and public work arrangements (which require false emotional displays). For Marx, Mills, and Crozier, this true/false distinction is enveloped by the broader proletarian/capitalist class distinction. The cultural dimension (the "superstructure") is therefore dominated by the economic dimension (the "base"). If we compare these definitions with the Japanese view of white-collar workers, the cross-cultural dimension can be brought back into the picture. The conceptualization of white-collar work in Japan clearly differs from that common in the United States. In Japan, the significance of Japanese-style management was acknowledged by means of a cultural conceptualization that also promoted, and was reinforced by, an autonomous "worker society" that separated itself culturally from the individualistic pursuits of capitalism. In contrast, in the United States, workers were not generally perceived as forming a "society" of their own; rather, they are seen as individuals striving for personal mobilization in a stratified market.

Crozier's concluding assertion in the passage quoted above is that to understand the real import of the smile (that is, to understand alienation), we must study subjectivity. This is quite agreeable in theory, yet in practice Crozier's methodology was based on questionnaires—hardly the ideal measure of subjectivity. Here again, it is interesting to introduce a comparative perspective, which I offer below through a discussion of Thomas Rohlen's 1974 ethnography of Japanese bank workers.

The Professional Practice of Japanese Management: An Overview

One of the main concerns of the preceding chapters is the managerial ideology of paternalism (*onjōshugi*). Those chapters treat managers as agents of this ideology and compare, for example, the different ideological orientations of Japanese and American managers toward small-group activities. In this chapter, I focus not on the ideology of management but on its practice and view managers and office workers not as agents but as subjects of workplace ideology. I examine the emotional themes inherent in such office practices as training, selection, promotion, job transfer, and decision-making patterns. My concern is to analyze such practices as emotional loci for normative control.

The beginnings of a "culture" of hired management are found at the turn of the twentieth century. In the late nineteenth century, the distinction between ownership and management was not yet clear in the majority of firms in the private sector. The spinning industry, in which companies had relatively large workforces, was probably the first to hire significant numbers of operational managers (Okazaki-Ward 1993: 6). These hired managers were usually graduates of local engineering and technical colleges. In the public sector, the graduates of the best universities became bureaucrats. This new breed of educated managers was the forerunner of today's salarymen. By the 1920s, the practices of hiring new graduates, internal promotion, in-house education, and life-time employment were already in place for some white-collar employees (see Morikawa 1987). The prewar period also saw the establishment of many groups within companies to study and discuss management, especially in the large conglomerates (*zaibatsu*). In 1914 Mitsubishi became the first business to create such a study group; participation in the Mitsubishi yōwakai (Mitsubishi Association for Promotion of Harmony) was limited to *shain*, full-time formal employees of the organization.

An interesting fissure developed between the practice of management by bureaucrats and white-collar workers in companies and the academic study of management. The notion of scientific management was "never considered seriously by the academics in Japan, who were critical of its pragmatism" (Okazaki-Ward 1993: 24). The major agents in the domestication of scientific management were consultants. The Japanese Management Association, the leading institution providing training in Taylorism, recruits mostly corporate participants (from over 2,000 firms) and runs some 1,400 courses for 60,000 students a year (Warner 1994: 520). In the United States, in contrast, Taylorism entered the academy through business schools and was re-adopted in the 1960s by the academic movement for systems rationalization. In Japan, management did not became an academic body of knowledge as it did in the American model of the business school. Management in Japan has been less of an independent project furthered by engineers and other professionals and more of an aid to capitalist-owners, with the strong and steady involvement of the state in the market.[3]

Academia and industry in Japan remained aloof from each other until very recently. In-house education substituted for professional or vocational schooling. Japanese companies tend not to place too much importance on academic degrees (except in science and technology). Greater emphasis is put on the ranking of the candidate's university and his personal qualities. New hires are expected to develop managerial skills after entering the company. Consequently, there is very little MBA or business studies education at the graduate level. MBAs are usually offered (by a relatively small number of universities) for those aspiring to stay in the academy rather than seeking employment in a company. The best-known accredited business school in Japan—that of Keiō University—formally conferred its first MBA degree only in 1978 (Okazaki-Ward 1993: 85). Almost all managers with an MBA received it from an American business school to which their company sent them. Many companies regard study in an American school more

---

3. In contrast, according to Adolph Berle and Gardiner Means (1932), American management studies began as the (successful) attempt of a new group or class of professional managers to develop an autonomous agenda significantly different from that of owners. Berle and Means envisioned professionals educated in business schools—rather than owners—in the role of corporate managers. In 1941, James Burnham identified "a drive for social dominance, for power and privilege, for the position of ruling class, by the social group or class of the managers" (Burnham 1941/1960: 71). Yehouda Shenhav (1999) stresses the role of mechanical engineers, who sought, at the turn of the twentieth century, ascendancy for their systems and themselves in a context in which capital and labor were much more powerful. Engineers triumphed, according to Shenhav's analysis, by redefining industrial conflict as a mechanical problem. The institutionalization of engineering systems for management legitimized the engineers as managers and as propagators of managerial curricula in business schools.

as a chance to build personal networks and to improve one's commu-nication skills than as an education in business.

White-collar workers are recruited under two quite distinct sys-tems: the *sōgōshoku* (a comprehensive job category in the integrated or career track) and *ippanshoku* (general job category).[4] Those recruited into the first track are graduates of the best four-year universities and are hired by the head office. This "management cadre" consists almost exclusively of men. The recruits for the second track, in contrast, come from a mixture of educational backgrounds and are hired by the personnel section of local offices. A large proportion of those in the *ippanshoku* category are women.[5] The members of the second group are not given the massive socialization and training that would-be managers receive. The non-career-track classification covers OLs, sales and customer-service jobs, and, in some cases, male employees engaged in front-line work. The two tracks perpetuate gender dis-crimination. At the beginning of the 1980s, the proportion of women in the total labor force (excluding the self-employed) was about 35 percent, but women in managerial jobs accounted for only 0.3 percent of the total labor force and 0.8 percent of employed women (Okazaki-Ward 1993: 51).[6]

---

4. Some scholars see the establishment of the "double-track personnel management sys-tem" as a direct result of the Equal Employment Opportunity Law of 1986. That is, compa-nies instituted the double track in order to continue to practice gender discrimination (see Wakisaka 1997; Shire 2000). This generalization seems to apply more to large firms with many branches. According to a 1995 Ministry of Labor survey, only 4.7 percent of all firms actually had a double-track system, but 52 percent of firms with over 5,000 employees had implemented the system (cited in Wakisaka 1997: 143).

5. Cannings and Lazonick (1994) suggest that *ippanshoku* was similar to the "mommy track" in the United States.

6. The 1986 Equal Employment Opportunity Law contains no penalties for contravening the rules. According to Okazaki-Ward (1993), the law did motivate a re-examination of dis-criminatory practices, and many competent second-track employees were offered a transfer to the first-track category. Some of these women were subsequently promoted and became managers. This phenomenon has been especially evident in the service sector. However, al-though many retail and service companies have abolished official discrimination on the basis of gender, a highly effective unofficial system nevertheless continues to exist through the sort-ing of regular employees into "national" (may be transferred anywhere in Japan) and "zone" or

Lifetime employment, although granted only to employees in the career track of large firms (a group constituting less than 30 percent of Japan's workforce), nevertheless motivates office culture. Lifetime (or long-term) employment affects the ways in which managers in large firms are recruited and selected, evaluated and promoted, socialized and motivated, and educated and developed. Lifetime employment means that the firm has to maintain a cadre of employees from which it can staff all managerial positions. Job switching, mid-career recruitment, and headhunting are minimized in such a system, and socialization, seniority, job rotation, and in-house education are maximized. New recruits are therefore hired into a closed society (the firm-as-family). They need to learn how to become a true "member of society" (*shakaijin*). This means behaving in the appropriate manner and internalizing the company ethos. The office, therefore, is also a hub of normative control.

For Harmony and Stress: Normative Practices in the Office

Thomas Rohlen's 1974 *For Harmony and Strength* is still unmatched in English as an ethnographic source on life in a Japanese office. When reading Rohlen, one is first impressed by the wealth of details. My suggestion for reading the book is to analyze Rohlen's larger picture into categories of organizational culture. The obvious point of departure is to locate Rohlen's description within a model of strong organizational culture, in which management-laden values, work norms, and office artifacts combine into one coherent reference system.[7] A closer look, however, reveals that the office is not totally integrated

---

"home" contracts. Employees with a "home" contract, usually female high-school graduates, have fewer chances for promotion (see, e.g., Matsunaga 2000).

7. I have in mind here Edgar Schein's (1990) pyramidal model of strong organizational culture. It is no coincidence to find this in a Japanese bank. Employment practices in the large urban banks feature lifelong employment and seniority-based wages for men, with young women hired for routinized clerical or supportive tasks. Typically women work for a short period before quitting at marriage. It is a paradigmatic example of Japanese-style management.

but is differentiated by job categories and gender distinctions.[8] A critical perspective undermines the integrative model by considering the discrepancies between ideology (values, ends) and actual practices (norms, means) as well as between the managerial message and its subjective interpretation by employees.[9]

The office is replete with the ideology of paternalism described in the preceding chapters of this book. Uedagin—Rohlen's name for the bank—is regarded as a "community of people organized to secure their common livelihood. . . . One often hears the company referred to as 'our house' (*uchi*). . . . People working in the bank are known as 'Uedagin people' while their occupational labels are of secondary importance" (1974: 14). "When a person enters the bank as a member he discards his independence and accepts the burdens of responsibility as a participant. It is also understood that in return Uedagin assumes the position of provider for the individual's security and welfare. . . . This general agreement, lacking details and specifications, is implicit" (1974: 18). This is another example of the anti-legalistic stance of Japanese-style management. Labor relations are said to be akin to the traditional relationship found among family members, with no notion of rights or obligations in the Western sense. Rather, the presumption is that the parties can rely on mutual understanding and trust.

The important ceremony of entering and joining the bank (the *nyūkōshiki*), in which newly recruited graduates are officially recognized as members, offers a concrete illustration of the emotional ideology of paternalism. The ceremony opens with everyone standing and singing the Uedagin song; next all those present join in reciting in unison the "Uedagin Principles." Finally, before sitting down, everyone recites the "President's Teachings" (Rohlen 1974: 36–37). These

---

8. An awareness of differentiation exposes the cracks in the (organizational) mirror and may bring about (and reflect) critical interpretations of the system; see Martin 1992 for an articulation of this perspective in the context of organizational culture(s).

9. The emphasis on discrepancies in the organizational system, particularly between employers and employees, seeks to uncover the domination of the former and the subjugation (and sometimes resistance) of the latter; for articulations of this perspective within the context of organizational culture, see Hochschild 1983; and A. Raz 1999a.

include harmony in the workplace, sincerity toward customers, kindness ("have a warm heart"), spirit ("let us work with all our strength"), unity, responsibility ("responsibility makes rights possible"), originality ("think creatively"), purity ("a noble character and proper behavior"), and health ("let us fulfill the Uedagin dream"). The list of management-approved traits demonstrates that the employees are indeed "moved by things spiritual."

Next comes the president's speech. Both the speech as well as the new employees' response, discussed below, are typical examples of the emotional discourse of paternalism. The president begins by saying that the new recruits are now *shakaijin*, adult members of society. "As a *shakaijin* working in this organization," he continues,

> you are expected to fulfill your individual responsibilities as well as you can, for the prosperity of each of us depends on the prosperity of the bank. I hope that you will be conscious and proud that you are members of this bank. . . . I sincerely ask you to get involved with your work in a serious and devoted manner. The bank is a public institution based on mutual trust. Our lifeblood is trust. Each of you in your heart must become worthy of the trust of others. Your character and skill must deserve their trust and for this reason you must learn every day. This will show that you have the correct spirit. (Rohlen 1974: 38)

As Rohlen notes, the president, "a large man of impressive posture and energy . . . has grown so emotional that his voice has broken off and tears have streamed down his face" (1974: 38).

The master of ceremonies next calls on the representative of the parents, who promises that the parents will support the bank. He requests that the bank discipline and guide their offspring, who are "yet immature and naïve." The involvement of parents in the ceremony is a uniquely Japanese phenomenon and attests to the importance of the firm-as-family. The bank is authorized, by the parents, to become a surrogate parent. The third group involved in this triad of fictive kinship, the new recruits, have so far been passive listeners. After the parents' representative has returned to his seat, the master of ceremonies calls the roll of new members, reading their names and the school from which they have just graduated. The list is ordered not alphabetically or by region but rather by the status of the schools. The representative of the new men then delivers his address, which is phrased in emotional words suitable for the occasion.

All 120 of us are extremely grateful for our three months of training. . . . At first, we were primitive and unaware of our responsibilities, but in a correctly ordered environment, we became aware of what Uedagin means, and a sense of devotion grew in our hearts. We know that Uedagin, for all its rigor and strictness, is, at heart, understanding and sympathetic, yet we are committed to a course of independent self-development within the bank. . . . We are young and as yet spiritually and technically underdeveloped. We ask our seniors to lead and educate us, for we know it is imperative that we become hardy and brave Uedagin men.

These three, well-coordinated speeches share a similar emotionality and address the same themes: the company-as-family, the coming of age of the young recruits as adult social beings, and the beginning of their lifelong commitment to the bank. Trust and interdependence are forged as the ideological building blocks of a strong organizational culture.[10] This is the ideological image of *daikazoku*, "one big family." The leaders of the company, like fathers, have the responsibility to watch over their employees. Older members of the company should advise and educate younger members. This is the ideological basis for the organizational practice of *senpai-kōhai* (senior-junior dyads). In time, each cohort or recruit advances from apprenticeship through in-house education and job rotation to responsibility. This is the ideological basis for the seniority system and lifetime employment.

The persuasive family metaphor is packaged in emotional rhetoric; the proper attitude toward the company-family is "love Uedagin," an

---

10. The ideological elements of paternalism and filial piety can be seen as echoes of Confucian tradition (see Bellah 1957; Bodde 1953; Rohlen 1974: 58–60). Uedagin and other modern Japanese organizations use Confucian values of harmony and age-set authority as ready-made explanations for organizational hierarchy. See also Dore's (1973: 234, 401–2) claim that the Confucian concept of innate virtue was consistent with the assumptions of McGregor's Theory Y and accounts for the organizational behavior of managers, supervisors, and workers in Japan.

often used yet rarely explained catchphrase of management. This attitude is commonly known as *aishashugi*, "love-one's-company-ism." Interestingly, this phrase is not a personal statement. Rather, it denotes a set of programs and ideological endeavors designed to bring the individual and his company into a close and effectual relationship. *Aishashugi* is therefore a central example of the emotional themes of Japanese-style management. Such emotional themes are social structures rather than personal realities. As such, they embody the Japanese blurring of the Western distinction between public and private.

Aishashugi cuts across the boundaries of public and private. It is a social structure that reflects on personal display. As Rohlen notes, when he interviewed Uedagin employees privately, they "expressed little interest in examining their own feelings about Uedagin in any depth, but they usually endorsed the general correctness and acceptability of the idea that one should feel affection for one's company" (1974: 50). To use the Japanese term, the idea of "love your company" was *tatemae*, front-stage behavior. It mattered little whether this expected emotional behavior was in line with inner, personal feelings.

Rohlen's attitude toward Uedagin's culture is also of interest. His view is aptly subsumed under "devotion" rather than under "defiance." Rohlen sees Uedagin's culture as a functionalist solution to the organizational paradox of maintaining unity within hierarchy (see 1974: 60). In his words, this paradox is "resolved through . . . organic unity. Hierarchy is natural and proper. It serves to order the organism" (1974: 45). Rohlen here revives the old Durkheimian rhetoric of organic unity, used in functionalist sociology to place Western industrialization and capitalism on a higher rung of the ladder of social progress. His view is contested by two of his own observations. First, organic unity is more of an ideological facade (*tatemae*) than a workplace reality. This is shown through a closer look at the normative practices of control, from the open-space, panopticon-like configuration of the office to small-group activities. Second, organizational culture in the office is not one unified system, but is differentiated along the lines of job categories and particularly gender.[11]

Recent workplace ethnographies have defied Rohlen's (1974) classic analysis. In many companies, the vast majority of workers are part-timers outside the career track. This produces a new "psychological contract" in which the employer does not have a responsibility to en-sure the continued employment of workers. Many female employees who remain with the company for ten years or more view this trend negatively, as an indication that they are either unmarried or childless. For example, in Matsunaga's (2000) ethnography of Nagasakiya, a re-tail company, she observed (in the early 1990s) all the "community ritu-als" mentioned by Rohlen (1974). However, her participant observa-tions "from below" focused on the reactions of employees in a way that severely undermines Rohlen's analysis of "organic solidarity." Matsu-naga describes induction training in which trainees (mostly female high-school graduates) evince no enthusiasm; the president's "arrival speech" elicits halfhearted giggling; and quality circle meetings are in-terpreted as "a front" and are considered neither popular nor effective. Nagasakiya's case appears to be a symptom of broader processes that have come to underlie (or perhaps undermine) the traditional Japanese employment system. Previous workplace ethnographies have centered on "community" as essential to the company and the epitome of its or-ganizational culture. In contrast, more recent studies invoke the con-cept of the "imagined community"—a rhetorical facade that is gener-ated, contested, and negotiated by different people in different contexts. Although the company-as-community may still be a ritual practice, it has become more a "dreamt-of" than a "lived-in" phenomenon.

The following section focuses on the male office worker, the ubiq-uitous white-collar employee informally known as the "salaryman."

---

11. Describing a typical office meeting, for example, Rohlen (1974: 97–98) writes: "Always the same people offer opinions. . . . All along, the women [sitting together in the rear] and several of the men have remained silent." The general view of "organic solidarity" seems ques-tionable in the context of such concrete descriptions. For a poignant account of the dark side of organic solidarity, see Kumazawa Makoto's (1996: 205–49) account of "twenty years of a bank worker's life."

This general job category is known in Japan as *shain* (staff). Male office workers in the management track enter the company after university graduation. They automatically become members of the company union, except when working in sensitive areas like personnel or the president's secretariat. During the first phase of acculturation (usually the first twelve months in large firms), the new recruits live in small groups in the company dormitory (see also Okazaki-Ward 1993: 127). Afterward they scatter throughout the corporate organization.

The Office Group as a Social World

The office group, while being the primary social unit of the white-collar organization, is not necessarily a locus of stable relationships. Rather, organizational practices such as job rotation[12] for men and job quitting upon marriage or childbirth for women turn the office into somewhat of a transit station. To be sure, it is the personnel who move; ideally the structure of the office group remains intact. The office group should therefore be analyzed not only as a group of people but also as an institutional structure. My argument is that the office group is maintained as a "people structure" through its normative practices. These practices channel and prescribe social and emotional behavior in a formalized manner that is independent of the people involved and the level of familiarity among group members. In other words, these normative practices and feeling rules turn the office group into a "social world."

The concept of social world is used here in its formal sociological sense. The "social world perspective" focuses on the abstract communicational channels and performative rules through which messages are relayed. Geographical-territorial parameters, formerly a must in

---

12. Job rotation usually occurs biannually; typically an employee serves for three years in a position before being rotated, according to a schedule devised by the personnel department. A promising employee in the management track may be rotated more often (Okazaki-Ward 1993: 170–71).

community studies, are treated as of secondary importance, and the focus on personal face-to-face interactions is replaced by structural rules that are autonomous of their human performers. Tamotsu Shibutani (1955) was the first to consider social worlds as configurations of shared communication in industrial societies, in which actors are engaged in a web of reference groups imbued with diversifying processes and meanings. Anslem Strauss (1978, 1982) further elucidated the theoretical foundations and the analytic properties of the concept and advocated its research potentials. The approach has since been employed as a core idea in numerous studies, such as analysis of worlds of art (Becker 1982), computers (Kling & Gerson 1978), alcoholism (Denzin 1977, 1978), and communities of the elderly (Unruh 1983; Hazan 1990; A. Raz 1993).

The social world of the office group is described below. This emphasis on performative rules is in line with my overall focus, in this book, on social structures that put emotion to work. The sociological study of emotion has a unique potential for emphasizing the role of emotion as a structure for action, emotion as a discursive theme in the order of things. A social world perspective similarly allows us to separate the institutional from the idiosyncratic, the discursive from the subjective, and the work group from the individual worker. Second, an emphasis on performative rules seems to match the Japanese work ethic of *katachi de hairu*, "to enter (self-fulfillment) through the rules." The concept of *katachi*, "rules and spirit," is crucial. Even as the rules formalize, they also spiritualize. Working on the external form transforms and redefines the internal, the spirit. Unlike Western thought, which sees what is below the surface as truer, the Japanese concept of *katachi* equates form with content. Such a perspective straddles, rather than separates, the public and the private. The social world perspective, which in Western sociological thought appears to represent a postmodern split in the life-worlds of participants, would be regarded as traditional wisdom in Japan.

Group Activities

Praised as one of the ideological pillars of Japanese-style management, teamwork is an office practice and a structure for emotion at work. Participation, one of the virtues of Japanese-style management, is encouraged through such practices as round-table discussions (*zadankai*). Eight to twelve office members are gathered (for example, by the firm's magazine) to discuss a common problem or experience. The discussion takes a particular pattern. According to Rohlen (1974: 56*n*10), "each participant seeks to offer opinions to the accumulating commentary without creating too much divisive argument. It is [more] important that a pleasant discussion ending in general agreement be held, than a logical debate be pursued." The round-table discussion is therefore also a norm-processor that cultivates the value of consensus. The expression of strong personal emotions is not allowed lest the "round-table" character be lost. The round-table discussion generates voluntary interest in offering solutions to the company's problems. In this sense, it is a quality control circle without the methodological design. Furthermore, the success of the round-table discussion is guaranteed—what matters is not the actual implementation of the ideas but the participation in the discussion. The discussion is an autotelic structure, a closed system or a language game, that takes its course irrespective of the personal character of participants. It is therefore a formal structure of the office group as a social world.

Additional performative structures for "doing things together" in the office, for example, are meetings, the *ringi* system of consensus building, on-the-job training, and the office party. Although these structures are quite different from one another, each includes a performative pattern that prescribes "trust" through emotional and social action while maintaining the hierarchies of rank, familiarity, and gender. Office life, in Japan and the rest of the world, is full of meetings. Some observers even see the work meeting as the most prevalent ritual of office life. In Japanese-style management, however, the meeting is elevated into an even more prominent position—in frequency, design, and social significance. A typical example is the *chōrei* (a daily or weekly morning information meeting usually attended by all employees).

The morning meeting is a ritual with a fixed starting time, attendees, and order. The positions assumed by attendees clearly reflect rank and gender—with the officers at the front, faced by the first line of ranking employees, and the lowest-ranking employees—usually women—at the back. A *chōrei* typically begins with a supervisor saying a few words about goals and announcing relevant information for the day. He then asks an employee to give a story for the day. This is particularly a feature of service-oriented companies that want to instill verve among their "front-line" workers. Employees take turns at this social duty, which is usually performed by men. The story is usually taken from the worker's school days or early days with the company. The story is usually humorous and ends with a moral on the importance of persistence. The employee then closes the meeting by leading a group chanting of the company song or some other corporate text.

Ringi is a process of decision making that "allows for ideas conceived in outline at senior management level to be worked out and developed on the 'shop floor'" (Okazaki-Ward 1993: 138). The section chief (*kachō*) is responsible for directing and overseeing the process, which culminates in a written proposal (*ringisho*). This "bottom-up" practice (which is nevertheless directed by middle management) provides a regular system for the generation of consensus. It is supported by the unofficial practice of garnering agreement (*nemawashi*, "root-binding") that accompanies the process. By the time the *ringisho* is drafted, the proposal "has been communicated to all affected parties, and their general acquiescence is assured" (Lincoln & Kalleberg 1990: 176). Like the round-table discussion, the *ringisho* is supposed to efface contradictions, not to heighten them. Generally speaking, no "minority report" is ever attached to the *ringisho*.

On-the-job training is regarded as the most important method of education by the majority of Japanese firms (Okazaki-Ward 1993: 229). Various surveys have shown that such training is much more prevalent in Japan than in the United States. In 1993, 90 percent of the workers in large Japanese companies had received some sort of in-house training, as compared with 52 percent in America (Brown et al. 1997). Considered a hallmark of Japanese personnel training, on-the-job training is a major form of "in-house education" in almost every Japanese company (Nakamura et al. 1994). In on-the-job training, experienced employees (*senpai*) teach the younger ones (*kōhai*) on the job.[13] Each new employee is assigned his or her first *senpai* immediately following orientation and thereafter with each job rotation. On-the-job training reproduces the gender stratification of the office—women are *senpai* for women, and men are *senpai* for men. On-the-job training also reproduces the managerial ideology of benevolence; it is a vertical relation of emotional responsibility similar to that found between parent and child.

Successful on-the-job training is geared primarily toward emotional stability: "a sense of achievement in both persons, contributing to a rise in the morale and confidence of the learner as well as the teacher" (Okazaki-Ward 1993: 229). According to Rohlen (1974: 127), *senpai* and *kōhai* "enjoy each other in a relaxed and intimate manner . . . based on trust and respect."[14] This is yet another normative practice that straddles instrumentality and affectivity. Rohlen (1974: 125) also writes that the *senpai-kōhai* dyad is a context in which "affection and hierarchy, rather than being contradictory, are understood as mutually reinforcing." Although the relationship in a given on-the-job training dyad range from genuine and warm to formal and perfunctory, it is precisely the formal, management-imposed structure—

---

13. The *senpai-kōhai* relation exists in almost every form of a Japanese dyad which is not merely collegial. It can be found in universities, corporations, and schools for martial arts. It denotes a relation of hierarchy—literally, the two concepts denote the one who comes before (*sen*) and the one who comes after (*go*). The senpai is not an official teacher (*sensei*) but rather a senior who becomes a guide.

14. Rohlen uses the *senpai-kōhai* relation as an example of the emotionality of the Japanese; according to his respondents, "people who rationally calculate self-interest would hardly choose to assume the burdens of a *senpai* since the possible benefits to one's career are hardly guaranteed. . . . The essential ingredients in any person's motivation to befriend and help a junior are emotional" (1974: 127).

the on-the-job training—that allows participants to realize the *senpai-kōhai* relationship and realize it anew in each and every job rotation.

Finally, one of the seemingly most unofficial group activities—the party—also has a management-prescribed performative pattern. In Rohlen's bank, office parties take place on the second floor. The chief, flanked by his deputies, sits at one end of the table. The other men take seats along each side of the table. The women sit at the back. This spatial arrangement of leaders, men, and women reflects the office hierarchy. Next, the chief opens the party with a toast (of beer) to the success of the coming months' work. Everyone sits down to eat. Turns are taken filling one another's glasses. Then the chief suggests that singing begin. Individual employees take turns singing a solo. By nine this "periodic meeting" (*teiki taikai*) closes. The women are urged to leave, and the men head off to a nearby bar. They start going home around eleven.

The office party (defined as a meeting) is another example of the blurring of public and private. Rohlen (1974: 100) asserts that "to the American observer accustomed to the homeward rush of employees at quitting time, these office meetings . . . seem profoundly exotic." Office groups hold six to a dozen such parties each year; some parties are more official, for example, the traditional year-end party or parties to welcome new employees or to send off old employees. Some parties grow out of Saturday afternoon recreation programs held for employees. According to Rohlen's calculations, a typical office worker spends 56 hours a week working and four to six hours socializing.[15] Martin Kilduff and his colleagues who observed a hi-tech R&D office in Japan, claimed that "group members sacrificed holidays, family life, and hobbies. . . . No one could afford to skip a day's work. So intense was

---

15. Michel Crozier's French office workers claim, in contrast, that they prefer a distance: "85 percent of them never get together with their colleagues outside of work, and the 15 percent who do seem to apologize for it. . . . Yet when one questions them about the character of employees, they do not fail to criticize them—as well as themselves—for their coldness, egoism, and distant character" (1965: 110).

the commitment to the group's work, that some of the engineers claimed they wouldn't know what to do with free time" (1997: 586).

The social world of the office also hinges on spatial structures. Although the office is usually arranged in an open-space manner with shared desks, hierarchy is maintained in the arrangement of desks and the positions around them. The office seating arrangement often reflects the organizational chart. Typically, the chief's desk is at the rear center of the main office. The rest of the staff is gathered in front of him. Desks within groups may be separated by dividers, and different groups may be separated by partitions. At each desk, the senior member sits at the end, and the others sit along the sides. The open-plan office serves normative purposes. It increases the visibility of workers and leaves no private place. Talk is easily monitored by others and therefore tends to concern company rather than personal business. The whereabouts of absent office workers is shown on the employee status board (see also Kilduff et al. 1997: 585 on similar arrangements in an engineering office). The board indicates which employees are in and where they are working. Employees move their markers accordingly when they arrive at work or leave. In Foucauldian terms, such an office layout is a panopticon—an overseeing structure of surveillance in which inmates, being aware of the existence of an ever-present yet illusive "big brother," become self-supervisors and monitor their own actions. This is reminiscent of the total quality management / just-in-time regime described in Chapter 3.

Character Building and Character Testing

The concept of character occupies a central role in the social world of the office. "Character" is continually being tested, built, and retested through selection, socialization, and promotion. In this case, however, "character" does not refer to individual personalities but to management expectations. More precisely, the rhetoric of character serves a normative purpose of social engineering. As stated in *Josei shain no shitsukekata* (How to discipline female employees), a publication of the Mitsui Bank Personnel Office (Mitsui Company 1994: 34): "It is now the workplace, not schools or home, that disciplines women. . . . Making them into grown-ups and a useful work force is a task that all managers have to assume." The disciplining of the workforce, as seen in this example, has clear paternalistic tones.

Selection

The formal recruitment process consists of a series of screenings. These include, for male office workers, a general aptitude test, the rank of one's university, and possibly a few personality tests. The job interview focuses on the candidate's interests, studies, and family situation. Many companies also investigate the family background of candidates. These investigations may include a visit to the candidate's home, inquiries in his neighborhood, and interviews of his teachers.

A representative of the personnel section explained to Rohlen the kinds of things the bank was most interested in learning from these inquiries (1974: 71). First was the health of all members of the family, and in particular, the presence of hereditary or mental diseases among relatives. This investigation—intrusive and probably illegal in most American states—should be viewed in terms of the "family" ideology of the management. A second concern was the proper socialization of the candidate. "If the household is not orderly, then the applicant's character and the thoroughness of his socialization are in doubt. One favorite technique is to visit the bathroom to see whether it is clean as a test of whether the mother is a good housekeeper and, by extension, a good mother" (Rohlen 1974: 71). A third was the nature of family relationships. Trouble between members of the family would make the candidate suspect. Conversely, a son who was slated to succeed to his father's position in a farm or a family business would be regarded as a poor choice for recruitment. Finally, the investigators considered the parents' character. "Do one or both of the parents seem particularly egoistic?" (Rohlen 1974: 71). Also of concern was the parents' attitude toward the company.

The company, then, goes to some length to establish the character of candidates. Interestingly, "character" is an attribute not of the individual but of the group. It is a social project in which relatives, teachers, and neighbors take part. The selection process, like many other office processes, calls for a social facade—one presents the appearance that will get one the job. It is also a means of normative control that precedes and empowers the disciplinary gaze of the organization.

The process also reveals a major difference between job interviewing for regular employment in the United States and in Japan. In the United States, the main concerns are the applicant's personal background and professional experience; in addition, the person is usually applying for a particular job. In Japan, the only background that matters is one's university and family. Previous professional experience is irrelevant in *shinsotsu saiyō* (hiring new graduates), which is "the normal interpretation of the term 'hiring' in Japan" (Karthaüs-Tanaka 1995: 39). Applicants are recruited not for a particular job but "into the company." To borrow the terminology used by Mitsui, graduates are "hired as 'raw material' to be trained and molded to suit the needs of the company" (Tung 1984: 30).

Douglas Lipp, an American human resource trainer who was sent by the Walt Disney Company to Japan when Tokyo Disneyland opened and later became an independent consultant there, has described some of the cultural breaches in communication between Japanese and American managers caused by Japanese habits of hiring new graduates (1994: 130–31). Lipp's account is based on his experiences in the service industry but is typical of job interviewing for any office work. He begins by quoting fragments from a job interview in which the interviewer is an American trainer.

"What did you study in your university?"
"Economics."
"What would you like to do in our company?"
"Anything will be fine."
"Isn't there any field which you are especially good at? What is the benefit for us hiring you?"
"I don't know about it very well, but I've been thinking that I would like to do a job like this."

"Then, 5 years from now, what would you like to be doing?"

"Well, I am ready to do anything that the company wants me to do."

(We then asked him what was his interest in Disney.)

"I've loved Disney since my childhood. Also, it is a big company in the U.S. and famous in Japan, too."

Lipp continues:

After every interview the American staff would have an evaluation meeting. We agreed that the person was not suitable. He did not have his own will, he was lacking self-promotion. One of my (American) colleagues was particularly disappointed about the passive approach of the applicant. In his opinion, this applicant was too unconcerned about his job. The American side therefore agreed that the person seemed to be unsuitable. Then, however, the Japanese personnel manager in charge said: "No. He is excellent. I think he will be able to adjust himself very well to the company. Definitely we should hire him. His school background is not bad, and we have received a recommendation from a professor at his university." We [the Americans] were simply astonished.

Lipp's account is not exceptional. As part of my own fieldwork, I heard similar descriptions from Japanese personnel managers, whose hiring decisions were based on impressions of friendliness and "personability," that is, character.

Self-declarations

Self-declarations (*jiko shinkoku*) are a standard personnel practice for assessing character on a periodic basis. Most large firms have each employee submit an annual report to the personnel department on his job history, self-development, and future preferences for rotation. Usually the form has sections for personal and family details, which are used to calculate family and travel allowances. Such reports are considered part of the personnel rating system (*jinji kōka*, sometimes also called *satei*), which supplies all the data needed to determine promotions and rewards. This system also provides assessments of the employee's performance and evaluations of his abilities by the em-

ployee himself and his immediate superior. The system uses standardized procedures and forms.

The appraisal system captures important norms that, although
characteristic of Japanese workplace culture, are nevertheless inconsis-
tent with its declared ideology of organizational culture. First, the appraisal system contains a significant element of personal competition,
despite the lip-service paid to teamwork and dedication as taken-for-
granted values in Japanese organizational culture. In practice, teamwork and competition are flip sides of the same coin. Second, contrary
to the claims of equal opportunities for all made by Japanese managers
and politicians, the self-evaluation system clearly differentiates and
discriminates between men and women. The format used for female
employees hired as general workers (*ippanshoku*) differs from that used
for male employees in the career track (*sōgōshoku*) category. Male employees' evaluations provide for a self-evaluation in which men rate
their job behaviors and attitudes (see below). There is often no such
component for female general workers (such as OLs, sales ladies, or
customer-service workers). In contrast, there is a special block on the
form reserved for information about "marriage and childbearing
plans." And although male employees in the career track are asked
about their preferences for future job transfers, female workers in the
general track are not.

I focus here on one form, a personal declaration used by the Mitsui
Trust and Banking Company. This annual form contains seven sections (see Fig. 4). The section asking for information on the type of
residence and the health of relatives would be regarded as intrusive by
Americans but is normal for a Japanese organization that pays family
and residence allowances. The most intriguing section is the third one,
the "personality inventory." Here, the employee is required to judge
himself either strong, normal, or weak with regard to fifteen personality traits, such as conformity, cooperativeness, cheerfulness, calmness,
and so on. His immediate supervisor is asked to confirm or reject
these self-ratings.

Personal Declaration

(For Ippanshoku)

Date: _____

	Self	Commentator	Checked by	General manager
Seal				

Division/branch	Name	Grade	Level	Office/section

Use a separate sheet if there is not sufficient space on this page.

1. Domestic information (circle as appropriate)
   (1) Marital status: married unmarried
   (2) Sharing the domicile: wife children ( ) husband father mother brother(s) sister(s)
   (3) Type of domicile: owner · company house · rented house · lodgings (public · private)
       family owned · company dormitory · other ( )
   (4) State of health: excellent normal needs care
       (self)   chronic illness or special medical treatment ( )
   (5) State of health: relationship ( ) · nature of illness ( )
       (family)
   (6) Others _____

2. Job experience

   (1) In the present division/branch: years   months (2) In the present post   years   months

   (3) Of all the jobs experienced   A. _____   for   years   months
       up to now, those in which   B. _____   for   years   months
       the employee excelled: C. _____   for   years   months

3. Personality inventory (✓ = marked by self   O = confirmed by superior)

	H	A	I		H	A	I		H	A	I
Conformity				Attention to detail				Creativeness			
Cooperation				Perseverance				Rationality			
Sociability				Stability				Calmness			
Cheerfulness				Carefulness				Tolerance			
Fastidiousness				Initiative				Earnestness			

H = High   A = Average   I = Insufficient

4. Specific expertise · qualifications · licence · language certification · various courses

   (1) Already mastered (circle appropriate items) Land and Property Conveyancing · English Cert : 1st, 2nd, 3rd level
       Banking Certificate: Banking Law Level 3; Accountancy Level 3; Taxation Level 3; Foreign Exchange Level 3
       Others _____

   (2) Study at present _____

   (3) Wishes to study in the future (courses, qualifications, licences etc.)
       _____
       _____

Fig. 4   Self-declaration form, Mitsui Trust and Banking

As a means of normative control, the personality inventory works on several levels. First, it represents—in a systematic, checklist manner—the ideal character of the company member. The list of traits moves generally from emotionalism in the first nine traits (conformity, cooperation, sociability, cheerfulness, fastidiousness, attention to detail, perseverance, stability, and carefulness) to rationalism (initiative, creativeness, rationality) and then back to emotionalism (calmness, tolerance, and earnestness). Only four of the fifteen traits are rational: attention to details, initiative, creativeness, and rationality. The other eleven traits (73 percent) are markedly emotional, which fits the Japanese-style management self-presentation.

Second, the personality inventory implements normative control by turning the employee into a supervisor of his own character. The employee knows that his marks will be confirmed or rejected by his supervisor. This is built into the form as a constant reminder of the nonpresent yet all-seeing "big brother." To minimize the discrepancy between his own grading and his superior's, the employee is likely to perform a double act of self-correction: aspiring to be "high" on character yet refraining from ranking himself too highly. Although the list of personal virtues subjects the employee to the company's view of ideal character (conformity, cooperation), the awareness of his superior's gaze makes the employee perform an act of self-objectification. He is forced to look at himself from the outside and try to foresee his superior's grading and anticipate it with his own. The self-declaration form is, at least on paper, part of the normalizing regime of a strong organizational culture.

Character Building as Spiritual Education

Character building is a matter of in-house education. In a survey of 458 large and medium firms, the Japan Management Association (Nihon nōritsu kyōkai 1988) found that more than half had their own training establishment away from the business site, ideally in a resort location. Since the 1988 survey, there has been an expansion in newly built corporate education establishments (Okazaki-Ward 1993: 294).

There are many courses specifically designed to teach "human relations" (*ningen kankei*), a ubiquitous concept in all Japanese human resources textbooks. In these courses, which constitute an elaborate attempt at socialization, supervisors and managers learn how to conduct group activities and discussions.

Rohlen subsumes such courses and educational activities under "spiritual education" (*seishin kyōiku*; see Rohlen 1974: chap. 9). The term refers to the practice of developing stronger character and respect for social requirements. According to Rohlen (1974: 194), about one-third of his bank's personnel receive some sort of training each year in the bank's training institute. Trainees sleep and eat in the institute during their training. They are divided into groups, choose their group leader (*hanchō*), and are assigned housekeeping chores (room sharing, cleanup, meals, roll checks) as part of the training. Strict attention is paid to the observance of detail and the proprieties, such as proper dress, hairstyle, sitting posture, walking on the right-hand side of the hallways, cordial greetings, and polite behavior. All these are strictly monitored and enforced under the general theme of "successful group living." Most programs last from two days to a week. Each morning, trainees are awakened at 6:30 and, dressed in athletic outfits, engage in exercises before breakfast. Usually this also involves cleaning up a section of a nearby park. During the daytime sessions, hierarchy is absent as a rule, and trainees spend their time in discussion groups, in reciting training songs, and in reviews of their diaries by the institute's teachers. The evening sessions are for group recreational activities. Every year, the fifty or so office workers with the poorest career records undergo a three-day reform session.

The act of diary writing and inspection as a formal exercise in self-reflection (*hansei*) is "nothing unusual as part of moral education in Japan" (Rohlen 1974: 198).[16] As part of their junior college education,

---

16. Merry White (1993: 200) describes how Japanese grade-school pupils learn the roots of social acceptability through *hansei*, critical reflection conducted in peer groups. According to White (p. 201), whereas "American ideas about healthy adolescence emphasize positive self-confidence, Japanese emphasize self-reflection and self-reliance."

future office ladies are required, as an aid to self-monitoring, to make a *jumon* (incantation) based on their weak points, to be repeated to themselves as a way of rectifying their faults (McVeigh 1997: 153). This is reminiscent of another organizational practice, *hansei*, the public apology used in Azumi's textile factory as a normative sanction devised to promote worker diligence. The public apology included a self-reflection on one's mistakes and what one planned to do to prevent it from happening again (Roberts 1994: 46, 74). Spiritual education therefore provides socialization in self-examination. In both cases, such socialization blurs the distinction between public and private. The fact that the diaries are read by the staff no doubt colors their contents; yet self-examination is practiced all the same. In a similar manner, the public apology is invoked more as an act of group solidarity than as a real expression of regret.

As an agent of socialization, the institute also reproduces gendered roles. A special theme in women's training is work as preparation for becoming good wives and wise mothers. Learning proper etiquette and polite language, as taught in the institute, for example, is touted as a means of making oneself more cultivated and therefore more attractive to a potential husband (Rohlen 1974: 198). Learning how to keep records and handle money likewise will aid women in their responsibilities as homemakers. Similar arguments are cited by Brian McVeigh (1997) in the context of women's junior colleges and by Jeannie Lo (1990) in the context of women workers at the Brother factory.

Special programs of spiritual education include *rotō* and the endurance walk (see Rohlen 1974: 203–6). In the former, a group of employees is sent to a training center in the countryside. Early in the morning, trainees are instructed to go individually into a nearby town and make an offer to work for a resident of the town, without pay, for the entire day, without giving any explanation of the reasons they are volunteering to help. This task challenges the Japanese convention of conducting interactions only within circles of attachment. It is supposed to create a state of insecurity that will shock trainees out of spiritual complacency (*rotō* can be translated as "bewilderment"). The usual experience is to be rejected a few times before being given work; at the end the day, the trainee has usually befriended the person he is working for and feels happy to be working for him. Trainees thus learn that work can be a source of security and attachment and accompanied by feelings of gratitude. This message is reinforced in a general discussion held at the center at the end of the day. Trainees come to agree that "enjoyment of work has less to do with the kind of work performed than with the attitude the person has toward it" (Rohlen 1974: 204). Even work that would normally be despised provides a sense of relief that can make it seem pleasant and satisfying.

The second program of character building, the endurance walk, is a long walk (about 25 miles) around a large public park. For the first part of the walk (about one-third of the whole course), all the members of the training group walk together; for the second part, they split up into smaller groups; the last part is walked alone and in silence. There is no time limit and no emphasis on competition between the groups or on finishing first. The walk begins early in the morning and ends some time in the afternoon. Its purpose is to create an understanding of the importance of participation, of endurance, and of spiritual strength.

Dorinne Kondo (1990: 78–108) describes a similar program for spiritual training at the family-owned confectionery factory in Tokyo where she worked. As part of her work, she and a group of other employees spent a week in an "ethics school" (*rinri gakuen*) facing Mount Fuji. Although Kondo's book describes a shop floor and not an office, her account of the ethics school describes programs that are offered by the Rinri (Ethics) movement[17] for regular employees, including seminars for managers, supervisors, and section chiefs. At the ethics school, trainees were organized in groups (*han*; "squads" is Kondo's term) that slept in the same room, ate at the same table, exercised together, and

---

17. The Rinri movement was established by Maruyama Toshio in the postwar years and had more than 100,000 followers in the 1980s, when Kondo did her fieldwork (see Kondo 1990: 78).

sat together in class; the position of group leader rotated daily. The school had "endless rules" and military-like bedroom inspections, with penalties publicly announced each evening by the squad.[18] The experience at the center was, according to Kondo, primarily emotional; it generated "profound feelings of warmth, anger, indignation, guilt, sadness, delight, frustration, and contentment" (1990: 81). Yet this experience was also meticulously planned and designed to foster a positive attitude toward work. The ethics center is another example of the blurring of the rational and the emotional in Japanese organizational culture. In Kondo's analysis, it was "precisely the combination of strong emotion and rigid form which provided the key to the interpretation of the ethics center program and its underlying assumptions about crafting disciplined selves" (1990: 81).

A typical day at the center consisted of the following schedule (Kondo 1990: 83):

5:00–5:40	Wake up, wash up
5:45–6:50	Cleaning, morning greeting and ceremony, vocalization practice
6:55–7:45	Exercise, cold water ablutions
7:45–8:30	Morning meeting, lecture
8:30–9:40	Breakfast
9:40–12:20	Lectures, tours, sports, special activities
12:30–1:20	Lunch
1:20–4:30	Recreation, lectures
4:30–5:30	Bath
5:30–6:30	Dinner
6:30–9:40	Lecture, *seiza*,[19] diary, closing ceremony, lights-out

During the morning ceremony, the teachers chose one person to share

---

18. Such group responsibility is a practice of normative control that should be familiar by now. An "infernally effective means of generating consent to the rules" (Kondo 1990: 80), this practice brings to mind the use of work teams as a normative solution to absenteeism, for example, on the shop floor or the assembly line.

19. *Seiza* is a formal sitting posture, legs folded (or lotus position), back straight, hands folded, used for example in meditation.

with the group a story of personal experience at work and praised each speaker for honesty and for taking the topic to heart rather than treating it as an intellectual exercise. The ceremony culminated in a "vocalization practice" in which each member stood in turn in front of the group, faced Mount Fuji, and screamed "Father! Mother! Good morning!" In the motivational seminars for salarymen, the participants were required to shout "I am the son of X company! I will make X company number one in Japan!" To counter embarrassment, every shouted word was rewarded with a shout of encouragement from the teacher and the group. The group applauded after each shouter finished.[20] The aim of this exercise, revealed by the head of the school in an interview with Kondo (1990: 87), was to "eliminate resistance toward responding positively toward authority."

Cold water ablutions (*misogi*), another part of the center's daily routine, are a traditional religious means of bodily mortification, a symbolic cleansing of selfishness. The ablutions were part of the center's emphasis on regimentation and perseverance, themes that were discussed in lectures. Another mortification ritual was the evening *seiza*. Trainees, sitting formally on the floor, were told to recall the faces of their mother and father. Filial piety was thus manipulated as a key to the "naïve heart" (*sunao na kokoro*), a state of emotional discipline that employees should strive for. The lesson, claims Kondo (1990: 94), was that "the realization of our indebtedness and obligation to our parents should create feelings of appreciation and regret for our thoughtlessness." A similar use of filial piety characterizes the managerial discourse of paternalism in general as well as particular company ceremonies such as the induction ceremony attended by new recruits and their parents. The ethics center also had its version of the "endurance walk." Trainees had to walk barefoot about a quarter of a mile over a path strewn with coarse gravel and rocks; they were instructed by the teacher not to look down while

---

20. The shouting performance—a group ritual of initiation through embarrassment—is reminiscent of the prescribed solo singing of embarrassed members during office parties described by Rohlen (1974: 97–99).

walking. "The pain," trainees were told, "will make you grateful for material things: shoes that cover your feet, clothes, all material objects. Most of all you should know that the pain you will feel is only one-thousandth of the pain your mother felt in bearing you" (Kondo 1990: 97).

Character building, as exemplified in the special training programs, matches the transmutated elements of Hochschild's emotion management. This match, we should note, contrasts with Hochschild's claim that emotion management is conducted primarily in the service sector and expressed in the representative-client dyad. First, emotion here becomes an organizational theme that binds employees and employers. Second, feeling rules prescribe the right emotional display at work. Cheerfulness and brightness, no matter what the difficulty, are a prerequisite for maintaining the social world of the office. Bodily movement and appearance (Hochschild's surface play) are indices of the *kokoro*, one's heart (emotional dispositions), and hence should always be stage-managed.

Whereas American service representatives learn that outward composure is a powerful symbol of quality service, Japanese office workers learn that a neat appearance is an index of their perfected inner self. Although both lessons have a similar organizational function, the ideological apparatus of the Japanese version seems much stronger. The significant other, for office workers, is not just the customer but first and foremost his or her colleagues as well as employers. Workers should therefore care for each other and cooperate so that harmony can be sustained. Happiness can be achieved only through good interpersonal relationships. Other people are our mirrors; everything we do is inevitably reflected in the behavior and responses of others. Expressing negative feelings only engenders negative responses. Working joyfully forces us to throw all our energy into work, making work into an end in itself, irrespective of its actual contents (which might be dull and normally despised). These feeling rules are formalized in workshops, training sessions, special activities, and manuals.

Commonsense Office Manners

Not all employees can be sent to training centers. The feeling rules of spiritual education must therefore be inculcated through more mundane, technocratic means. In addition, not all companies have the time, experience, and money to invest in in-house education. Standard manuals for emotion management in the office are therefore good business. Such manuals represent and reinforce the transmutation of the private/public that Hochschild discussed in the context of American service. They also signify a blurring of the emotional (feelings) and the rational (protocols and checklists). The office manuals also blur the global (the manual as an American invention entered Japan with the arrival of transnational organizations such as McDonald's) and the local (the domestication of the manual within Japanese organizational culture). One such typical manual, in video form, is *Office Rules and Commonsense Manners* (*Shokuba no rūru to manā no jōshiki*).

Office Rules and Commonsense Manners is a 23-minute video, Part I in the "Start Dashing" Series for new recruits. It was produced by a subsidiary of the Japan Management Association in 1992, when it was priced at ¥45,000. Personnel managers in various organizations have told me that this video, which is a typical example of its genre, has grown quite popular for the training of new office members. The video opens up with two new recruits, a salaryman and an office lady, walking together into their company's office building. "Soon they will realize the meaning of becoming company people / adult members of society (*shakaijin*)," exclaims the narrator in a ceremonial, manly voice.

A sequence of episodes then presents the dos and don'ts of office conduct, covering such topics as greeting one's co-workers, entering and leaving the office, walking in hallways, grooming, sitting around the office desk, organizing one's portion of the desk, speaking and listening, interacting with *senpai*, and using polite language in the office. The pedagogic method is to present a demonstration of wrongful conduct; the viewers are asked to define what makes it wrong. Then the correct answer is given, and the example is re-enacted properly. At the end of each topic, summaries appear in the form of checklists. The examples enforce attention by dramatizing the embarrassment felt by the wrongdoer through a close-up on his or her embarrassed and then tormented face followed by a close-up on his or her colleagues' sealed, scornful faces. The same embarrassment will be yours if you don't learn how to behave properly, the video seems to imply. The correct examples, in contrast, end with close-ups of affirmative, benevolent faces. Israeli students who watched the video told me they experienced a strong feeling of infantilization and consequently resistance. Japanese viewers did not report experiencing such critical reactions.

The "office rules" video brings together the two central issues of this section: the social world of the office and emotion management. The standard behaviorial procedures, display rules, and checklists that the video teaches are a form of disembodied emotion management suitable for a social world based on generalized performative patterns. As an artifact, the video illustrates the commodification of spiritual education in (post)modern Japan. The rules (*kata*) are in the video, but the spirit is mostly gone. The video, in its neat presentation, does away with the ideological baggage of self-cultivation through work and other spiritual exercises. The video's makers left this aspect of training to traditional, "hands-on" training activities. The video is a symbol of organizational instrumentality, a mass-produced artifact for fast consumption and instant utilization.

The Office Lady

No matter how valuable a worker she may be, a woman must play the part of a woman. This includes showing deference to men (even those younger), serving them tea, preparing food for parties, taking responsibility for brightening up the office with flowers and other decorations, and being cheerful. Women leave drinking parties early, act as hostesses for guests to the office, are expected to arrive at the office early, and are permitted to go home before the men. In all of these examples, they act the conventional part assigned to women in the home.
—Rohlen (1974: 103).

Office ladies (OLs) are young women in their twenties who are hired as regular employees for office work. Even so, OLs cannot expect promotion or lifetime employment. They are known as *shokuba no hana* (flowers of the office)—"pretty to look at and decorative but in-substantial and transient" (Iwao 1992: 156). The average OL stays em-ployed for five years and then usually marries. In 1990, 75.1 percent of Japanese women age 20–24 worked—the first and highest peak of la-bor force participation rate for Japanese women (Iwao 1992: 163). More then one-third of this labor force work as OLs (McVeigh 1997: 147). OLs emerged as a distinct work (and later, social) category fol-lowing World War II. Their emergence thus coincided with the crys-tallization of Japanese-style management.

Many OLs live at home with their parents as long as they are single (Iwao 1992: 165). They can therefore use their income primarily for clothing, hobbies, and vacations. Although paid relatively low wages, OLs usually enjoy the privilege of using their salaries freely. A survey conducted by the Prime Minister's Office in 1989 found that the pri-mary reason (57 percent) women in their twenties worked was "to make money to use freely" (Iwao 1992: 166). OLs consequently attract massive marketing efforts through the media (see Kinsella 1995), which in turn reinforce their image as easygoing, leisure- (and husband-)seeking "moratorium people." The rich imagery associated with the OL was artfully depicted in a manga by Risu (1980), which was later translated into English. An important part of this image is the behavioral and appearance code known as *burikko*. *Buri* means pretense; *ko* is child. A *burikko* is a grown-up (usually a woman, often an OL) who acts like a child. As Merry White describes the phenomenon, "A caricature of a burikko girl has a high-pitched voice, giggles helplessly when ad-dressed, and squeals '*kawaiiii!*' (cute) or '*iyaa!*' (I hate it) when asked her opinion on a boy, a new drink, or a cartoon on TV" (1993: 129). Acting like a child is evidently linked to the paternalism of managers toward OLs at work.

The OL's workday starts officially at 9:00 A.M. OLs usually take turns preparing the office: wiping the telephones and desktops, boiling water for tea, tidying up the kitchen, and turning on the lights, copy machines, and the air conditioning. These domestic duties are per-

formed by the "on-duty OL" beginning at 8:30 A.M. (see Lo 1990: 40–
48 for a detailed description of a typical OL workday). Upon entering
the office, OLs and salarymen go to the ubiquitous magnetic board
and move their nameplates to the proper heading: "present," "out of
the building" (conducting business in the city), or "business trip." On
another column of the board, people can write notes on exactly where
they are. Such organization is necessary for the OLs who answer the
phone. During the workday, most OLs do light clerical work, answer
the phone, operate the photocopier, and serve tea. The workday usually ends at 6:00 P.M. Although many salarymen work extra hours,
OLs are supposed to leave a few minutes after 6:00 to go shopping or
return home.

Learning to Be an Office Lady

Stand in front of a mirror and introduce yourself. What is your first impression of yourself?
—from *The New Company Employee*, a women's junior
college workbook (McVeigh 1997: 153).

Most OLs are graduates of two-year women's junior colleges. These
colleges are the training ground and socialization agents for OLs
(McVeigh 1997; see also Kameda 1986). Brian McVeigh's book provides a detailed ethnography of one such college. His findings regarding the ideology of self-cultivation and the practices of training are
read here through the perspective of emotion management. According
to McVeigh (1997: 60), women's junior colleges have two primary
purposes: general education (*kyōyō*) and employment (*shokugyō*). The
ideology of general education is linked to self-cultivation and the self-
realization of femininity and womanly virtues.[21] School mottoes
promise to "educate women who have hearts of sincerity, harmony
and love . . . in the spirit of obedience, courtesy, deep respect, and service" (McVeigh 1997: 61). The second, more practical purpose of education for employment provides semi-professional training in clerical

---

21. The college studied by McVeigh also stipulated an ideology of "internationalization"
(*kokusaika*). McVeigh sees this ideology as a marketing ploy that covers a nationalistic worldview.

work. The ideology and practice of the women's college therefore per-
fectly complement the managerial ideology of paternalism and the
practice of gender segregation in the office. The college arguably produces an annual quota of standardized OLs socialized to know their
place as flowers of the office. They are too poorly and narrowly
trained to be promoted to more challenging work; brought up to look
on the office as a way station on the road to marriage, they are socialized not to aspire.

The training of OLs includes, in Hochschild's terms, elements
of both deep and surface play. Deep play can be seen in the commodification of "womanly feelings" as appropriated by the ideology of
self-cultivation. Office ladies are expected to internalize the feeling rules of "obedience, courtesy, deep respect, and service" required
for self-presentation in the office. These feeling rules are no doubt
needed to cope with the daily on-the-job boredom that is inevitable
for many OLs. Jeannie Lo (1990: 47) describes the story of a young
OL who sat in a chair from 9:00 A.M. to 6:00 P.M. and answered the
phone. She sat in front of her division chief so she could not read or
pass her time doing other things. In an anonymous letter to Lo, this
OL wrote: "It's horrible. . . . I wonder if you have this in America"
(1990: 47).

Surface play complements the ideology of self-cultivation through
service by formalizing numerous protocols of appearance and interaction. These protocols constitute a major portion of the college training described by McVeigh and others and far exceed those found in
American service training. Moreover, the emphasis that colleges put
on these protocols blurs the American (or Hochschild's?) distinction
between "surface" (public) and "deep" (private) play. According to
McVeigh,

In the texts that teach students how to be OLs, there seems to be an attempt
to merge subjective, unseen states with objective, observable behavior. The
type of training students receive indicates a deeply ingrained belief that the
"outside" world should ideally somehow shape the "inside," that the line between what is exterior and what is interior is mutable and contingent on the

social situation. The proper attitude is discussed along with correct conduct. (McVeigh 1997: 150)

In the end, Hochschild's distinction between surface and deep play has little relevance to Japanese-style emotion management. In the case of Hochschild's American flight attendants, the surface-deep distinction was related to the more basic ethno-moral distinction between a false self and the true self. It was the false self—the emcee, the attendant, the occupational role—that was involved in either surface or deep play. These kinds of play were understood by workers in practical terms, as a means of reducing stress, rather than in ideological terms, as steps toward self-cultivation. A comparison of the training practices will illustrate this point.

Hochschild cites a training instructor for Delta Air Lines who explained that "dealing with difficult passengers is part of the job. It makes us angry sometimes. And anger is part of stress. So that's why I want to talk to you about being angry." The recommended strategy he then offered was to imagine a reason that excuses the passenger's annoying behavior, from the general (all people have a latent fear of flight) to the particular (imagine this passenger had lost his/her child in a car accident three months ago). Instructors traded tips on the least offensive ways of expressing anger when these "deep play" strategies for producing empathy fail: "flush the toilet repeatedly," and "chew on ice, crunch your anger away" (Hochschild 1983: 113). In another American shrine of service culture, the Disney University, the manuals stress: "At Disneyland we get tired, but never bored, and even if it's a rough day, we appear happy. You've got to have an honest smile. It's got to come from within. And to accomplish this you've got to develop a sense of humor and a genuine interest in people. If nothing else helps, remember that you get paid for smiling" (cited in A. Raz 1999a; see similar citations in Van Maanen & Kunda 1989).

The OL manuals and workbooks, in contrast, insist that one's dress, demeanor, deportment, and speech signal not just "good service" but, more important, "one's true character." There is no surface or deep play; all performance is ideally both surface and deep, since it is supposed to reflect one's true (not false) character. Boredom and stress trouble only those who do not cultivate their self through work. In the words of an OL manual, "Aren't there many OLs who say, 'Simple tasks such as preparing tea and making copies are awful'? But wait a minute. The task of preparing tea certainly appears simple, but because it is indeed simple, isn't the manner in which you live and carry your heart directly expressed on the outside?" The emotional ideology of self-cultivation thus effaces the American distinction between surface and deep play as well as between true and false self.[22] Yet to accept this emotionalism at face value would be to miss its true character. Like the managerial discourse of *onjōshugi*, the emotional discourse that surrounds the OL is a male-made ideological facade supported by various normative controls. OLs are not just serving tea; they are learning how to bring out their feminine character and how to be good Japanese women. On the other hand, OLs are not "really" working (in terms of pursuing a career); rather, they are entrusted by their families to the company until they marry and quit their office. The sad truth is that for the most part OLs perform low-paying, unchallenging work that reproduces their official image as "dutiful daughters and suitable wives."

The life of the OL is regimented by numerous protocols that constitute a form of what Bourdieu terms "habitus" and that enforce proper conduct through greetings, facial expression, appearance, speech, and attitude. This is illustrated in Figure 5, a checklist of OL behavior, from a college manual. This "five basic principles" checklist is one of many contained in the *New Company Employee: Notebook for Company Life*, a workbook with written exercises used in the college

---

22. I am comparing OLs in Japan and service workers in the United States (flight attendants, ride operators). This is because (1) there are no OLs in the United States, and (2) OLs do embody, in Japanese eyes, the organizational ideal of service (serving employees as well as visitors and customers). The available sociological studies of secretaries, who technically resemble OLs, do not deal with emotion management (see, e.g., Pringle 1988, 1989). In the next chapter, I turn to a more direct comparison of Japanese and American service cultures as they relate to emotions at work.

Items to be Checked		CHECK
Formal greetings (*aisatsu*)	(1) Do you smile and say in a cheerful voice "Good morning" and "Good afternoon"?	___
	(2) When you greet someone do you look at that person's eyes?	
	(3) Are you always careful to take the initiative in greeting others?	___
		___
Facial expression	(1) When asked to do something, do you respond with a smile and "certainly"?	___
	(2) When you receive an important order, do you listen with a serious look on your face?	
	(3) The way you feel at any given moment doesn't show on your face, does it?	___
		___
Personal appearance	(1) Are your clothes appropriate for the workplace? Is your hair neat?	
	(2) Are you wearing your uniform neatly?	___
	(3) Have you been taking care of your shoes, briefcase, and pocketbook?	___
		___
Choice of words	(1) Do you speak clearly and with a cheerful voice?	___
	(2) You haven't unintentionally used student slang, have you?	___
	(3) Have you learned the appropriate polite language for each situation?	
		___
Attitude	(1) Is your back straight?	___
	(2) Do you look at the other person's eyes as you speak?	
	(3) Do you take the other person's position into account and think of the whole situation?	___
		___

Fig. 5   The five basics checklist for OLs

studied by McVeigh. This workbook, with its emphasis on checklists, exercises, and charts for evaluation (by self and others), is a Taylorist behavior manual representing a meticulous normative regime. Its formalization of feeling rules suggests a fusion of design and devotion, surface and deep play, public and private, rational and emotional.

The following exercise from the *New Company Employee* will illustrate the point (see McVeigh 1997: 152). Entitled "One Day in the Life of Miss Heisei: What would you do in these situations?" it requires the student to "correct" various mistakes. The exercise presents an

OL's worst nightmare. Miss Heisei oversleeps and puts on the same clothes she wore the day before (error no. 1). Arriving at the company entrance exactly at 9:00, she barely greets her department head (no. 2). Without saying anything to her colleagues, she starts preparing for work (no. 3). When her boss asks her to work on another project, she answers with a frown (no. 4). Heading toward the cafeteria in the afternoon, she leaves documents and materials spread all over her desk (no. 5). When a colleague leaves the office and everyone says "Come back soon," she is too busy and ignores him (no. 6). Finally, when it is 5:00, she decides to leave early because she promised to meet a friend (no. 7). Miss Heisei's mistakes and the situations she encounters are identical to those appearing in other manuals, such as the Japan Management Association video on office manners. Similar lists of dos and don'ts appear in books put out by other colleges. For example, *Guidance for Job Hunting—Junior Colleges*, a text given to each student by the college, emphasizes self-evaluation charts in which one awards oneself points for attitude and behavior, clothes, speech, cooperativeness, positiveness, sincerity, sense of responsibility, and sense of service.

The college's manuals represent an "ethnomorality of etiquette" (McVeigh 1997: 153) that can be read as a cultural variant of emotion management (Hochschild 1983), or—to use the college's terms— defined as part of *jiko shindan* (self-diagnosis) and *jiko kanri* (self-management). Like the salarymen's "spiritual training" and the regular workers' "cultivation of self through work," the OLs also have an ideology of self-commitment. They are told that the basic point of their education is to learn empathy (*omoiyari*) for others. According to McVeigh (1997: 155), "empathy" is the most common term women hear in secretarial classes.[23] The point of empathy is to sympathize with the other so as to be able to anticipate his or her wishes (often called *sasshi*, guessing). The resemblance to Delta Air Line's feeling rules for flight attendants is self-evident. Indeed, the college employed a former Japan Airlines stewardess as a teacher. The global and the lo-

---

23. See Lebra 1976: 38 for a similar account of *omoiyari* as a keyword of Japanese culture in general, indeed one of the virtues of being "really human."

cal again seem to blur. *Sunao*, another college keyword, is translated by McVeigh as "obedient"; *sunao na kokoro*, the "obedient heart," is a corollary of Hochschild's managed heart and a relative of Kondo's "naïve heart," the heart that sympathizes, the heart that is so pure that it can reflect (anticipate) others' wishes.

The body, as an interface between the internal (private) and the external (public), has to be closely managed. Indeed, so many behavior protocols—appearance, posture, facial expression, bowing, serving tea—are aimed at and realized through the body, it is almost as though the body, not the person, is the locus of socialization. The OL manuals illustrate how "empathy" is *embodied*—internalized, processed, and then externally presented. For example, by performing the proper farewell greetings when seeing guests off, OLs ensure that the guests depart with a favorable memory. Students are hence taught that feelings are reflected on the body.[24] This notion of "bodily habitus" may seem strange to the Western mind, which is largely conditioned on the (Cartesian) mind-body split. As McVeigh (1997: 160) puts it:

An assumption of western ethnopsychology is that people first possess a thought or attitude, which is then expressed through bodily action, but in the materials under examination, this assumption is sometimes reversed. For example, when depressed, students are advised to "look into a mirror and form a smile with your eyes and mouths. Mysteriously, as you look at your own smile, a feeling of cheerfulness gradually grows. Forgetting your unhappiness, the smile seen in the mirror then becomes the real thing."[25]

---

24. Jacob Raz (1992) has a fascinating chapter on *mie*, the concept of bodily display among the *yakuza*, of which the famous tattoos are but one, although quite eye-catching, indication.

25. In fact, America has recently discovered similar techniques of self-induced "change of heart." For example, a promotion blurb for "emotion management tapes" advises potential customers to "practice daily affirmations: Choose one that will work for you, for instance, 'I am interesting because I am interested,' or 'I love to meet new people.' Write it down 20 times a day. Put it where you can see it, like a bathroom mirror or car dash board, somewhere you will be reminded of your affirmation." My point is that there is nothing intrinsically unique about the Japanese emphasis on role taking. Psychological evidence based on laboratory research shows that the act of publicly expressing a given emotional state can induce a corresponding change in felt emotion (Baumeister 1982). Hochschild (1991: 121) was well aware of this when she argued that "in surface acting, we do not simply change our expression; we

In addition to body management, another realm of continuous self-monitoring is language and speech. All OL texts have chapters on speech manners, and there are courses on speaking style in which one learns voice training, public speaking and greetings, polite language, the role of the emcee, and audience analysis. The ethno-moral principle underlying speech manners is *keigo* (honorific language), a grammatical and lexical framework for expressing in-group/out-group status and degrees of emotional formality: respect, humility, and politeness. "Your words, spoken carefully, add a comforting feeling to the atmosphere of the workplace," exclaims an OL workbook (cited in McVeigh 1997: 163).

Honorific language is gender specific, with women traditionally occupying the inferior end of the dyad, at home and at work. Although both salarymen and OLs study honorific language, the latter's subordination is much more apparent. OL workbooks instruct students to use "cushion words" during unfavorable situations and to change negative phrases into positive ones and orders into requests (for example, "may I humbly receive your doing" instead of "please do"). Although salarymen are familiar with such speech and may, on very formal occasions, use it to address a senior, they are not expected to use such language when addressing an OL.

Interestingly, the justification for using polite speech is not merely pragmatic (for example, succeeding in a company interview) but ideological. Polite speech distinguishes young people from adult members of society. Many company trainers with whom I spoke regarded polite speech as one of the hallmarks of company socialization. According to one trainer, "Polite speech is one of the things that a *shakaijin* (company person / adult member of society) has to master. To be a *shakai*-

---

change our expression in order to change our feeling." Adler and Adler (1991) described how college basketball players who publicly conformed to their "star" image while privately retaining a less inflated view of themselves gradually came to think of themselves as stars: role playing had become role taking. Similar teachings characterize American workshops on "personal empowerment." This new brand of popular psychology know-how, which is yet to be researched, seems to challenge the "western ethnopsychology" regarding the primacy of the inner/true self.

jin means to understand the status system. A correct usage of polite speech is the ultimate proof that one has such understanding" (cited in A. Raz 1999a).

The OL as Subject

So far I have described the OL as an object, defining her from the point of view of work ideology and office manuals. Arguably there is also a subject behind all these masks. Do OLs oppose or resist their socialization and their assigned role in the office? According to McVeigh (1997: 238n1), "As a rule, students did not overtly subvert the dominant cultural codes at the women's junior college. . . . Resistance was rarely visible." His position as a teacher employed by the college, however, probably made it unlikely that McVeigh would observe resistance or hear from students about it. Ogasawara Yūko (1998), in her recent book on OLs at work, provides many examples of their irritation and discontent. Many of her respondents said that men get on their nerves, for example, in the context of tea pouring:

"Sure, what we do are all simple tasks—serving tea, making copies, typing documents. After all, our job is different from men's jobs. But that doesn't mean we feel all right to be bothered to bring tea. I mean, an OL has her own way of doing things. You think of the procedures, for example, that you'd make copies first, then type this letter, and next that document. In the middle of all that, you're suddenly told to bring tea, and you're supposed to smile cordially and say, 'Yes, I'm coming!' Every time you serve tea, you interrupt your job and serve for others. It may sound funny to talk about *your* job, when all the jobs are ordered by men. But once you accept them, they become your jobs." (An OL in an interview with Ogasawara; 1998: 41)

Why then do OLs remain, or seem to remain, passive about their situation? There are several reasons. First, solidarity among OLs is usually weak. To the outsider, OLs may look the same, but in fact each group consists of women with different educational backgrounds. This creates conflicts of rank since OLs with more tenure may be less educated than newly hired OLs. In some cases, an OL who is senior yet less educated would resent it if a junior yet more educated colleague were "promoted" to a desirable secretarial position. In contrast, a junior OL who is more educated finds it unpleasant having to yield to a *senpai* with less education. Second, OLs often accept their provisional status and regard the possibility of rebellion as unrealistic. Finally, OLs are not union members and hence lack a formal venue for expressing their grievances collectively.

One of the detailed descriptions focusing on conflict among female office workers is Susan Pharr's 1984 article on the "rebellion of the tea pourers" in a Kyoto City Office. These female office workers were aggrieved by the gendered distribution of chores, such as serving tea to men, cleaning men's desks, and emptying ashtrays. Other issues raised by women centered on the problem of taking their menstruation leave days, since custom in the City Office required that employees asking for time off state the reason on a publicly displayed sign-up sheet. Still another problem was the women's need for a place to change in and out of uniforms. There was no such place because restrooms in the office, following Japanese custom, were for both men and women. It took the women a few years to develop "collective consciousness" through meetings and discussions, since the union did not step forward to help their cause. Several of their requests (for example, a room to change in) were granted, and they felt courageous enough to tackle the problem of tea serving. The suggested compromise was that the women make tea at agreed upon times and then leave it for the men to serve themselves. Although some of the younger men complied, Pharr reports that many women continued to take tea to their immediate bosses. The conflict "faded out" when several of the women leaders quit to get married.

The "rebellion" of the tea pourers illustrates the extent of normative control in the office. As Max Weber noted, social consensus is possible only as long as the existing status relations are seen as legitimate. In the Kyoto City Office, the consensus was disrupted. However, since the rebellion did not change the status relations of the existing power structure, its achievements faded.[26] Normative control was consequently restored.

Unable to change the power structure in the workplace, OLs turn to alternative forms of self-expression. Part of the stereotype of an OL is the cute behavior style termed *burikko*. It celebrates "sweet, adorable, innocent, pure, simple, vulnerable, weak and inexperienced social behavior and physical appearance" (Kinsella 1995: 220). A *burikko* may be sexually active, but she feigns innocence.

The *burikko* style is not restricted to OLs, although it has certainly been elaborated by them. Several phrases—such as *kawaiiko burikko* ("mock cutie-pie," that is, someone who pretends to be a cute child)— developed in the context of high school students and OLs. The performance of *burikko* also constructs a cultural space for shopping, consumption, and media coverage. The Sanrio novelty company, which specializes in cute items, found in a market survey that "items sold to Japanese girls between the age of five and the time of marriage would be bought in America only by girls from four to seven years old" (White 1993: 126). One popular OL magazine, covering the latest in fashion and merchandising, is called *Cutie for Independent Girls*. Consistent with their zeal for cuteness, OLs have become avid consumers of Disney merchandise. Women older than eighteen constitute more than 60 percent of the visitors to Tokyo Disneyland, and the customer profile of the Disney retail stores in Japan shows that the largest group of consumers (around 33 percent) is between 20 and 29 years old, and that 53 percent of customers are single females (A. Raz 1999a). In the United States, the Disney Stores' major market consists of a different group—married people over 25 with children.

Jeannie Lo (1990: 42) also describes how many OLs act *burikko* in the workplace when men are present. This is encouraged by the men, who regard cute young women as "nice to have around" (Lo 1990: 43). The *burikko* act is an exaggeration of the OL's role. Among researchers,

---

26. In organizational development terms, only "single-loop learning" took place, not "double-loop" learning (see Argyris & Schon 1979).

burikko is dually interpreted—as a symbol of social authority and compliance as well as of the counterculture and implicit resistance. Although described by Japanese media in terms of an exotic and longed-for world of individual fulfillment and by older Japanese observers as "leisure-seeking moratorium people," the OLs are in fact caged in a social niche prescribed for them by patriarchal, middle-age Japanese society (see also Sievers 1983). Many of them resent their socially enforced moratorium, which prevents them from having their own careers and inevitably pushes them into marriage. Being "cute" is, as Kinsella (1995: 237) puts it, "an act of self-mutilation: posing with pigeon toes, dieting, acting stupid, squeaking and giggling" (see also Shimamura 1990).

On the other hand, the cute act is also viewed as a rebellion by youth against adulthood. "Rather than acting sexually provocative to emphasize their maturity, Japanese youth acted pre-sexual and vulnerable in order to emphasize their immaturity" (Kinsella 1995: 243; see also Silverberg 1991). According to Karen Kelsky (1994: 20), the OL work experience is "not one of unrelieved victimization, but constructive play in a society of oppressive work, a venue for exploration and self-expression in a culture that encourages conformity and obedience, and an opportunity to explore the 'foreign' in a country that elevates the native." At the end of the day, however, *burikko* seems to reproduce the normative control of the office, rather than to defy it.

The portrayal of OLs in Japan's popular culture strengthens their image as subjects of normative control. Although salaryman comedies have long been a staple of Japanese films, and a special genre of salaryman comics have been thriving since the 1960s,[27] OLs have usually played a subordinate role in these comedies and other pop-culture representations of office life. In the past decade there have been some satirical portrayals of OLs in pop culture. In 1989 a young cartoonist named Chūsonji Yutsuko created a series called "Sweet Spot." Instead

---

27. For essays on and examples of selected salarymen and OL comics, see Schodt 1983: 113–15; and Silverman 1995.

of decorative office flowers, her OLs were "long-haired, miniskirted toughies who played golf, bet the ponies and otherwise acted like middle-aged men on a spree" (Schilling 1998). Dubbed *oyaji gyaru* (*oyaji* is an informal term for "middle-aged men" or "uncle," and *gyaru* is Japlish for "girls"), they created a sensation, even though they were, as Chūsonji herself admitted, hardly representative of real OLs.

OLs also feature in a host of popular columns published in weekly magazines. Among the most popular of these columns is the series *Ojisan kaizō kōza* (Lessons for transforming "middle-age strangers,"i.e., male co-workers), published since 1987 in *Shūkan Bunshun*. Authors Shimizu Chinami and Furuya Yoshi try to be as candid and realistic as possible; they discuss subjects such as men's poor taste in clothes, their repellent physical characteristics, and their annoying habits, and so on. It is an exaggerated version of OLs' real-life gossip, backed up by questionnaires and surveys.

Researchers of organizational culture have yet to recognize what OL comics have known all along, namely, that the image of the OL combines deference and resistance. Despite overt discrimination, OLs rarely organize to challenge the official hierarchies of their male-dominated workplaces. Such "collective bargaining" would require union and class-consciousness. OLs, however, are characterized by the provisional nature of their occupational role and by internal division due to disparities between organizational status (based primarily on tenure), educational background, and age.

The academic literature on OLs is generally divided between more structural analyses of personnel systems that have concluded that OLs are powerless, and more ethnographic-minded studies that see OLs as exercising power over the men they serve. In Ogasawara's (1998) recent ethnography, OLs rarely challenged structural arrangements, but they did resist, individually and sometimes collectively—through gossip, popularity polls, and withholding cooperation—the authority of men they deemed arrogant or discourteous.

In reality, OLs are neither completely powerless nor the hidden tyrants of the workplace. They are somewhere in between. The combination of creeping feminism and a lingering economic slump may eventually lead to changes in the consciousness and status of OLs. At the moment, however, the OL subculture is too vast, too powerful, and too emotionally bound to male-dominated Japanese (organizational) culture to be changed by a mere economic recession.

CHAPTER FIVE

Part-time Service Work and the Consummation of Emotion Management

Since younger Japanese cannot reasonably be expected to follow the traditional pattern and sacrifice themselves for duty's sake, the manual system ensures cheerful service from all employees.

—Awata 1988: 60

[In Japan] the smile is to be used upon all pleasant occasions, when speaking to a superior or to an equal, and even upon occasions which are not pleasant; it is part of deportment. The most agreeable face is the smiling face.

—Hearn 1894: 658–59

When Japanese mask or conceal emotions, the expression most often used is the smile.

—Matsumoto 1996: 60

The First World shift from industries that produce to industries that perform has attracted much economic, political, and sociological attention. According to Daniel Bell (1973), the "postindustrial" society begins when employment in tertiary industries, such as the service sector, exceeds 50 percent of the total workforce. By 1990, the manufacturing sector in Japan accounted for only one of every three employees and one of every five companies (Sano 1995: 40). The rise of the service sector in Japan was accompanied by an exponential growth in leisure activities from 1980 to the 1990s (Harada 1994; Linhart 1988). In the 1980s, Japan thus underwent a process that had begun in the United States in the 1960s. According to Bell, postindustrial society is also a leisure society. This transformation is often characterized in Japan as the shift from an "industrialized" to an "information-oriented" society and from "hardware" to "software" (Kakita 1984: 4).

The service sector has the highest rates not only of part-time employment but also of turnover; these two are connected. Such institutional conditions call for a special organizational culture. In Japan, student part-timers are generally called *arubaito* (from the German *Arbeit*, "work"); *pāto* is the standard term for working housewives. In bureaucratic company jargon, both groups are termed *junshain*. The dual structure of part- and full-time work is a prominent example of the control exerted by companies on their internal labor market. The distinction between part- and full-time workers is particularly pronounced in Japan, where the three pillars of the Japanese system—seniority, lifetime employment, and company union membership—are limited to regular workers. Part-timers are the first to feel the effects of an economic downturn: in the oil shock of 1973, for example, they were the proverbial "first fired" (Nakamura 1981: 171; cited in Kondo 1990: 275). In general, however, the part-time labor market has grown considerably in Japan since the end of World War II, particularly with the increased entry of both unmarried and, later, married women, into the paid labor force, usually as part-time workers and usually into the retail and service sectors (Ichino 1989; Japan Rōdōshō 1996). For the employer, part-time labor offers savings in wages, a solution to labor shortages (of permanent workers), and flexibility in responding to fluctuations in the work pace and in the demand for a product or service. For the employee, the opportunity to work on a part-time basis accommodates the need to earn supplemental income without disturbing the focus on family or school. Employers, in turn, generally cite these attitudes to justify the low pay and dead-end nature of part-time work.

Given the dynamic and fast-changing and often unique quality of service encounters (sales representative–customer interactions), it is usually difficult for organizations to regulate encounters through such conventional controls as direct supervision or remuneration. Although service representatives are expected to be considerate, organizations cannot mandate an emotional rapport between their agents, who are usually part-timers, and the potentially demanding customer. As a result, many companies in the American service sector have developed forms of emotion management as a hallmark of their so-called service culture (for a review, see Ashforth & Humphrey 1993). The service sector has thus proved to be fertile ground for the emergence and crystallization of normative controls for the proper display of emotions.

The McDonaldization of the Japanese Service Industry

To many Japanese managers, the introduction of an American-style service culture was a fall from grace. Traditional service in Japan, the argument goes, developed in intimate, one-on-one situations such as a stay in a *ryōkan* (inn), an encounter with a *geisha*, or the daily visit to the neighborhood *sentō* (public bath), *chaya* (teahouse), or *nomiya* (drinking place).[1] Traditional service professionals, in this view, served apprenticeships and received many years of training and were consequently committed to and took pride in their work.

Christine Yano's (2002) description of the *enka* (traditional Japanese popular song) industry captures the essence of emotion management and traditional showmanship in Japan. *Enka* singers, like Disneyland cast members, are trained to be part of a show. Their output, like that of the service person, is intangible, and their performance is part of an elaborated economic system. *Enka* singers are trained by the traditional system of *minarai* (see and practice) and *detchi* (apprenticeship); they often live for a year with an established singer and learn by watching and listening. One of the tricks of the trade to be learned is the patterning of emotional expression. These patterns (*kata*) include

---

1. For a description of these places and the services they offer, with a focus on their Japaneseness, see Takahashi 1994; his essay is evocatively entitled "You Can't Have Green Tea in a Coffee Shop."

"the smallest nuance of breathiness, the lifting of a heel, and the streaming of tears, as well as the sounds, sights, and situations that evoke those tears" (Yano 2002: 25).

Enka is an emotion business. Lyrics are nostalgic, full of yearning, and sad. The music is evocative. The singer, as part of the performance, must embody and re-present these feelings. In *enka*, tears play a role similar to that played by the smile in the service industry. The tears, like the smile, are to appear in the performance at the right time and must be produced sincerely. Professional *enka* musical scores contain both musical and emotional instructions. These are the industry's manuals. The emotional notation, usually printed above the musical score, calls for such patterns as "sobbing pitch," "guttural rasp," "grunt," and "gasp."

The Western observer might regard such training and its ensuing performance as programmed and false. To use Hochschild's terminology, which is culturally representative of this view, this is "surface play" at its maximum pitch. Yet to the Japanese observer, emotions in *enka* are at once raw and cultivated, private and public, personal and social. It is their very cultivation over time that provokes moral and aesthetic admiration. The singer is expected to perfect the emotional display to the point where the *kata* vanishes, the individual becomes the form, and the form becomes individualized.

The ideology of self-cultivation through patterned work, still very much alive for OLs, has diminished and faded in many contemporary service organizations, particularly for part-time employees. The service manual is, according to the view that idealizes traditional Japanese service, the opposite of the apprenticeship system of *minarai*. The service manual, which is seen as a symptom of mass-consumed, anonymously delivered, American-style modern service, represents the deskilling of service workers.[2] The American concept of service is rendered in Japanese in katakana (the syllabary used for the transliteration of Western words) as *sābisu*, denoting its foreign and poten-

---

2. American society is often "characterized by Japanese businessmen and engineers as being a *manyuaru* (manual) society" (Schodt 1994: 170).

tially alienating nature. The story of Japan's incorporation of the service manual in the 1980s is a replay of Japan's domestication of scientific management in the 1920s and 1930s. In both cases, lip service to the beautiful customs of tradition was coupled with pragmatic implementation of new managerial systems of control.

The rhetoric of tradition facilitated the introduction of the new systems of service since it legitimized their implementation as an inevitable sign of the times. Part-timers in the service sector, managers argue, find themselves at a certain place for a limited amount of time. Whether sales go up or down, their pay remains the same. There is no promotion or bonus to be gained by doing more. This is hardly a work environment that encourages the traditional Japanese commitment and "sacrifice for one's company, section chief or superiors, or the sacrifice of present for future" (Sengoku 1985: 5–6). It is the kind of environment, according to trainers, that requires manuals. Manuals are also necessary, it is argued, because the job rotation system in large service companies frequently replaces an experienced supervisor with an inexperienced one.

The fall from grace in Japan's modern service is occurring throughout the world. It is a local response to the global process George Ritzer (1996) calls "McDonaldization." This process, which not surprisingly bears the name of a fast-food chain, features such basic elements as efficiency, calculability, predictability, and control. Efficiency, in the service industry, means the optimum method for getting the worker from one point to another. These methods are inscribed in training manuals and enforced by direct supervision. McDonald's also offers calculability; the size and cost of the product, as well as the service offered (the time it takes to get the product), are connected and standardized. Predictability assures the customer that the product and services are the same at all times and in all locales. Even the sales scripts are predictable. As Robin Leidner (1993: 82) notes, "McDonald's pioneered the routinization of interactive service work and remains an exemplar of extreme standardization." Finally, control means that workers and customers do a limited number of things in precisely the way management wants. Lines, limited menus, drive-through windows, and uncomfortable seats represent a subtly controlled environment in which diners are expected to eat quickly and leave.

The McDonald's formula has proved successful around the world, Asia included (Watson 1998). It is successful because it provides a solution to the global problems of consumerist society. For consumers around the world, McDonald's is the best available way to get from being hungry to being full. As Ritzer (1996: 9) argues, in a society in which both parents are likely to work and people usually rush by car from one spot to another, the efficiency of a fast-food meal is undeniable. McDonaldization epitomizes the economic logic of mass consumption. The keyword of the business is turnover—of customers as well as workers. Customers must be controlled to ensure a smooth and continuous flow. Every customer must receive prompt and proper service, so as to make way for the next customer. This is the job of front-line service employees. The problem is that such workers seldom remain with the company for long; turnover in the service industry in the United States (about 60 percent annually) is the highest of all employment sectors.[3]

The need to deal with the high turnover rate has generated an emphasis on design: the engineering of an efficient assembly line. Management sees this line, on which the product is assembled and served, as the one stable framework in a world of rushing customers and temporary employees. The logic of turnover promoted a return to Taylorism and its "efficiency expertise" and emphasis on work standards and assembly lines. The formalization of service production, human interaction included, brought a recognition of the importance of emotion management. Emotion management, however, was also to be pro-

---

3. In Japan, data collected by the Ministry of Labor (Rōdōshō) on the job tenure of part-time workers (workers whose contracted working hours are shorter than those of regular workers) show that 30.8 percent of male part-timers and 25.8 percent of female part-timers keep a job for one to three years; the next largest group (20 percent of the men, 12.5 percent of the women) stay for six months to one year. The average job tenure of part-time workers is 2.6 years for men, 4.3 years for women (cited in Wakisaka 1997: 146).

grammed by the logic of turnover. It was to be another instrument in an organizational culture whose goal is profitability.

Emotion management has recently become a fad in counseling circles in the United States. The wide adoption of emotion management demonstrates that its use is not limited to the service industry. Emotion management is not bound by the logic of turnover. There are other cultural reasons for its popularity. Emotion management is sold to Americans as a do-it-yourself method for all kinds of "positive change management" in organizations, teams, and one's personal life (see Fig. 6).[4]

"Emotion management" and "emotional intelligence" have become new slogans in the development of managerial skills (see Miller 1999; Laabs 1999). According to the new gospel, today's managers must learn to manage the emotional climate of their organizations with the same proficiency that they use to manage tasks and resources. The "good news" is that emotional intelligence and its associated competencies can be acquired through training. According to the Consortium for Research on Emotional Intelligence in Organizations— which was founded in 1996 by Daniel Goleman in conjunction with the Graduate School of Applied and Professional Psychology at Rutgers University—thousands of consultants and human resources professionals are engaged in efforts to promote social and emotional competencies in employees. Interestingly, American consultants argue that emotional intelligence training works best in small groups; usually 15 to 25 people is considered optimal. Although emotional intelligence training is not intended to be team building, it is sold as potentially promoting that important outcome.

Emotional intelligence training, like other fads, will probably die out soon. In that sense, even though it has transcended the boundaries

---

4. Figure 6 is an internet ad that appears on the homepage of an American consulting company. The name of the company has been deleted. The potential customer that surfs the homepage is urged to buy the company's product: "emotion management tapes" that help practice positive affirmations daily.

EMOTION MANAGEMENT
For Bottom Line Results in a World of Change

EXPERT IN:

- Positive Change Management
- Communication and Conflict Resolution
- Team Building
- Custom Service
- Gender Diversity
- Workplace Violence

TEAM & SERVICE Management

- Team Esteem: Healing Corporate Wounds
- Customer Service, Not Lip Service
- The Service Ethic: Selling It To Your People
- How to Manage Difficult (Different) People
- Back to the Family: Creating a Winning Team

PROFESSIONAL Management

- The Super Leader Concept: How It Can Work for Your People
- Earning a Living: The Power of Self-Direction
- Overcoming Sexual Politics at Work
- Women as Leaders: Widening the Window of Opportunity
- No More Hot Water: Emotion Management at Work
- Coach, Not Critic: The Essence of Performance Management

PERSONAL Management

- Permanent White Water: Staying Afloat in Rapid Change
- You Don't Have to Be Perfect to Be Excellent
- You, Me & We: The Wisdom to Know the Difference
- Addiction-Free: Positive Coping in a Negative World
- Mint Condition: Wellness for Life
- The New Prime Time For Women Over Fifty
- Spice Up Your Spouse: How to Stay in Love Forever

Fig. 6   Emotion management

of the service industry, it reflects the logic of turnover. In the mean time, this fad demonstrates the American propensity for practice without ideology. Emotion management is sold in the United States as a practical manual, without the elaborated ethical ideology of "the cultivation of self" found in Japan.

"Smile Training" in the United States and Japan

The smile has become a trademark of service training. Service representatives are asked by their companies not only to smile at customers but to smile sincerely. Many training programs urge service workers: "Be happy and people will be glad they came to your store. . . . Smile! Service with a smile and a friendly attitude will keep them loyal and keep them coming back."[5] McDonald's menus used to include the line "The smile is free of charge." Kōrakuen, an amusement park in the heart of Tokyo, has a part-timers' orientation video called "Smile on You." Hochschild (1983) cites the following excerpt from a Delta Air Lines manual for flight attendants: "Did the flight attendant hand out magazines? How many times? How were the magazines handed out? With a smile? With a sincere smile?" The Disney manuals refer repeatedly to the "Disney smile." The smile is integrated into cast members' behavior protocols: "At Disneyland we get tired, but never bored, and even if it's a rough day, we appear happy. You've got to have an honest smile. It's got to come from within."

The smile concept is also found in the translated manuals for cast members at Tokyo Disneyland. Consider, for example, this statement in the manual for a Tokyo Disneyland restaurant:

Stand straight. You are the representative of Plaza Pavilion. Make a big smile. The smile is necessary. When you speak up, pretend as if you were meeting somebody you love or haven't seen for a long time. Pay attention to eye contact. You should see the eyes of the guests you are addressing. Say the introduction of the restaurant clearly ("Hi. This is Plaza Pavilion Res-

---

5. This quote is from "Effective Customer Service Increases Sales," a 7-Eleven training program (cited in Sutton & Rafaeli 1988: 461).

taurant. This is a buffet-type restaurant. We have cold drinks, hot drinks, desserts. We have spaghetti, grilled beef.") Be friendly. Say: "*Konnichi wa.*" Be friendly to children. Say: "*Kyō wa genki?*" (Feeling good today?) If they are taking a picture, offer to help. Say: "Would you like me to take your picture?"

The standardization of service smiles has also depreciated their value, however. As a result, the concept of "smile training" now has a negative connotation in the United States. Karl Albrecht and Ron Zemke, the prophets of service management, warn readers away from "smile training": "By all means, let's use training. . . . But let's not insult our employees with smile training or 'be nice' training. Let's treat them like adults" (1985: 181–82). The Disney University is similarly disdained by Schickel for "training employees in the modern American art forms of the frozen smile and the canned answer delivered with enough spontaneity to make it seem unprogrammed" (1968: 318).[6] American workers respond to "smile training" as a form of deskilling that promotes alienation. And American observers, from Hochschild to Ritzer, regard service management as a hegemonic program that subjects individuality and emotion to social structure and instrumental rationality.

In contrast, in Japan, "smile training" encountered little resistance. This incorporation of this behavioral protocol was facilitated by a local, pre-existing cultural construction of "the smile" as the primary mask of emotion (Matsumoto 1996: 60).[7] One of the earlier Western

---

6. Schickel's criticism of Disney is linked to the critical outlook of the Frankfurt School's view of the culture industry. Theodor Adorno, for example, saw Disney as the site for American cultural imperialism. In Horkheimer and Adorno's chapter on the culture industry in *Dialectic of Enlightenment*, we find that "Donald Duck in the cartoons, like the unfortunate in real life, gets his beating so that the viewers can get used to the same treatment. . . . This 'iron bath of fun' administered by the culture industry does not inspire a conciliatory laughter that would echo the escape from power, but a *Shadenfreude*, a terrible laughter" (cited in Hansen 1993: 34). The terrible laughter is Adorno's consumerist mirror-image of Schickel's mass-produced canned smile.

7. See Ekman and Friesen 1982: 239 for an experiment that demonstrated that Japanese and Americans showed the same facial expressions when experiencing fear, disgust, and distress if they were alone. However, when they were in social situations, quite different expres-

commentators on the ubiquity of the Japanese smile, the Irish-Greek writer Lafcadio Hearn, who spent his last years (1890–1904) in Japan, argued:

A Japanese can smile in the face of death, and usually does. But he then smiles for the same reason that he smiles at other times. There is neither defiance nor hypocrisy in the smile; nor is it to be confounded with that smile of sickly resignation which we are apt to associate with weakness of character. It is an elaborate and long-cultivated etiquette. It is also a silent language. But any effort to interpret it according to western notions of physiognomic expression would be just about as successful as an attempt to interpret Chinese ideographs by their real or fancied resemblance to shapes of familiar things.

. . . The stranger cannot fail to notice the generally happy and smiling character of the native faces; and this first impression is, in most cases, wonderfully pleasant. The Japanese smile at first charms. It is only at a later day, when one has observed the same smile under extraordinary circumstances— in moments of pain, shame, disappointment—that one becomes suspicious of it. Its apparent inopportuneness may even, on certain occasions, cause violent anger.

. . . The smile is taught like the bow, like the prostration. . . . But the smile is to be used upon all pleasant occasions, when speaking to a superior or to an equal, and even upon occasions which are not pleasant; it is part of deportment. The most agreeable face is the smiling face; and to present always the most agreeable face possible to parents, relatives, teachers, friends, well-wishers, is a rule of life. . . . Even though the heart is breaking, it is a social duty to smile bravely. (Hearn 1894: 658–59; cited in Matsumoto 1996: 60).

What Lafcadio Hearn is describing here is the extensive use, in Japan, of the smile as social glue. Every emotion has three major dimensions: expression, motivation, and social glue (Matsumoto 1996). Emotion as social glue (or more generally, as social structure) emphasizes the cultural given-ness of emotion, the fact that various emotional scripts exist as "social facts" prior to the individual. The "smile,"

sions were evident. The Japanese covered negative emotions with a smiling mask much more often than did the Americans.

in Lafcadio Hearn's description, is culturally constructed as a sign of the agreeable and the conformist. It therefore serves as social glue. This is not to say that behind every "smile" there is always agreement. In Paul Ekman and Wallace Friesen's (1972) original study, Japanese participants smiled in the presence of a higher-status experimenter to hide what they later conveyed were intense, negative feelings.[8]

The possible discrepancy between the smile as social glue and the real negative feelings behind it relate to the second dimension of emotion, motivation. Emotion as motivation denotes the subjective experience of feelings and stresses individual resources and intentions. By constructing the smile as the primary mask for emotions, the Japanese have made this discrepancy culturally acceptable. When smiles are used in this fashion, they become "signs of something other than true joy, or happiness, or positive emotion. . . . Japanese people learn that the smile does not necessarily mean that one is happy" (Matsumoto 1996: 109).[9] As a result, "smile training" is part of normative socialization. This is also evident in the training for OLs, described in the previous chapter.

"Smile training" has become a global fad because the smile is universal. Emotional expression consists of the spoken and bodily, mainly facial, display of emotion and is, according to research, universal. The smile is one of the easiest expressions to produce; everyone can voluntarily engage the muscles used in the smile to pull the corners of the lips up. A sincere smile, trainers were quick to learn, should also include the muscles surrounding the eye. Laboratory research has shown that this lip-eye configuration is cross-cultural, too (Ekman et

---

8. The use of the smile as a mask is not unique to the Japanese. The smile is used for similar purposes in a variety of situations in many cultures (see Ekman 1985; Ekman & Friesen 1982).

9. Among the anecdotal evidence mentioned by Matsumoto (1996: 109) to show differences in the significance of the smile in Japan and the United States is the role of smiles in photographs. In the United States, it is common for people posing for photographs to smile ("to say cheese"). In Japan, it is more common to see posers with a serious expression. Japanese children are socialized to pose not with a smile but rather with their right hand making the "V" sign (called *piisu*, "peace"). According to Matsumoto, smiles are bad because a posed smile would be interpreted as a sign of negative feelings.

al. 1990). Interestingly, the smile has become so much a global expression of the service culture that cultural differences in the motivation and social structuring associated with the "smile" have been ignored.

The Japanese, in general, respond to "smile training" not as being shallow, but as being too *weak* rather than too *strong*. Trainers and managers look down on service culture (*sābisu bunka*) and criticize American service manuals as lacking spirit, as *kata* without the *chi*. This has not stopped managers and trainers in the Japanese service industry from using manuals, however. Like the Japanese managers who adopted industrial management, service managers mouthed ideological objections to manuals while actually using them. Recently, as "spiritual education" becomes more and more detached from the contemporary reality of service culture, such objections have been fading. Spiritual education has been reduced to a behavior campaign.

The Warm Heart: Tokyo Dome's Behavior Campaign

How, then, do Japanese service companies manage "undisciplined" part-time labor? In this section, I offer a bottom-up, backstage view of a labor-management conflict. In contrast to the classless image of "Japan, Inc." and the prevailing image of harmony and strength in Japanese-style management, this case study highlights a fissure between managers (regular workers) and front-line employees (part-time workers). In the end, the problem was solved and order restored—an outcome that reinforced the superiority of Japanese-style management.

The Tokyo Dome Corporation was founded in 1936 as Kōrakuen Company, Ltd., for the purpose of constructing and operating Japan's first baseball stadium (Tokyo Dome Company 1995: 1). In the early 1950s, the Kōrakuen amusement park—Japan's first urban amusement park—was built near the stadium. The company was a pioneer in the leisure industry and a typical representative of that tradition (Yoshimitsu 1970). In 1988 the baseball stadium was rebuilt as the Tokyo Dome, Japan's first all-weather stadium. Known as the "Big EGG" (Big Entertainment and Golden Games), the Tokyo Dome hosts events ranging from concerts and exhibitions to baseball games and other sports matches. In 1995 Tokyo Dome had 1,200 regular employees and about 5,000 part-timers. Big EGG hosts about 10 million visitors per year. The organization and role of Tokyo Dome's large personnel department are typical of the Japanese service sector.

On November 16, 1992, Kōrakuen's Service Division launched a "Behavior Campaign." A special memorandum, issued that day, described the campaign's objective of establishing a service code and the schedule for implementing that code. Every three months another theme would be declared. The first was the "smile," to be followed by greetings (*aisatsu*), appearance (*midashinami*), behavior (*taido*), manner of speech (*kotobazukai*), cleanliness, safety, customers' complaints, and so on. Three videos were produced for the campaign, and various newsletters, posters, stickers, and telephone cards were published. The campaign is re-enacted every year. The posters for the 1994 campaign were especially impressive. On one, half the poster was occupied by a large title in gold ink reading: "Declaration of Customer Principles" (*kasutoma nizumi sengen*). Below the title, over a white illustration of the Tokyo Dome, a diagonal question printed in yellow challenges the employee: "Are you customanist?" (*kasutomanisuto ka?*). Below that, a salaryman standing in Uncle-Sam-Wants-You pose points his finger at the viewer.

The Behavior '93 poster was more modest. A vertical sentence printed in black over a background of red hearts stated: "To begin with, warm heart" (*hajimari wa, wōmi hāto*). The extensive use of katakana Americanisms ("warm heart," "behavior campaign," "customer") illustrates how the new service culture is being reproduced and marketed in Japanese organizations. *Wōmi hāto* ("warm heart") is not an original Japanese idiom. It is a borrowed Americanism, rendered in katakana. Tokyo Dome's "warm heart" is the *sunao na kokoro* ("naïve heart," the traditional ideal of cultivating selfhood through work) of the 1990s. Like Taylorism in the 1920s and quality control circles in the 1960s, "CS" (customer service) and "service manuals" are the American imports of the 1990s.

Tokyo Dome's Behavior Campaign coincided with a few labor-management incidents. A typical incident took place in 1994, after the campaign had been under way for two years. The campaign was thus not a foolproof answer to Tokyo Dome's problems. The backdrop for the incident can be briefly described. In 1994, sales at the Tokyo Dome baseball specialty shop outside the stadium fell 10 percent, despite an increase in the number of visitors to the games (Tokyo Dome Company 1995). Yamada (a pseudonym), then a young salaryman (*tantō*) in the sales division, was appointed to study the problem:

I was told that we are not expected to increase sales, because of the recession. Our goal was to keep sales at the same level, as much as possible. We couldn't introduce new goods to our baseball specialty shop, because the Tokyo Giants (our sponsoring baseball team) controlled all the merchandise. Our strategy was to improve management on the one hand and service on the other. We knew there was a problem with service, because shop personnel did not say "*irasshaimase*" (please come in) or "*arigatō gozaimashita*" (thank you very much)—at least they didn't say it when a large number of customers was coming in after the baseball game in Tokyo Dome.

Yamada's first step was to collect evidence of what he considered the staff's unprofessional behavior. He videotaped the shop personnel at work by placing a camera behind the registers. This was a relatively easy task since in Japan, as Yamada explained to me, all companies may legally videotape everything on their premises. On crowded Saturday nights, the video showed the four cashiers talking among themselves while many customers waited in line. In addition, when the cashiers handed the merchandise to the customer, they did not say thank you. Both the regular worker in charge and the part-timers exhibited the same behavior when the store was crowded. According to Yamada, they later explained that "so many customers were coming anyway that we didn't think we had to worry about *greetings*."

Convinced that he had pinpointed the problem, Yamada's second step was to organize a general meeting of representatives from a consulting company, his boss, and the shop's staff. The meeting was held at Tokyo Dome's instruction center. Following an opening address by the department chief, which focused on the worrisome fall in sales, Yamada showed his video. The employees were embarrassed in public. Yamada: "They were really ashamed. I edited the video, pasting in all the material that showed unprofessional behavior among the workers. Many lowered their heads because they were ashamed to look at it."

The word he used to describe the workers' reactions was *hazukashii*, a semantically loaded term in Japan. According to McVeigh (1997: 53), this word denotes "anything from the Japanese penchant for reticence, reluctance to express one's opinion, Japan's *haji no bunka* (shame culture), to an inability to master foreign languages." This semantic field makes sense in Japan, where "ethics are often equated with etiquette . . . [and] breaches in manners, besides eliciting embarrassment, may also cause shame" (McVeigh 1997: 53). Yamada's disciplinary strategy vividly exemplifies the Japanese culture of shame as an important emotional vehicle for fostering commitment (Benedict 1946; Sakuta 1967; Lebra 1976; Doi 1973; Pelzel 1986). Yamada's campaign illustrates the argument I made in the Introduction that Japan as a "shame society" reveals the power of emotion as a social sanction and shows how social norms and feeling rules may have a profound impact on the subjective emotional experiences of individuals.

Following the video presentation, the department chief announced an "off-JT" seminar for the shop's personnel. "Off-JT," a derivative of "off-the-job training," refers to unpaid, mandatory, after-hours training. The seminar consisted of voice lessons, training in the correct use of greetings, role-playing, and the use of a script to explain goods. A year later, business had returned to normal. In 1995, Yamada and another trainer involved in the campaign were transferred to other jobs, following the usual career-development procedures for white-collar workers in Japan, and lost contact with the shop. Apparently the shop's revenues increased enough to direct the management's attention to other, more pressing problems. Note, however, that the Behavior Campaign did not make use of the ideological baggage of self-cultivation or paternalism. In its repetition and its emphasis on normative control by the book (the manual), Tokyo Dome's Behavior

Campaign illustrates the logic of turnover that has come to characterize the global service sector.

In 2000, the theme of the Behavior Campaign was customer satisfaction, which was ceremonially presented in the now-familiar set of posters, banners, and memos. A new addition to the campaign, however, was a company-wide system to monitor service performance, managed by the service division. The system included a customer service audit by "mystery" shoppers and culminated in a "Malcolm Baldrige award contest." The audit checklist and the award criteria were not Japanese but adopted from an American service manual (found in Christopher 1994). According to a Tokyo Dome service manager, the monitoring system was designed after international service standards such as the BS 5750 in the United Kingdom and the ISO 9000 of the International Standards Organization.

In 1987, the U.S. Congress created the Malcolm Baldrige National Quality Award. It has since become accepted as defining the criteria of total quality for any organization seeking to improve its service. The Baldrige examination categories include leadership, quality planning, human resource utilization, quality assurance, and customer satisfaction. Each category is assigned a maximum number of allowable points; the combined total of all items is 1,000.

Tokyo Dome hired some thirty mystery shoppers to do the monitoring. These were nonprofessional outsiders hired to test the quality of service. Each shopper files a report that includes subjective impressions as well as quantitative ratings; the service division conducts group interviews with the shoppers and integrates the data; the division's report is sent to a special customer service committee, which is composed of representatives from all divisions in the company. The customer service committee issues a final report and grants the award. According to a Tokyo Dome service manager:

We don't actually distribute the grades or ratings in the report, just a bottom line saying "good" or "not good." The divisions would get mad at us if we compared them using a test score, and everybody would hate the service division. The whole process is very expensive . . . and results in huge amounts of data. In the future, we are thinking about using it as part of the knowledge management of the service division, putting it on the Internet, and so on.

Many of the service personnel with whom I discussed the monitoring system expressed a hope that this system would some day be managed internally by a "service quality center." Currently, the company hires an external consulting agency to manage the monitoring system. Future plans include the implementation of quality control circles for service workers. This is also part of the trend of applying to service work statistical and normative control schemes developed in manufacturing. It also signals the return of scientific management to contemporary people-intensive workplaces such as service companies.

Tokyo Dome Hotel

Overlooking the Dome, the Tokyo Dome Hotel—with 43 stories containing more than a thousand guest rooms—is the newest addition to Big EGG City. Company managers are anxiously watching their new investment. To finance the hotel, the company sold portions of the traditional amusement park and several shopping centers. Construction began in 1997, and during 1999, 400 new employees were hired to work in the hotel. One hundred of these were hired as regular employees, and 300 as part-timers. The hotel's "identity" is publicly presented in four words—"Satisfaction, Tenderness, Amusement, Relaxation"—which appear over a background of three stars in official company publications. A period of intensive training for all new front-line employees began about one month before the opening of the hotel on June 1, 2000. The following description of the training is based on an interview I had with the head of the training program.

All employees were given the latest edition of a trade textbook on "basic manners," which contains the conventional sections on appearance, polite language, courtesy, smiling, and so on. Employees also attended seminars on walking, role-playing, modulating the voice (vol-

ume, tone, tempo), smiling (the trainees used mirrors to learn to smile
with the eyes as well as the mouth), and bowing (15 degrees when the
other person is of similar status; 30 degrees when the other person is
of higher status; 45 degrees when the bower has made a mistake). The
employees practiced in groups. Employees also received a "service
leadership handbook," prepared by the company, that repeats the contents of the lessons. The handbook ends with encouraging and enthusiastic comments by hotel trainees. The last page of the handbook reproduces the Tokyo Dome company song.

Tests were administered during the seminars using checklists that
workers had to fill from their memory. Did the new part-time employee object to this service training? Not at all, according to the man
in charge of training: "Of course, many were members of the younger
generation (*shinjinrui*), but there was no problem. Those who came
with light or brown hair corrected their appearance after we mentioned it to them. Everyone got along fine. If someone doesn't like polite language or appearance management, they don't choose to work in
a hotel."

An interesting part of the training consisted of teamwork games,
such as reassembling a booklet cut into pieces or forming a circle in
the order of the team members' birthdays, without talking. Teamwork
games, however, were limited to regular workers only; temps were excluded. When I asked why, a Tokyo Dome trainer said: "Because we
don't have enough time and money for that." Her supervisor, who was
present at that time, added: "Temps will learn teamwork when we
[meaning the regulars] take them drinking with us after the work day.
This is the Japanese way."

The training program at the Tokyo Dome Hotel is a direct continuation of the service culture described in the context of the Behavior Campaign and the incident in the Tokyo Dome shop. In all these
situations, regular workers disciplined the emotions of part-time
workers. Common features of this emotional discipline included formal guidelines, detailed training, direct supervision, and indirect
monitoring. Emotion management focused on manuals and surface

acting. There was little reference to the ideology of self-fulfillment through work. This is quite different from Rohlen's (1974) depiction of "harmony and strength." First, he and I approached the subject from different points of view. Rohlen's analysis largely subscribed to the values of management and took management's declarative rhetoric as a depiction of workplace reality. My approach, in contrast, is to distinguish the declared values of management, actual norms in the workplace, and the interpretations of groups within the organization. Second, he studied white-collar, professional (and usually regular and male) bank workers, whereas I focus on nonprofessional, part-time, and usually female workers in the service industry. Third, nearly thirty years have elapsed since Rohlen's observations, and during this period there have been changes in work values and intergenerational relationships. Rohlen's analysis reflects the organizational culture of regular, male office workers and their codependent female workers in a Japanese bank during the 1970s. Mine reflects the contemporary service culture of front-line part-timers. The underlying structure of this new and global service culture can be substantiated further through a comparison to similar service workplaces in the United States.

"Service with a Smile": An American Convenience Store Chain

The emotions at work in 7-Eleven stores, a large nationwide chain of convenience stores in the United States, provides a basis for comparison with the Japanese Behavior Campaign.[10] Inspired by Thomas Peters and Robert Waterman's *In Search of Excellence* (1982), the human resources staff of the Southland Corporation, the owner of the chain,

---

10. My discussion of this report is based on Sutton & Rafaeli 1988. At the time of the research (1984), the 7-Eleven chain was owned by the Southland Corporation, with about 7,000 stores in the United States and Canada, 36 percent of which were franchises. The research was conducted in a sample of 576 convenience stores. The typical store had eight–ten employees who worked in three eight-hour shifts (morning shift, swing shift, and night shift). Stores carried small inventories of food, drinks, cigarettes, and magazines because of the lack of storage space.

conducted this research as part of a chain-wide effort to enhance employee courtesy. One year before the evaluation was made, the human resources staff had revised the employee handbooks and the classroom training given to new recruits. The changes consisted of instructing the clerks to greet, smile at, establish eye contact with, and say "thank you" to every customer. Store managers received new handbooks, entitled—for example—"Effective Customer Service Increases Sales," and containing lectures, readings, and suggestions for role-playing exercises and group discussions. In addition, clerks were informed that "mystery shoppers" would be used to observe them. In some regions, clerks who were found displaying the required good cheer received a $25 bonus. The corporation also held a contest, costing over $10 million, in which store managers could qualify to enter a drawing for a $1 million if their clerks consistently offered good cheer to customers. The corporation also awarded a bonus of 25 percent of base salary to regional managers when a high percentage of salesclerks in the stores in their region were observed displaying good cheer to customers. These individual incentives are themselves a cultural difference (or a difference in organizational culture) between the United States and Japan. At Tokyo Dome (and other Japanese service organizations) no individual incentives were offered to managers or employees.

"Incognito participant observers" who coded clerks' behavior during transactions with customers measured the display of emotions. The firm did not hire special observers for this task but used members of its human resources staff. Observers visited each store in pairs. They acted independently and did not communicate with each other while in the store. They walked around the store for a few minutes, noting how well it was stocked and whether the clerk was wearing a nametag and a clean smock. Typically, the observers then walked to the magazine rack and observed the clerk's behavior from that vantage point. The observers then selected a small item like a candy bar and stood in line, continuing to note the employee's behavior toward customers. The amount of time in each store varied from four to twelve minutes.

The company required its clerks to express a "warm outward de-meanor" during transactions with customers. The performance of this requirement was formalized in handbooks and manuals that broke the task down into four required elements: greeting, thanking, eye contact, smiling. This is Taylor's "job analysis" at work: finding the one best way of performing a particular task by dividing it into its basic units. The procedure is typical of the American service industry, whose organizational culture emphasizes ground (rather than surface) rules[11] to design and control the emotional behavior of front-line employees. McDonald's, for example, has a similar checklist: front-line employees are instructed that every transaction with a customer must follow seven orderly stages: (1) establishing eye contact, (2) greeting, (3) taking the customer's order, (4) calculating the bill and informing the customer, (5) collecting the order, (6) collecting the payment, and (7) saying "thank you." These checklists epitomize Taylor's scientific management. The checklist deals with devotion in the form of design. There is no ideology of self-fulfillment here.

At 7-Eleven, the formalization of feeling rules was matched by the quantitative measurement of displayed emotions, and the clerks' displayed emotions were operationally defined. Only "Hello," "How are you today," or another polite phrase at the outset of a transaction was considered a greeting. Anything else was not coded as greeting. In thanking the customer, the clerk had to use the word "thank" or a derivative. A smile was defined as a noticeable uptwisting of the lips. And a direct gaze by a clerk counted as a sincere attempt at eye contact. Note that all these definitions are unilateral; they do not take into account the behavior of the customer. Contrary to Figure 2 (p. 45), the company disregards customer feedback. (This unique aspect of "service acting" is discussed below.)

The 7-Eleven observers assigned a value of 1 if a behavior were displayed and a value of 0 if it were not. The data were aggregated at the store level to create an index of the display of positive emotions as a store attribute. For each store, a score was computed for each of the

---

11. For ground and surface rules, see the discussion of Fig. 2, pp. 44–45.

four emotional expressions by calculating the proportion of transactions in which the behavior was displayed to the total number of transactions coded. Observers also gathered data on the following control variables: (1) the gender composition of the clerks (operationally defined as the proportion who were women); (2) the gender composition of the customers (again, calculated as the proportion who were women); (3) the clerks' image (the degree to which clerks in a store observed the dress code specified in corporate guidelines—that is, wore a clean smock and a name tag); (4) the stock level in the store (the extent to which the shelves, snack stands, and refrigerators were fully stocked); (5) average length of the lines at the cash registers; (6) store ownership (corporation-owned or franchised); and (7) store supervision costs (the amount of money spent by the corporation on salaries, benefits, and training).

The criterion variable used in the study was total store sales. Multiple regression analyses were performed to determine the relationship between the display of positive emotion and total store sales. The direction of the observed relationship, however, contradicted the original hypothesis—higher levels of displayed positive emotion were associated with lower, rather than higher, levels of sales. The modest positive relationship between line length and sales, along with a modest negative relationship between line length and the display of positive emotions, led the researchers to consider the difference between busy and slow settings.

Like the clerks at Tokyo Dome dealing with the rush of customers following a game, convenience store clerks were less courteous when the store was crowded and busy. During busy times, it was not unusual to hear a customer asking "Can I please have a plastic bag for my merchandise?" and a salesclerk answering: "Lady, we don't have time for your please and thank you. Can't you see how busy we are? Just say what you want."[12] Like the Tokyo Dome clerks, American clerks

---

12. This exchange, quoted in Sutton & Rafaeli 1988: 473, reflects a transaction between one of the researchers and a clerk in a very busy store. At this stage the study was conducted using qualitative methods, i.e., interviewing and unstructured observations.

contended that friendliness and warmth were unnecessary when customers "just want to get in and out quickly." Can we then conclude that the norms of the surrounding cultures give way, in the service context, to a common global culture, whose "carriers" are part-time service employees?

The answer is not clear-cut. Although common features are evident, there are also cultural differences, for example, in the reaction of customers and management. Both studies—in Japan and the United States—revealed that store pace is the cause, rather than an effect, of expressive behavior. For American and Japanese salesclerks, the number of customers in the store provides a cue for norms about expressed emotions. Did customers also share this cue? Here we see some cultural variation. In the American study, during busy times both clerks and customers tacitly agree that the expression of pleasant emotions is not essential, whereas both clerks and customers tacitly expect that pleasant emotions should be expressed during slow times.[13] In Tokyo Dome, however, "customer satisfaction" forms have shown that customers expected clerks to be courteous even during busy times.

Similarly, Japanese managers reacted differently to what they saw as the failure of clerks to display positive emotions during busy times. American managers tacitly accepted that at busy times customers are inputs to be processed rapidly. Managers also tacitly encouraged workers to forgo the programmed courtesies during busy times by redefining the resulting behavior as being "more task-oriented" rather than being "less friendly." The argument advanced by the researchers (who published their research in an American managerial journal) was that displays of courtesy prolonged transactions. A "no-nonsense" clerk was less likely to irritate those waiting in a long line. Apparently for managers and clerks in American convenience stores, efficiency overrides courtesy during busy times. Conversely, managers at the Tokyo Dome corporation thought that clerks should always remain

---

13. This conclusion remains to be proved. Data on customer reactions were not gathered as part of the American study, and the authors of the study could only speculate about the "tacit agreement" between customers and clerks. I rely on their interpretation in this matter.

courteous. The resulting off-the-job training, with its shaming sanctions, was uniquely Japanese. The annual behavior campaign, although a ritualized importation of an American organizational practice, was also strikingly different from the individual incentives used by the American corporation.[14]

The Case of Disneyland

Unlike the customers of convenience stores, where efficiency is valued more highly than courtesy at busy times, visitors to Disneyland expect employees to be cheerful even when the place is crowded. This expectation is encouraged by Disney management. Indeed, Disney employees know that persistent discourtesy is grounds for dismissal. Unlike Tokyo Dome or the convenience store, however, Disney allows employees very little discretion about which emotions they convey and how. Disney has repeatedly been selected as one of the top five American service companies in many American surveys and industry magazines (Carey 1995; Castoro 1995; Peters & Waterman 1982). In 1983 Tokyo Disneyland opened in the Tokyo Bay area and quickly became a huge success. Tokyo Disneyland is a transplant—a service organization licensed by the Disney Company yet owned and operated by a Japanese firm in Japan. Like the auto transplants, Tokyo Disneyland provides a unique comparative viewpoint from which to examine emotion management in the United States and Japan.

In Japan Disney is considered as a model for service in the same way McDonald's is the model for retail fast-food operations. Disney manuals for part-timers have been hailed by many Japanese commen-

---

14. It would have been interesting to compare the American study with the organizational culture of 7-Eleven Japan. 7-Eleven convenience stores entered Japan around 1974, where they were operated by the Ito-Yokado Company under license from the Southland Corporation. The convenience store (*conbini*) has been a huge success in Japan. 7-Eleven Japan actually got so big and rich it took over the American chain in 1990. However, the *conbini* are quite different from the American original. These stores are nearly all franchise operations, typically held by a married couple. Instead of relying on company-owned distribution centers as Southland did, 7-Eleven Japan uses Japan's regular wholesale network (for additional comparisons, see Sparks 1995; and Bernstein 1994).

tators as "the secret of Tokyo Disneyland's success" (Komuya 1989; Tadokoro 1990). One Japanese executive said:

Japan has very little more to learn about management from the U.S. There is one exception, though. We have been impressed with Disneyland. Do you know that when Disneyland was opened in Tokyo, they had a book this large which explained everybody's job completely? The book also explained policies and procedures for the park. Everything ran smoothly when it opened, with no problems and no uncertainties in job assignments. (Eberts & Eberts 1995: 185)[15]

According to Awata Fusaho (1988: 60), "There are manuals— manuals detailing the ways the cast should stand and sit, wave and whistle—which are undoubtedly at the heart of the Disney management system. . . . Since younger Japanese cannot reasonably be expected to follow the traditional pattern and sacrifice themselves for duty's sake, the manual system ensures cheerful service from all employees."

Sociological accounts of work in Disneyland and Walt Disney World have focused on its mechanisms of normative control. To American managers and businessmen, Disneyland is the Sistine Chapel of service culture: an American model for training and people management. Much has been written—by business journalists and sociologists—on the Disney University in Anaheim, California, at which all employees—or cast members—take two courses called "Traditions 1 and 2." There is a copious literature on the Disney manuals, in which work procedures and scripts ("spiels") for courtesy talk are meticulously prescribed, as well as on the emotion management practiced on, and by, the employees of this smile factory.[16] Dis-

---

15. For similar conversations regarding Disney as model management, see Drucker 1992: 182–83.

16. Fjellman's 1992 monograph on Walt Disney World is the most wide-ranging scholarly treatment of a Disney theme park. The discourse of Disney films is examined in Smoodin 1994. Disney and postmodernism are the subject of an anthology (Willis 1993) titled *The World According to Disney*, whose contributors later published a treatise on Walt Disney World composed by a collective forum called "The Project on Disney" (1995). Several sociologists have dealt with the indoctrination of Disney values, language, and stories as means of corporate con-

ney's worlds are fertile grounds for a sensitive and critical sociology of emotions. Indeed, the Disney view of human nature is basically emotional; according to Tokyo Disneyland's trainer's manual, the correct answer to the question "What moves people?" is "20 percent reason, 80 percent emotion."

Since its opening on April 15, 1983, Tokyo Disneyland has annually attracted well over 10 million visitors (16.5 million in 2000), which makes it the most popular diversionary outing in Japan and relatively more successful than the two Disney theme parks in America. Owned and operated by a Japanese company (Oriental Land Company), Tokyo Disneyland is a big organization. As of April 1, 1995, it had 12,390 cast members; 2,540 of these were regular employees and 9,850 part-time employees (TDL 1995: 2). The proportions have remained the same in following years. Every day, over 600 entertainers appear in stage shows, musical performances, and parades.

Tokyo Disneyland employees are divided into two groups: part-time and regular workers. This division of the work force exists at both Walt Disney World and Disneyland, as well as in Japanese organizations. The regular workers consist of supervisors ("leads," in DisneyTalk) and office workers. This is the Japanese world of salarymen and OLs described in the previous chapter. The world of part-timers, in contrast, is governed by the Disney manuals and the "Disney Way." This is the world of front-line employees ("cast members," in DisneyTalk), and it embodies the global culture of service.

The world of Disney's cast members, in Japan and the United States, is governed by both design and devotion. In terms of design, Taylorism provides the conceptual and practical system for front-line

---

trol (e.g., R. Smith & Eisenberg 1987; Boje 1995). John Van Maanen, in a series of four innovative papers, made Disneyland a case study of strong organizational culture (Van Maanen 1989, 1991, 1992; Van Maanen & Kunda 1989). The tremendous success of Tokyo Disneyland has similarly spawned a thriving genre of "how does it really work" books in Japanese (for example, Komuya 1989; Tsuromaki 1984; Tadokoro 1990; Awata & Takanarita 1984; Kanō 1986; and, most recently, Lipp 1994). Many of these books explain the success of Tokyo Disneyland in terms of its human resource management and service manuals. This outline of the social science literature on Disney does not include articles, of which there are several hundreds.

work at Tokyo Disneyland. All of the original four components of Taylor's "job analysis" can be found at work here (see also Howard & Crompton 1980 as well as Sterle & Duncan 1973 for a discussion of how to implement Taylorism in recreation and leisure management):

1. *Finding the best way of performing any particular task by dividing every task into its basic units.* This is the focus of Disney training as well as the cast members' shift schedule. Every job at Tokyo Disneyland (or at any Disney World for that matter) is carefully defined and broken down into checklists that workers have to memorize. Shift changes are punctually defined. The work schedule and procedures (how many plates to carry at any one time, which table to start with) are closely defined, almost like the timing of the various attractions. This is the Disney version of Taylor's time and motion studies.

2. *Standards.* The park is obsessed with time standards based on the most efficient way of doing the job. Attractions are timed in seconds and half-seconds. Lines are timed, and retimed, in minutes. There is also an obsession with standardizing the requirements for materials, machines, tools, working conditions, and the people to fill the job. The wage charts for various hours and shifts are meticulously standardized.

3. *Planning of work.* Taylor was one of the first organizational innovators to glorify the manual as the epitome of standardization, efficiency, and rationality in the workplace. Disney takes after Taylor in its wide range of manuals and their significant role in organizational culture.

4. *Maintenance of standards.* A system of inspection and control assures adherence to standards. This system is daily at work in the park, in the form of visible and invisible supervisors, leads, and "shoppers" (a Disney term for supervisors disguised as customers).

In terms of "devotion," cast members are normatively controlled and emotionally managed. The "Disney Way," imparted to the "Disney Family," can be seen as part of a managerial discourse of paternalism. The Oriental Land Company scrapped several socialization practices found in the American versions of the manuals because Japanese managers saw them as "too much fussing about what the Americans call 'getting an emotional buy-in to the Disney culture.'" The practices abandoned at Tokyo Disneyland include, for example, Disney's "pixie dust" decor in the training center, the orientation video, the teamwork quiz, and (in part) DisneyTalk.

At the Walt Disney World training center, new hires are greeted by fifteen Disney characters that stand atop twelve pedestals (Heise 1994). Illustrations on the ceiling show Peter Pan and Tinkerbell flying across the sky. There are no such decorations ("pixie dust") at Tokyo Disneyland's training center. The structure of the job interview is also different. Every applicant for an hourly job at Walt Disney World is given a preliminary eight-to-ten-minute interview (Blocklyn 1988) that is meant to make sure that the applicant "understands" the requirements of the job. An explanatory video has recently been used for the same purpose (Heise 1994). Mike McGuffey, a hiring supervisor at Walt Disney World, says that "the unusually strong corporate culture at Disney means that a career at the resort is not for everyone" (cited in Blocklyn 1988: 30). The introductory process therefore "saves face" (Heise 1994: 18). This preliminary interview is omitted at Tokyo Disneyland. Company managers claim that since Japanese part-timers are already accustomed to working during holidays and vacations as well as adhering to strict grooming standards, there is no need to prepare them for all this.

During the "Traditions 1 and 2" orientation classes, the new hires at Walt Disney World are asked to take a quiz answering questions about the company's past, present and future.

After . . . [the new employees receive] their instructions, the instructor leaves the room. As they begin working, someone realizes that an answer is on the wall, they let someone else at their table know the answer. Then someone at the next table hears it and shares the answer. They soon realize that they are not in competition with each other, but they are actually working all together. Teamwork is the key. (Heise 1994: 19)

The "teamwork quiz" is missing from the Tokyo Disneyland orienta-

Table 6
The Domestication of DisneyTalk in Tokyo

Regular organizational terminology—"taboo words" at Disneyland	DisneyTalk	Tokyo Disneyland Talk
Front-line employees	Cast members	*Casuto* (D)
Part-timers	Seasonal cast members	*Arubaito* (J)
Hiring	Casting	*Shinsotsu saiyō* (J)*
Supervisors	Leads	*Senpai-shain* (J)**
Customers	Guests	*Gesuto* (D)
Training Center	Disney University	*Dizunii unibāshiti* (D)
Information	Spiel	*Jōhō* (R)†
Amusement park	Onstage	*Suteiji* (D)
Office space	Backstage	*Shokuba* (R)‡

NOTE: Words at Tokyo Disneyland are categorized as (D) = domesticated (i.e., katakana version of the original DisneyTalk); (J) = Japanese (i.e., Japanese replacements of the original DisneyTalk that embody different cultural meaning); and (R) = reversal (i.e., Japanese replacements of the original DisneyTalk that serve as equivalents to regular organizational terminology).
*Meaning "hiring of new graduates"
**"Senior regular worker"
†Literally, "information"
‡Literally, "office"

tion. Tokyo Disneyland employees thought it a strange idea. A manager in the Oriental Land Company's personnel department confirmed that they had scrapped that quiz because "Japanese employees are socialized for teamwork from a very young age."

Finally, DisneyTalk—a powerful means of socialization and normative control in the U.S. parks—has been domesticated at Tokyo Disneyland. Many Disney concepts have been modified through Japanese pronunciation or abandoned altogether (see Table 6). The changes in DisneyTalk, which reflect a cultural adaptation of the manual, also result in changes in interpretation—how workers respond to the socialization effects of organizational language. Disney language, like all language, plays a crucial role in socialization and emotion management (see Eisenberg & Goodall 1993 for a discussion of the organizational role of Disney language). As Jane Kuenz (1995:

112) argues, "most [employees] have internalized the Disney terms; they never say uniform, but costume, just as they always say cast, on-stage, and backstage." R. C. Smith and E. M. Eisenberg (1987) similarly report that in their interviews with employees at Disneyland, no one used such taboo terms such as "customer," "amusement park," or "uniform." Tokyo Disneyland cast members generally find it easier than their American counterparts to distance themselves from Disney language; it is, after all, a foreign language for them. They learn it, use it, and play with it, but they leave it behind them when they go home.

Disney and Emotion Management

The Disney Way demonstrates the character of normative control in the service industry. The fact that Tokyo Disneyland is viewed as a model of exceptional service in Japan illustrates the globalization of American service culture, which is reproduced throughout the world (DiMaggio and Powell 1983). Emotion management in the worlds of Disney begins as early as the first day of orientation, when instructors beseech recruits to wish every guest "a nice day" (*otanoshimi kudasai,* "please enjoy," in Tokyo Disneyland's spiel). The service motto printed on the front cover of the "Tips on Magic" manual is "We create happiness." Even more direct emotional manipulation is involved in the prohibition, first uttered in orientation, not to talk with visitors about what goes on behind the scenes. Disney's culture is replete with "magic moment" stories, such as the ever-popular "popcorn story":

Emerging from the theater, a mother buys her young son a box of popcorn from an open-air stand. Seconds later, the lad, who looks to be about four, trips and falls. The popcorn spills, the boy bawls, the mother screams. A costumed Cast Member on his way to another attraction happens by. Barely breaking stride, he scoops up the empty cardboard box, takes it to the popcorn stand for a refill, presents it to the shattered child, and continues on his way. (Walt Disney World trainer Robert Sias; cited in Henkoff 1994: 115).

I have heard the same story told about ice-cream cones and balloons. The magic is always "spontaneous." A number of lessons about emotions are instilled in these stories. The first is that everything in the park should be controlled, every mishap quickly taken care of, because this is the meaning of "happiness." Cast members learn that everything they do on stage is meaningful and should therefore be under total control. It is a show, but everything—including the production of spontaneity and the stage-management of emotion-conveying behavior such as smiling, welcoming, or thanking—must look real. Furthermore, emotion-management training cleverly uses these vignettes in two important ways. First, by emphasizing such magic moments, trainers try to impart verve to jobs that are otherwise tightly regimented. Second, the magic moment implies that emotional rewards can be gained from doing your job, as monotonous as it is. This is explicitly suggested in "The Tokyo Disneyland Show," a manual handed to new hirees during orientation. It begins with the following recommendation (written inside a Mickey Mouse–shaped frame and signed by the president of the Oriental Land Company): "The key to happiness is communicating with Guests. . . . We also hope you will be able to find your own happiness through working here."

Many cast members, in the United States and in Japan, soon realize the sleight of hand behind such stories and the commodification of emotion underlying their work environment. While discussing the magic moments stories, one Japanese cast member said:

You know, they have a message service in the park, the one you usually hear Disney music coming through. It's not supposed to be used as a message service, though. The leads realize we know it exists, so they tell us, if a guest comes to you in panic because she hasn't seen her baby for an hour, don't mention the message system. They tell us, using the message system too often will destroy the atmosphere of dreams and magic. It's there only for emergencies, you know. In the bottom line, the "atmosphere" is more important than actually helping out people.

Other workers have experienced emotional dissonance in the context of company prohibitions about speaking with family members visiting the park, attending to a visitor who has had an accident, and refraining from arguing with customers.

Against management-told magic moment stories, Disney employees tell their own brand of horror stories. A Japanese cast member
in the foods division told me the following story. "There's this rumor:
We have a restroom next to the Plaza Pavilion Restaurant. One day a
lady was screaming 'help me,' her kid was stuck in the toilet. A supervisor went to see what happened and pulled out the kid. She was
dead already because it was too late and nobody could help her. It's a
tragic story." Hochschild's flight attendants, in a similar counter-
emotional response, spoke of "anger fantasies" with a strong oral component, such as "befouling the passenger's food and watching him eat
it" (1983: 114).

Unlike the American employees, Japanese cast members did not
seem to resent emotion management. Employees did not speak about
experiencing "phoniness" or a "false self." The manuals had a lot to say
about the cast members' role in the show, and employees took it for
granted that they were supposed to be acting. As cast members (and
most other service providers) know too well, the "acting" and "cast"
image are not *real*. It is something the company sells them, a rhetorical
facade made to keep them enthusiastic. There are, however, no conflict and no "re-definition of self" involved in this recognition. Employees regard the Tokyo Disneyland manuals for appearance management or etiquette as quite normal and reasonable, no tougher, for
example, than other companies' manuals or even high-school guides.

Sales Ladies and "Counter Culture"

Similar compliance with emotion management in the service sector
can be found among Japanese saleswomen (Creighton 1996; Matsunaga 2000). The organizational culture of American department
stores is also dominated by a malestream ideology of unquestioning
obedience, similar to the social discourse of domestic service (Benson
1993, 1996). In both the United States and Japan (and every capitalist
country for that matter), the customer has the higher status. In Japan,
the cultural role of the customers as "guests" of the store also contrib-
utes to their higher status. Millie Creighton (1996) argues in this con-

text that Japan's "vertical society" legitimizes such status relations, and that Japanese salesclerks must exhibit the subservient behavior consistent with their inferior status. Susan Benson (1993: 107–8), in contrast, describes how American managers have historically tried to ease the potential of status conflict by giving their employees a veneer of bourgeois culture. However, "most of their efforts were absurd and superficial, such as requiring saleswomen to memorize a few French words and the names of chic Parisian streets" (1993: 108). Such programs, writes Benson, often backfired, as saleswomen intentionally bungled the minutiae.

Benson's ethnography contains a rich typology of resistance strategies used on the selling floor. As Benson contends, "saleswomen had an ingenious variety of tactics for manipulating managers, customers, and merchandise to their own advantage" (1993: 110). For example, clerks refused to take on extra duties that would eat into their "spare time," and when they felt threatened, they fought back by doing sloppy work stocking the new displays. The informal work group also covered up for a certain amount of theft of merchandise. Their most effective tactic, however, was restricting output and limiting intradepartmental competition. Each department had a concept of the total sales that constituted a good day's work. Saleswomen used various tactics to keep their "books" (sales tallies) within acceptable limits. They would, for example, avoid customers late in the day when their books were running high in order not to run extraordinarily high books and be considered "grabbers" by their peers. Management's attempts to break worker solidarity through the use of monetary incentives proved ineffective.

The absence of conflict in Creighton's ethnography is particularly astounding (in Western eyes at least) given two additional factors: the relative strictness of the training the Japanese clerks received and their relatively high educational status. According to Creighton, although the majority of Japanese companies refuse to hire female graduates of four-year universities, department stores were willing to make use of their talents. However, to meet customers' expectations, a saleslady has to undergo a particularly demanding training. Stores often regulate female dress and mannerisms (bowing, for example) more strictly than male dress because, according to Creighton (1996: 202), "customers have more exacting standards for female clerks. . . . According to one personnel director, if female clerks wear too much makeup or jewelry, do not dress according to expectations, or behave in ways considered inappropriate for women, Japanese customers will complain."

A possible explanation for the absence of reported conflict is that department stores are regarded in Japan as a "women-oriented" workplace (cf. Wakisaka 1997). Department stores are unlikely to pressure women to resign if they marry or even if they are pregnant—something many other companies would not allow (Creighton 1996: 198). Some department stores have even instituted in-house childcare facilities for employees. Department stores are also more likely to promote women to managerial positions, although Creighton suggests that most of these women are single (1996: 211). This confirms James Valentine's (1990: 43) statement that "the most obvious case of marginality at work is the professional women." It is also no coincidence that the first female executive director in Japan was Ishihara Ichiko of the Takashimaya department store. Ishihara, by the way, became famous for her slogan: "Think like a man, act like a lady, and work like a dog" (Creighton 1996: 197, cited in Sugahara & Takeuchi 1982).

The Practice of Service Acting

Figure 2 (p. 45) suggests that factors affecting the display of emotions at work can be subsumed under two categories: "ground rules"—sociocultural, organizational, occupational, work-group, and individual norms; and "surface rules"—the specific properties of the setting, the target person, and the employee's "real" feelings on the job during a particular emotional transaction. The emotions displayed in a transaction may also change as the interaction unfolds. Depending on feedback from the target person, the employee may maintain, abandon, or revise the emotions he or she initially displayed. Such transience depends on "defining cues," that is, the attributes of the setting and the target person. Cues from the target person that can influence displayed emotions include gender, age, race, dress, and so on. Cues from the setting include temporal features (whether it is night or day), interactional (the number of customers), and spatial and atmospheric features.

The descriptions of service organizations given above present a variety of test cases. The description of the convenience stores and the Tokyo Dome shop exemplified the viability of all the factors suggested by Figure 2. Salesclerks operated within pre-established ground rules (organizational definitions of proper emotional displays on the job). These ground rules led to surface acting: saying thank you, establishing eye contact, smiling, and so on. The display of emotions was operationalized through service manuals, checklists for employees, and measurement protocols for mystery shoppers. These Tayloristic elements of service culture became global and now characterize the organizational cultures of many service organizations around the world. The globalization of service culture is partly explained by what I term the logic of turnover: the need, common to many service organizations, to discipline part-time workers who remain on the job for only a short time.

The convenience stores and the Tokyo Dome shop also demonstrated the role of "defining cues" (surface rules) in the display of emotions at work. Salesclerks in these service settings modified their emotional display according to interactional cues. At busy times, clerks acted in a less friendly and more no-nonsense manner. This modification of the employee's emotional display was influenced, for example, by feedback from impatient customers in a long line. It was probably also influenced by the employee's real feelings on the job during busy times.

In the case of Disney, however, things look different. There was no room for such transience. Cast members are expected to follow only

the ground rules of the organizational culture, and defining cues are
not to affect the expected display of Disney emotions. Appearances
have to be kept up in the face of crowds or negative feedback from
angry visitors who have been standing in line for two hours, or even
when the employee's true feelings are negative. The same logic applies
in other organizations with a strict service code, such as Delta Air
Lines (Hochschild 1983). Unlike a convenience store or a fast-food
restaurant, where efficiency can override courtesy, customers of theme
parks and airlines expect employees to respond to them cheerfully
even when the place is crowded. Disney allows its employees very little
discretion about which emotions they convey and how. As we saw,
the Disney Way—the ground rules of the Disney organizational culture—has also become global.

Despite these variations, service cultures are characterized by
common features that distinguish them from other organizations in
terms of emotion management. Compared with the Japanese office
and its ideology of self-fulfillment and self-cultivation through work,
the global service culture appears to be geared toward surface play.
The main difference between cast members and salesclerks boils down
to the issue of transience or feedback. According to Figure 2—which
presents a generalized scheme of emotional display—feedback from
the target person may also influence the display of emotions as the
transaction unfolds. At this level of emotional display, behavior is dynamic and involves mutual negotiations and interactions. The employee usually relies on such feedback to determine the "next round"
of emotional behavior. However, in a strict service culture, the employee is supposed not to negotiate. This is a unique work situation;
critical employees and scholars refer to it as "going into robot" or as
"emotional lobotomy."

I suggest that what we are seeing here is another conceptualization
of acting, different from either surface or deep acting. The emotional
display that is inculcated and practiced at Disney and other strict service organizations can be defined as *service acting*. Such service acting is

built on paradigms of behavior that are embodied by participants through a fixed set of performative practices. This way of acting was not invented by strict service organizations, but they are unique in having formalized it as their organizational culture. Service organizations have appropriated age-old cultural constructs. Consider, for example, the roles of Harlequin or the Rogue. They are theatrical (rather than organizational) roles, but they also represent prescribed emotional displays and acting that are not altered by feedback or other defining cues. We say about such roles that they "live in a world of their own." In a way, service acting is also such a role.

Richard Grathoff (1970) suggested the concept of "symbolic types" as a replacement for the conventional conception of roles. This concept was further elaborated by Don Handelman (1986, 1992), who defined symbolic typing as coming into existence when, and only when, a person ceases to modify his or her behavior in response to the reactions of others. Symbolic types, then, are roles that do not depend on social give-and-take. Other roles are continuously modified, produced, and reproduced through interpersonal give-and-take; they are always constituted through perspectives that combine "self" and "other." Symbolic types, in contrast, are stable, permanent performative patterns of behavior that through their inner consistency, self-referentiality, and independence of social context serve to create a reality of their own.

Whereas everyday roles are subject to the social flux and uncertainty that enliven human interaction, service acting is meant to regulate and control that flux. Many service jobs involve fixed performative patterns, and the procedures of symbolic typing are laid out in service manuals. Spiels, the set menu, the smile, all enable and dictate a ritualized performance. This is why front-line employees are warned never to talk back to an angry customer. Instead, they must alert a supervisor. When reality evades the manual, part-timers are no longer fit to deal with reality (unless they are "empowered" by the company to do so under well-defined circumstances).

Service culture, enacted through symbolic typing, is a patronizing performance. It habituates and conditions us, the customers (patrons). It colonizes our mind through indulgence. As patrons, we must cooperate with the spiel, follow it, and choose from it (try asking for something not on the menu, even a different combination of existing items). Social interaction becomes a big Nintendo game, with prizes awarded to those who push the right buttons and route their character through the pre-designed maze. Otherwise, order is lost, and we are back into the flux. Symbolic typing, as inculcated by the service manual, abolishes one of the basic constructs of symbolic interaction: the "looking glass self," a term coined by Charles Cooley (1922: 183) to describe how our awareness of our own experience is shaped by what others around us think, say, and do about it. Significant others are the "looking glass" in which we see our reflection. In contrast, symbolic typing—and hence service culture—is locked in a mirror stage. Service attendants are attentive to facial expressions and to a basic vocabulary of linguistic expressions, but this "awareness" must be only skin-deep. In symbolic typing, there are no more "looking glass selves," only "mirroring bodies"—Arthur Frank's (1991) conceptualization of the body in consumerism (see also O'Neill 1985: 23; Falk 1993). This is perhaps the consummation of service culture and its oracle, the service manual. It is a Taylorist world whose influence on the postmodern self is not totally ephemeral.

The following story illustrates the nature of service acting. It is taken from Tokyo Disneyland's biweekly "communication newsletter," *Line* (May 15, 1996, p. 8). Under the headings "From cast to cast" and "Hello, this is Oriental Land," Saitō Yoshiko of the general service division of the Oriental Land Company recounts the official story of three telephone operators.

We, the three operators—they say our voices, at least, are beautiful—are working with big smiles every day.

When making telephone calls to big hospitals or hotels, have you ever had a suspicion that the operator was an android because the way she answered you was too mechanical?

In a way, telephone operators don't need emotions to do their job. But we, the operators of the Kingdom of Dreams and Magic, do our job with human kindness and warmth. . . .

Sometimes, of course, too much humanity can cause accidents. One day I remember hearing a new fellow operator receiving a call by saying "*Osewa ni natte imasu!*" (Thank you for giving me this service).[17] Instead of preaching, I gave her a big hand saying, "That's a good one!" I think I heard the man laughing over the line. . . . When you receive phonecalls, try to smile, too. Your smile will no doubt go through the telephone wire and reach to the other person.

The story could apply to the work of OLs as well. However, it embodies several elements that tie it to the context of service. The telephone operator is primarily concerned with providing a service to customers. Thousands of such service representatives work in Japan and elsewhere. In contrast, the OL is concerned primarily with producing a service for the members of her work group. Consequently, the OL's education, orientation, and training are aimed at perfecting her skills for working in an office group. As Lo (1990: 99) concludes, "OLs experience more pressures from the social network (*shigarami*) of company relationship than do their sisters in the factory. The OLs, who have much more contact with others in their work group, are careful not to damage relationships with coworkers."

Contact is a key concept here. OLs and other office members must handle eye contact, ear contact, and interpersonal contact on a daily basis. For this reason they are trained in managing their appearance, in speaking and listening, and in "guessing" (*sasshi*)—anticipating the other's requests before that person even utters them. Moreover, OLs are told that they are cultivating, through such trained performance, a culturally defined feminine identity. Like the salarymen's "spiritual training" and the regular workers' "cultivation of self through work," the OLs have an ideology of self-commitment.

---

17. The new operator failed in her speech. The expression she used should have been slightly different: *Osewa ni natte orimasu.*

The service training of telephone operators is different. There is no longer an emphasis on the cultivation of self. That elaborated ideological baggage has been replaced with a general rhetoric of "human kindness and warmth." This rhetoric, however, creates an inevitable discrepancy, given the status-laden formalities of telephone language. Telephone operators are consequently asked to do their spiel properly, and no more. Service manuals for part-timers rarely contain elaborated reflections on the ethno-morality of etiquette, empathy, or guessing. Service acting is a praxis—it certainly reproduces the relations of production—that has done away with culturalist ideologies. This praxis is a reflection of the logic of turnover, of course. In the case of the OL, the office group provides a close-knit social world in which social feedback abounds, in the form of either harmony or stress. Service workers, in contrast, are dealing with strangers. Telephone operators interact with a disembodied voice.

Within the office, OLs and newly hired salarymen are the subjects of paternalistic consideration. The management-employee dyad is framed by the overarching emotional ideology of paternalism, benevolence, and the company-as-family. Seeing the OLs and blue-collar women workers as "daughters" of the company is a corollary of the family metaphor.[18] The service sector, in contrast, is built around the company representative–customer dyad, which is essentially different. Since customers are strangers, the family metaphor is out of place. Moreover, interactions are Taylorized, since service organizations strive to keep the lines moving. The service dyad is seen as involving not the *whole* person but a particularly managed portion of their social identity—for example, the voice (telephone operators), the look

---

18. The family metaphor is not unique to Japan. Pringle (1989: 161), for example, describes how the family metaphor is used to characterize the workplace relations of secretaries and bosses. Secretaries are situated as office wives, mothers, or daughters, depending on the situation and on the personality of the people involved. Such variability does not characterize the use of the family metaphor in Japan, where it is a part of a rigid organizational ideology rather than of personnel idiosyncrasy.

and the voice (elevator girls), or the look, the voice, and a certain procedural knowledge (salesclerks). The recognition that only a portion of one's self is involved in service acting delineates a gap between internal and external, private and public, self-identity and role-identity. The American distinction between external and internal, public and private, might become global as it travels aboard the Trojan horse of service culture.

Consider also the stark example of the elevator girl, perhaps the height of service acting. According to Creighton (1996: 202), this position is thought by many new employees to be an extremely glamorous job. However, being an elevator girl can be tiring and boring. According to a spokesperson for the Mitsukoshi department store, "the elevator girls get a lot more break time. . . . They have an extremely tiring job. They have to stand all the time and use their voice continually. It gets boring too. They are primarily there to give a good, sparkling impression to the customers. They can't express much of a happy smiling condition if we keep them at the elevators for more than forty-five minutes each time" (Creighton 1996: 202).

The elevator girl is a living, *ad absurdum* proof of the power of symbolic acting. Her behavior is entirely programmed. Her "social interaction" is reduced to pushing elevator buttons and uttering spiels (floor descriptions). This is a job that could equally—if not more efficiently—be performed by an automaton. Although the technology for installing "speaking elevators" is available, department stores like Mitsukoshi prefer to keep organic elevator girls because they give a "good, sparkling impression to customers." Management, however, openly acknowledges that the performance of elevator girls consists of a tiring, boring facade. This is service acting: a one-dimensional, unilateral display (or praxis) that turns the employee into an instrument. The elevator girl, as an instrument of service, cannot sustain its performance for more than 45 minutes. She is a machine that cannot be operated too long lest it overheat. The manual therefore recommends a break every 45 minutes. The machine is turned off in order to cool it down; then it is turned on again. No doubt OLs or salarymen are also service instruments. In their case, however, this is covered by ideology. In the service industry, the ideology is no longer required. Here we find the true "end of ideology" and the culmination of instrumental rationality.[19]

---

19. Karl Albrecht and Ron Zemke concluded their best-selling manifesto *Service America!* with the following words: "Does the recruiting and hiring process attract people who can fulfill service roles effectively? Does the orientation program for new employees instill the service strategy in their minds right from the start? Does the company newsletter preach the same gospel that the chief executive preaches?. . . . At some indistinguishable point, the service management program ceases to be a program and becomes the basic orientation of the organization. . . . The organizations that make that investment most effectively will be the ones that thrive and grow" (1985: 180). I have searched Albrecht and Zemke's book for an ideological framing of service and found none. This quotation represents the kind of "ideology" provided by the authors. It is an "ideology" of instrumental rationality, of effectiveness, profitability, and growth. When the authors speak about service as a way of life, they refer to organizational goals. The whole orientation is toward rational organization rather than to the self.

CHAPTER SIX

The End of the Road?

John Barth's 1958 novel *The End of the Road* opens with a description of the Remobilization Farm, a private therapy center where the book's protagonist, Jacob Horner, is treated for mental paralysis whose outward symptom is a complete inability to decide what to do; he hence does nothing. In the opening scene, Horner and his doctor/mentor are seated in the Progress and Advice Room of the Remobilization Farm. In the center of the room are two straight-backed, white wooden chairs facing each other; there is no other furniture.

The doctor sits facing you ... and leans a little towards you. You would not slouch down, to do so would thrust your knees virtually against his. Neither would you incline to cross your legs. ... The masculine manner, with your left ankle resting on your right knee, would cause your left shoe to rub against the Doctor's left trouser leg, and possibly dirty his white trousers; the feminine manner, with your left knee crooked over your right knee, would thrust the toe of your shoe against the same trouser leg, lower down on his shin. To sit sideways, of course, would be unthinkable, and spreading your knees in the manner of the Doctor makes you acutely conscious of aping his position, as if you hadn't a personality of your own. Your position, then (which has the appearance of choice, because you are not ordered to sit thus, but which is chosen only in a very limited sense, since there are no alternatives) is as follows: you sit rather rigidly in your white chair ... and keep your legs together. ... The placing of your arms is a separate problem. (1958: 1–2)

The End of the Road is a Western novel about emotion management. The (self-proclaimed) doctor treats Horner with various role-playing therapies such as mythotherapy or agapotherapy, all of which are intended to induce action through acting and motivation through a pretense at emotion.[1] These "therapies" train the patient to choose a course of action by assuming a role—by becoming a symbolic type, to use the concept introduced in Chapter 5. In approaching an attractive woman, for example, the patient overcomes his paralysis by assuming the symbolic type of "the seducer." Although assuming the right sitting position would be "surface play" in Hoshschild's terms, assuming a symbolic type would be "deep play." Horner's reactions to the layout of the Progress and Advice Room illustrates the patient's hypersensitive "me" or "looking-glass self." It also demonstrates the power of normative control through self-monitoring and self-supervision.

The Remobilization Farm is reminiscent of the Japanese training centers mentioned in this book (Kondo's Ethics Center is a blatant example). In these orderly environments, employees are taught the rules of proper behavior and self-monitoring. Barth's "therapies" are equivalent to the *kata* promoted in such training for the cultivation of self through work, and the self-monitoring of Barth's patient brings to mind such organizational practices as the individual self-declaration. The analysis of self through others' expectations is prescribed in the layout of both the Progress and Advice Room and the personality inventory section in the self-declaration. In both situations, one's decisions have the *appearance* of choice, but the individual chooses *only in a very limited sense*. Interestingly, the doctor urges Horner to get a job as a necessary step toward rehabilitation. As the doctor notes, the workplace is a sheltering environment because its normative programs are already in place.

Despite the surface similarities between the Japanese workplace and the Rehabilitation Farm, *The End of the Road* also throws into relief deep cultural differences. To begin with, it illustrates the Western

---

1. The Latin stem of both "emotion" and "motivation" is *motere*, "to move."

emphasis on psychological individuality. Emotional training is performed by a doctor, using psychological procedures, which is the legitimate way in the West to "fix" someone's personality. In Japan, such emotional training is performed by parents, schoolteachers, managers, and trainers. This difference highlights the disparities in the cultural construction of emotion between the United States and Japan. Moreover, as an American morality tale, *The End of the Road* also warns its readers against emotional intervention. This is arguably why the "doctor" is actually a witch doctor, the patient suffers from pathological alienation, and the treatment ultimately ends in disaster. In the final analysis, the novel warns against meddling with the public-private or I-me distinction, on which the Western paradigm of the self is built. In Japan, in contrast, emotion management is not the *end* of the road but rather the very beginning of it. It is integrated into a socialization that takes place both within organizations and outside them, in the surrounding culture.

As White (1993: 97) put it in the context of teenage socialization:

The Japanese teen is, by the end of middle school, acutely aware of the distinction between private propensities and values (*honne*) on the one hand, and correct social performance (*tatemae*) on the other. . . . American teens, too, are aware of this, but they see more often the distinction as disillusioning: their sensitivity to what they see as hypocritical is conditioned by a cultural norm which favors "being yourself" over an accommodation to others through self-discipline and sensitivity.

The *honne-tatemae* paradigm, translated approximately as the difference between public and private or appearance and reality, is not unique to Japan; it is a universal ideal type of human psychology (see also Moeran 1989: 3), as George Herbert Mead's (1932) famous distinction between the "I" and the "me" shows. However, sociologists of Japan have long argued that Japanese society has taken the "I/me" duality much further and created a "relational self." As the analysis in this study has shown, organizational identities are indeed more "relational" and have to conform to feeling rules that are more uniformly and closely scripted within emotionally binding workplace ideologies.

The integration of emotion management into Japanese ethical conceptions, however, does not occur without conflict and involves an abundance of normative controls. I have argued throughout this book that organizational identities are molded within matrices of design and devotion and that categories such as the emotional and the rational, the global and the local, and the public and the private are narrative conventions. I analyzed these categories in regard to specific organizational settings in the preceding chapters; here I will use the results of these analyses to highlight the common denominators of emotion at work and re-emphasize the comparison between Japan and the United States.

The central issues of this book can be subsumed under two themes: institutional and cultural. The first is concerned with variations in emotion management in different work settings; the second, with the influence of local culture on organizational and workplace culture. I argue that emotion management is influenced both by the type of workplace (the service encounter, the factory, the office) and by the local culture (Japanese/American). Further, these two themes blur, rather than reproduce, the grand oppositions of global and local, public and private, and rational and emotional.

Emotion Management Across Work Settings

It was in the service industry that emotion management was initially "recognized" in the United States, first by managers and then by scholars. The sociology of emotions inspired by Hochschild's seminal study on flight attendants therefore centered on the service industry. The argument developed in this book, in contrast, is that emotion management in the service industry should be read as a continuation of, rather than a break from, previous managerial systems of "devotion." The American recognition of emotion management took shape within a managerial discourse dominated by "design." Within Japanese-style management, in contrast, emotions have played a recognized role at least from the turn of the twentieth century.

The role of emotions in Japanese-style management is clear in such dominant ideologies as paternalism and mutual trust. Although paying lip service to emotions such as trust, benevolence, and harmony, managers and employees have also used these ideologies to promote their own interests. These "emotions" became prominent within Japanese-style management because they served as a social structure that locked cultural blueprints of socialization into the political and industrial interests of the groups involved. Historical research has revealed the melding of paternalism with Taylorism as well as with workers' quest for dignity in the context both of blue-collar work and, more recently, of the shop floor and the office.

In my discussion of shop-floor practices, at the Toyota plant in Japan as well as in the American auto transplants, I tried to show how an emotionalist ideology must also be implemented through mechanisms of normative control. On the shop floor, I focused on small-group activities. Quality control circles, as instruments of normative control, have three major aspects: the development of personal responsibility, worker evaluation, and foreman education. Within the office group, I emphasized the normative practice of character building as exemplified in special training programs. These programs match the transmuted elements of Hochschild's emotion management and contrast with her claim that emotion management is conducted primarily in the service sector and expressed in the representative-client dyad. Through character-building programs, emotion becomes an organizational theme that binds employees and employers. Moreover, feeling rules prescribe the right emotional display at work. Cheerfulness and brightness no matter what the difficulty are prerequisites for maintaining the social world of the office. Bodily movement and appearance are indices of the *kokoro*—one's heart (emotional dispositions)—and hence should always be stage-managed.

The institutional comparison of different work settings illustrates that even though emotions are at work in all sectors, the precise way they are managed is connected to the dyad involved as well as to the institutional conditions of work. Within the office and on the shop

floor, regular workers, salarymen, and OLs are the subjects of paternalistic consideration. The management-employee dyad is framed by
the overarching emotional ideology of paternalism, benevolence, and
the company-as-family. The view that OLs and blue-collar women
workers are "daughters" of the company is a corollary of the family
metaphor. The service sector, in contrast, is built around the representative-customer dyad. Since customers are strangers, the family
metaphor is largely out of place.

Moreover, the service dyad is informed by what I have called the
"logic of turnover." Employees are usually part-timers who "await instructions" and cannot be "expected to sacrifice themselves for their
company." Interactions are Taylorized, since service organizations
strive to keep the lines moving. The service dyad is seen as involving not
the *whole* person, but a particularly managed portion of their social
identity—for example, the voice (telephone operators), the look and
the voice (elevator girls), or the look, the voice, and a certain procedural
knowledge (saleswomen). All these elements require a certain state of
mind, a "service state of mind," which is nevertheless seen as artificial—
in the United States as well as Japan. The American distinction between external and internal, public and private, has arguably become
global as it traveled aboard the "black ship" of service culture.

Putting emotion to work occurs through three major, interrelated
processes: commodification, formalization, and reduction. *Commodification* takes place when emotions become a company ideology, no
longer a private sentiment but rather a public "social glue." The remaining two processes provide concrete mechanisms for sustaining
these ideologies. Feeling rules regarding the employer-employee dyad
are *formalized* through manuals, workshops, checklists, and spiels. In
addition, social interaction within the representative-customer dyad is
reduced to standardized service tasks that embody the feeling rules of
the organization.

The shop floor, the office, and front-line service encounters combine these processes in different ways. The shop floor, where the ideology and practice of both paternalism (in Japan) and human relations

(in the United States) were developed, is colored by commodification. It was on the shop floor in Japan that emotions such as trust, harmony, participation, benevolence, and dignity became "social glue" and were molded into structures of managerial control. These emotions were at work in the context of the firm-as-family, without reference to customers.

The office is a slightly different station along the road of emotion management. In terms of ideology, the office is firmly located within paternalism, directed in this case toward managers, office workers, and the "company daughters"—the OLs. Yet the office group also involves social interactions, both among its members—for whom it serves as both a primary social unit and a way station—and with customers. As a result of these institutional conditions, office life has become replete with formalized practices of character building and display rules concerning appearance, emphatic behavior, and even the meticulous—but no less ethically important—protocols for serving tea.

It is in the front-line work of service representatives that an interesting twist has taken place. Here, where formalization and reduction are at their extreme, there is much less emphasis on ideology. I have referred to this phenomenon in the context of Japan as a "fall from grace." The American concept of service is rendered in Japanese as the katakana *sābisu*, denoting its foreign and potentially alienating nature. The ethics of self-cultivation through work is largely out of place in the modern service manual.

The Influence of Local Culture on Organizational and Workplace Cultures

As this book has demonstrated, the local culture influences both management systems (organizational culture) and workers' responses (workplace culture). This finding has implications for three major issues: (1) conventional theories of organizational culture, (2) organizational theories of contingency and isomorphism, and (3) the positioning of our sociologies of emotions.

Emotions at work and normative controls are widely considered to be elements of organizational cultures. Conventional theories of organizational culture hinge on a top-down, functionalist model in which the "culture" is a managerial project and ends-means chains are complemented by values-norms chains. Edgar Schein's (1990) conventional model represents organizational culture as a pyramidal structure. Values and ideological premises are found at the top of the pyramid, norms are in the middle, and the base contains artifacts of various kinds. In this view, emotion management is regarded as a human resource practice (or norm) that may reflect, for example, the corporate value of quality service. Manuals, business cards, name tags, and uniforms are the relevant artifacts. This view focuses on managerial functionalism and places little importance on workers' voices.

An alternative view replaces the hegemonic gaze of the top-down pyramidal structure with a bottom-up ethnographic perspective that stresses the worker's point of view. Critical sociologists such as Arlie Hochschild (1983) and labor scholars such as Mike Parker (1993) have focused on workplace cultures in order to highlight workers' resistance to their subjugation by management. Despite their acute differences, however, both the organizational-culture and the workplace-culture models define and examine "culture" as a dependent variable bound by organizational rules and labor conditions.

The view presented in this book, in contrast, sees both organizational and workplace cultures as two complementary entities that are influenced by a local, surrounding culture. In my argument, the concept of "culture" is also an independent variable. This analytical turn is compatible, to a certain extent, with broader theorizations of organizations, such as contingency theory. This theory holds that organizations operate in different institutional and cultural settings and seek to maximize their "fit" with those environments and thereby enhance their viability (Scott 1987).

The three-circle model presented in Figure 1 (p. 9) is illustrated in this study across a variety of work settings and cultures. In regard to Hochschild's two paramount constructs, surface versus deep play, for example, the discussion showed that the distinction loses much of its relevance in Japanese-style emotion management. For Hochschild's American flight attendants, the surface/deep distinction relates to the more basic ethno-moral distinction of the surrounding culture between the false and the true self. It is the false self—the emcee, the attendant, the occupational role—that is involved in either surface or deep play. American workers approach these kinds of play in practical terms, as means of reducing stress, rather than in ideological terms, as steps toward self-cultivation.

The OLs' manuals and workbooks, in contrast, insisted that dress, demeanor, deportment, and speech signal not only "good service" but also "one's true character." There is no surface or deep play; all performance is ideally both surface and deep, since it is supposed to reflect one's true (not false) character. Boredom and stress trouble only those who do not cultivate their self through work. The emotional ideology of self-cultivation thus effaces the American distinction between surface and deep play as well as between true and false self. However, there is nothing here that is culturally "unique." Like the managerial discourse of paternalism, the emotional discourse that surrounds the OL is a male-made ideological facade supported by various normative controls.

Many sociologists and anthropologists have written about Japan's schools as the primary agents of socialization behind the cultural fit between organizational and workplace cultures and between managerial paternalism and workers' devotion.[2] If education is behind the success of management in Japan, then the Japanese system of moral education is behind the success of emotion management.

There is a link between many of the management practices studied here and Japanese school life. The fact that in Japan nearly everyone is a high-school graduate provides a homogenous normative baseline of school socialization. Many key management practices are based on values and attitudes that characterize the Japanese schooling process.

---

2. For key works in English on Japan's schools in sociological perspective, see Rohlen 1983; Rohlen & Letendre 1996; Duke 1986; Dore & Sako 1989.

The organizational practice of teamwork and job rotation is consistent with educational habits of group work, in which students continuously rotate within and among small groups (*han*). Union procedures for grievances reflect the habit of discussing and analyzing mistakes in a productive manner, a habit cultivated by schoolteachers as part of small-group activities. Working in small groups thus becomes part of socialization, a sort of *forma mentis* for the Japanese student (Peak 1991). The sense of unity cultivated by Japanese organizations is an important part of school life, where it is practiced through various extracurricular activities.

On a more general level, school socialization also concerns rule-related behavior. At schools, students are socialized to acknowledge the duality of *tatemae* and *honne*. The fine line that divides public appearance and personal feelings is also taught at school, for example, through the practice of "public apologies" to group members and to one's class. As an American teacher working with Japanese students in Japan observed, "While we tend to view Japanese students as academically lax or dishonest, Japanese students tend to observe manners of respectful dress, gesture, and speech which Americans overlook or misinterpret as 'sucking up'" (Hill 1996: 105). School cultivates a culture of "shame," or other-oriented and rule-informed behavior, rather than a self-oriented culture of "guilt." Indeed, this form of socialization begins in the pre-school years.

Compared to U.S. schools, Japanese schools are allocated more responsibility for the moral education and discipline of children. Moral education consists of formal and intentional teaching of normative values, taboos, and imperatives. The Japanese term for citizenship classes is *dōtoku*, "the path of virtue": these classes often feature authoritarian training in public comportment with the declared objective of character building. The organizational "ethics" of training, character building, and the cultivation of self through work is a continuation of moral education at school. Moral education is a distinct area of instruction and is built around such themes as the importance of order, participation, endurance, trust, and harmony. These lessons do not remain in the classroom. It is customary for Japanese schools to set curfews, to prohibit the acquisition of a driver's license, and to forbid part-time work, decisions that in the United States are typically regarded as the moral responsibility of the student's parents.[3]

The importance of rule-governed moral and emotional conduct in organizational life is mirrored by the importance attached to moral education at school. Recently it has become common among managers, politicians, educators, and trainers in Japan to lament the lack of discipline and devotion found in the "new breed" (*shinjinrui*), the present generation of Japanese young people. The responsibility for this failing is attributed squarely to problems in moral education. Whether the new breed is morally bankrupt is not an empirical but an ideological question. It is not a question this study can answer. Whatever the answer may be, the concern demonstrates the public importance accorded moral education in Japanese society.[4] The dictum that other people are our mirrors is brought home to the Japanese child at an early age; it is stressed with growing intensity and formalization in organizational life. It is indeed one's entrance into regular work that marks, in Japanese eyes, the culmination of one's socialization and the final stage in one's transformation into an "adult member of society" (*shakaijin*).

I began this study with the observation that organizations are emotional cauldrons. I hope that I have demonstrated the truth of this view. I also hope that this study has illustrated how to analyze "emotions" as normative control. In my view, organizational culture is not something we should buy into, but something that needs to be deconstructed, questioned, and confronted. I have tried to provide both

---

3. Not everything is bright in this picture of school life. Japanese education, just like Japanese-style management, has its dark side of abuse, punishment, and bullying. On this aspect of Japanese schooling, see Schooland 1990; and Shields 1989.

4. For more on the historical development and importance of Japanese moral education, see Khan 1998; Tu 1996; and Tsurumi 1974. In Japanese the literature is much more varied. See, e.g., Khan 1998: 255–57 for a list of primary sources; Kaigo 1962 on ethics textbooks; Murai 1990a, b on the principles of moral education; and Owatari 1989 on ethics schools.

a rationale for analysis and a variety of ethnographic illustrations that can be used as a map for critical reading and to suggest useful paths for further studies of emotions in organizations. A culturally sensitive perspective of emotions at work provides an unexploited conceptual basis for research that treats emotions as properties of individuals, groups, and organizations. The service industry is obviously not the end of the road for such research. Many more ethnographies of emotions at work are waiting to be written.

Reference Matter

Works Cited

Abe Takao. 2000. "Case Study of Shinano Pollution Laboratory Co., Ltd." Paper presented at the Twelfth World Conference of the International Industrial Relations Association. Tokyo. May 30.

Abegglen, James. 1958. *The Japanese Factory*. Glencoe, Ill.: Free Press.

Adler, Patricia A., and Peter Adler. 1991. *Backboards and Blackboards: College Athletes and Role Engulfment*. New York: Columbia University Press.

Adler, Paul. 1993. "The 'Learning Bureaucracy': The United Motor Manufacturing, Inc." *Research in Organizational Behavior* (annual series), pp. 111–94. Greenwich, Conn. JAI Press.

Ahmad, E. 1991. "Racism and the State: The Coming Crisis in U.S.-Japanese Relations." Special Issue: Japan in the World. *Boundaries* 2, 18, no. 3: 21–28.

Albrecht, Karl, and Ron Zemke. 1985. *Service America!* New York: Warner Books.

Albrow, Martin. 1992. "Sine Ira Studio—Or Do Organizations Have Feelings?" *Organization Studies* 13, no. 3: 313–29.

Allen, Matthew. 1994. *Undermining the Japanese Miracle: Work and Conflict in a Coalmining Community*. Cambridge, Eng.: Cambridge University Press.

Ando Kiyoshi. 1994. "Japanese View of Self—Is It Unique?" *Japan Institute of Labour Bulletin* 33, no. 3: 1–5.

Argyris, Chris, and Donald Schon. 1979. *Organizational Learning*. New York: Addison-Wesley.

Ashforth, Blake, and Ronald Humphrey. 1993. "Emotional Labor in Service Roles: The Influence of Identity." *Academy of Management Review* 18, no. 1: 88–118.

Awata Fusaho. 1988. "Disneyland's Dreamlike Success." *Japan Quarterly* 35: 58–62.

Awata Fusaho and Takanarita Tōru. 1984. *Dizuniirando no keizai gaku* (An economic study of Disneyland). Tokyo: Asahi shinbunsha.

Babson, Steve. 1993. "Whose Team? Lean Production at Mazda U.S.A." *Labor Studies Journal* 18, no. 2: 3–24.

Bachnik, J. M. 1986. "Time, Space and Person in Japanese Relationships." In J. Hendry and J. Webber, eds., *Interpreting Japanese Society*, pp. 49–74. Oxford: JASO.

Baritz, Loren. 1960. *The Servants of Power: A History of the Use of Social Science in American Industry.* Westport, Conn.: Greenwood Press.

Barley, Stephen, and Gideon Kunda. 1992. "Design and Devotion: Surges of Rational and Normative Ideologies of Control in Managerial Discourse." *Administrative Science Quarterly* 37: 363–99.

Barth, John. 1958. *The End of the Road.* New York: Bantam Books.

Baumeister, R. 1982. "A Self-presentational View of Social Phenomena." *Psychological Bulletin* 91: 3–26.

Becker, Howard. 1982. *Art Worlds.* Berkeley: University of California Press.

Befu, H., and J. Kreiner. 1992. *Otherness of Japan.* Munich: Iudicium.

Bell, Daniel. 1973. *The Coming of Post-Industrial Society.* New York: Basic Books.

Bellah, Robert. 1957. *Tokugawa Religion: The Values of Pre-industrial Japan.* Boston: Beacon Press.

Bendix, Reinhard. 1963. *Work and Authority in Industry: Ideologies of Management in the Course of Industrialization.* New York: John Wiley.

Benedict, Ruth. 1946. *The Chrysanthemum and the Sword: Patterns of Japanese Culture.* Boston: Houghton Mifflin.

Benge, Eugene. 1918. "Grouping Workers to Get Best Results," *Factory* 24, no. 8: 1332–33.

Bennet, John, and Ishino Iwao. 1963. *Paternalism in the Japanese Economy.* Minneapolis: University of Minnesota Press.

Benson, Susan P. 1983. "'The Clerking Sisterhood': Rationalization and the Work Culture of Saleswomen in American Department Stores, 1890–1960." In James Green, ed., *Workers' Struggles, Past and Present: A "Radical America" Reader*, pp. 101–16. Philadelphia: Temple University Press.

————. 1986. *Counter Cultures: Saleswomen, Managers, and Customers in American Department Stores, 1890–1940.* Urbana: University of Illinois Press.

Berle, Adolph, and Gardiner Means. 1932. *The Modern Corporation and Private Property.* New York: Macmillan.

Bernstein, J. 1994. "Convenience Store Retailing in Two Countries: Southland and 7-Eleven Japan." Harvard Business School Case N9-794-121. Boston: Harvard Business School Publishing.

Besser, Terry. 1996. *Team Toyota: Transplanting the Toyota Culture to the Camry Plant in Kentucky.* New York: SUNY Press.

Blocklyn, Peter L. 1988. "Making Magic: The Disney Approach to People Management." *Personnel* 65: 28–35.

Bodde, Derk. 1953. "Harmony and Conflict in Chinese Philosophy." In Arthur Wright, ed., *Studies in Chinese Thought*. Chicago: University of Chicago Press.

Boje, David. 1995. "Stories of the Story-Telling Organization: A Post-modern Analysis of Disney as 'Tamara-land.'" *Academy of Management Journal* 38, no. 4: 997–1035.

Bramel, Dana, and Ronald Friend. 1987. "The Work Group and Its Vicissitudes in Social and Industrial Psychology." *Journal of Applied Behavioral Science* 23, no. 2: 233–53.

Brandes, Stuart. 1976. *American Welfare Capitalism, 1880–1940*. Chicago: University of Chicago Press.

Braverman, Harry. 1974. *Labor and Monopoly Capital*. New York: Monthly Review Press.

Brinton, Mary. 1993. *Women and the Economic Miracle: Gender and Work in Postwar Japan*. Berkeley: University of California Press.

Brody, David. 1993. "Workplace Contractualism in Comparative Perspective." In Nelson Lichtenstein and Howell J. Harris, eds., *Industrial Democracy in America: The Ambiguous Promise*, pp. 176–206. Washington, D.C.: Woodrow Wilson Center Press and Cambridge University Press.

Brown, Clair; Yoshifumi Nakata; Michael Reich; and Lloyd Ulman. 1997. *Work and Pay in the U.S. and Japan*. New York: Oxford University Press.

Burawoy, Michael. 1979. *Manufacturing Consent*. Chicago: University of Chicago Press.

————. 1985. *The Politics of Production*. New York: Verso.

Burnham, James. 1941/1960. *The Managerial Revolution*. Bloomington: Indiana University Press.

Cannings, Kathleen, and William Lazonick. 1994. "Equal Employment Opportunities and the Managerial Woman in Japan." *Industrial Relations* 33, no. 1: 44–69.

Carey, Robert. 1995. "5 Top Corporate Training Programs." *Successful Meetings*, Feb., pp. 56–61.

Castora, Amy. 1995. "A Passion for Service Excellence." *Credit Union Management*, June, pp. 28–31.

Christopher, Martin. 1994. *The Customer Service Planner*. London: Butterworth-Heinemann.

Clawson, Dan, and Mary Ann Clawson. 1999. "What Has Happened to the US Labor Movement? Union Decline and Renewal." *Annual Review of Sociology* 25: 95–118.

Cole, Robert. 1971. *Japanese Blue Collar: The Changing Tradition*. Berkeley: University of California Press.

———. 1985. "The Macropolitics of Organizational Change: A Comparative Analysis of the Spread of Small Group Activities." *Administrative Science Quarterly* 30: 560–85.

———. 1992. "Some Cultural and Social Bases of Japanese Innovation: Small-Group Activities in Comparative Perspective." In Kumon Shumpei and Henry Rosovsky, eds., *The Political Economy of Japan*, vol. 3, *Cultural and Social Dynamics*. Stanford: Stanford University Press.

Cooley, Charles H. 1922. *Human Nature and the Social Order*. New York: Scribner.

Creighton, Millie R. 1990. "Revisiting Shame and Guilt Cultures: A Forty Years Pilgrimage." *Ethos* 18, no. 3: 279–307.

———. 1996. "Marriage, Motherhood, and Career Management in a Japanese 'Counter Culture.'" In Anne Imamura, ed., *Re-imaging Japanese Women*, pp. 192–220. Berkeley: University of California Press.

Crozier, Michel. 1965. *The World of the Office Worker*. Trans. David Landau. Chicago: University of Chicago Press.

Daitō Eisuke. 1989. "Railways and Scientific Management in Japan, 1907–30." *Business History* 20: 1–28.

Dale, Peter. 1986. *The Myth of Japanese Uniqueness*. London: Croom Helm.

Davis, Mike. 1983. "The Stop Watch and the Wooden Shoe: Scientific Management and the Industrial Workers of the World." In James Green, ed., *Workers' Struggles, Past and Present: A "Radical America" Reader*, pp. 83–101. Philadelphia: Temple University Press.

Delbridge, Rick. 1998. *Life on the Line in Contemporary Manufacturing*. New York: Oxford University Press.

Denzin, Norman K. 1977. "Notes on the Cuminogenic Hypothesis: A Case Study of the American Liquor Industry." *American Sociological Review* 42: 905–20.

———. 1978. "Crime and American Liquor Industry." In Norman K. Denzin, ed., *Studies in Symbolic Interaction*, 1: 87–118. Greenwich, Conn.: JAI Press.

Dickson, William J. 1945. "The Hawthorne Plan of Personnel Counseling." *Journal of Orthopsychiatry*, 15: 343–47.

DiMaggio, Paul, and Walter Powell. 1983. "The Iron Cage Revisited: Institutional Isomorphism and Collective Rationality in Organizational Fields." *American Sociological Review* 48: 147–60.

Dobbin, Frank. 1994. "Cultural Models of Organization: The Social Construction of Rational Organizing Principles." In Diana Crane, ed., *The Sociology of Culture*, pp. 117–41.

Dohse, Knuth; Jürgens Ulrich; and Thomas Malsch. 1985. "From 'Fordism' to 'Toyotism'? The Social Organization of the Labor Process in the Japanese Automobile Industry." *Politics & Society* 14, no. 2: 115–47.

Doi Takeo. 1973. *The Anatomy of Dependence*. Tokyo: Kodansha.

Dore, Ronald. 1973. *British Factory, Japanese Factory: The Origins of National Diversity in Industrial Relations.* Berkeley: University of California Press.

———. 1984. "Goodwill and the Spirit of Market Capitalism." *British Journal of Sociology* 34: 459–82.

Dore, Ronald, and Mari Sako. 1989. *How the Japanese Learn to Work.* London: Routledge.

Drucker, Peter. 1992. *Managing for the Future.* New York: Truman Talley Books / Dutton.

Duke, Benjamin. 1986. *The Japanese School: Lessons for Industrial America.* New York: Praeger.

Eberts, Ray, and Cindelyn Eberts. 1995. *The Myths of Japanese Quality.* Upper Saddle River, N.J.: Prentice-Hall.

Edwards, R. 1979. *Contested Terrain.* New York: Basic Books.

Eisenberg, E. M., and H. L. Goodall, Jr. 1993. *Organizational Communication: Balancing Creativity and Constraint.* New York: St. Martin's Press.

Ekman, Paul. 1985. *Telling Lies.* New York: Norton.

Ekman, Paul, and W. Friesen. 1972. *Unmasking the Face.* Englewood Cliffs, N.J.: Prentice-Hall.

———. 1982. "Felt, False, and Miserable Smiles." *Journal of Nonverbal Behavior* 6: 238–52.

Ekman, Paul; R. Davidson; and W. Friesen. 1990. "The Duchenne Smile: Emotional Expression and Brain Physiology II." *Journal of Personality and Social Psycholoy* 58: 342–53.

Elias, Norbert. 1978, 1982. *The Civilizing Process.* 2 vols. Oxford: Blackwell.

———. 1983. *The Court Society.* Oxford: Blackwell.

———. 1987. "On Human Beings and Their Emotions: A Process-Sociological Essay." *Theory, Culture, and Society* 4, no. 2/3: 339–61.

Endō Koshi. 1989. *Nippon senryō to rōshikankei seisaku no seiritsu* (The occupation of Japan and the making of labor relations policy). Tokyo: Tōkyō daigaku shuppanbu.

———. 1994. "Satei (Personal Assessment) and Interworker Competition in Japanese Firms." *Industrial Relations* 33, no. 1: 70–83.

Ewing, Katherine. 1990. "The Illusion of Wholeness: Culture, Self, and the Experience of Inconsistency." *Ethos* 18, no. 3: 251–78.

Falk, Pasi. 1993. *The Consuming Body.* London: Sage.

Feigenbaum, Armand. 1961. *Total Quality Control: Engineering and Management.* New York: McGraw-Hill.

Ferguson, K. 1984. *The Feminist Case Against Bureaucracy.* Philadelphia: Temple University Press.

Fineman, Stephen, ed. 1993. *Emotion in Organization.* Newbury Park, Calif.: Sage.

Fjellman, Stephen M. 1992. *Vinyl Leaves: Walt Disney World and America*. Boulder, Colo.: Westview.

Florida, Richard, and Martin Kenney. 1991. "Transplanted Organizations: The Transfer of Japanese Industrial Organization to the U.S." *American Sociological Review* 56: 381–98.

Foucault, Michel. 1980. *The History of Sexuality*. New York: Vintage.

Fournier, Susan. 1998. "Consumers and Their Brands: Developing Relationship Theory in Consumer Research." *Journal of Consumer Research* 24, no. 4: 343–73.

Fowler, Edward. 1996. *San'ya Blues: Laboring Life in Contemporary Tokyo*. Ithaca: Cornell University Press.

Frank, Arthur. 1991. "For a Sociology of the Body: An Analytical Review." In M. Featherstone, M. Hepworth, and B. Turner, eds., *The Body: Social Process and Cultural Theory*, pp. 36–103. London: Sage.

Fruin, W. Mark. 1982. "From Philanthropy to Paternalism in the Noda Soy Sauce Industry: Pre-Corporate and Corporate Charity in Japan." *Business History Review* 56, no. 2: 168–91.

———. 1983. *Kikkoman: Company, Clan, and Community*. Cambridge, Mass.: Harvard University Press.

Fucini, Joseph, and Suzy Fucini. 1990. *Working for the Japanese: Inside Mazda's American Auto Plant*. New York: Free Press and Macmillan.

Fujimori Mitsuo and Ouchi Akiko. 1996. "Japanese Uchi Society—And Its Historical Relationships to Japanese Management." *Keio Business Review* 34: 29–50.

Fujita Wakao. 1972. *Nihon no rōdō kumiai* (Japanese labor unions). Tokyo: Nihon rōdō kyōkai.

Fukaya Masatoshi. 1977. *Ryōsai kenboshugi no kyōiku* (The teaching of the doctrine of good wives and wise mothers). Nagoya: Reimei shobō.

Garon, Sheldon. 1987. *The State and Labor in Modern Japan*. Berkeley: University of California Press.

Garrahan, Philip, and Paul Stewart. 1989. "Working for Nissan." Unpublished paper. Sunderland Polytechnic, Oct.

———. 1992. *The Nissan Enigma: Flexibility at Work in a Local Economy*. London: Mansell Publishing.

Gaugler, Eduard. 2000. "Co-partnership Management." Paper presented at the Twelfth World Conference of the International Industrial Relations Association. Tokyo. May 30.

Gercik, Patricia. 1996. *On Track with the Japanese*. Cambridge, Mass.: MIT-Japan Program.

Giacalone, R., and P. Rosenfeld. 1991. *Applied Impression Management*. Newbury Park, Calif.: Sage.

Giddens, Anthony. 1991. *Modernity and Self-Identity*. Stanford University Press.

Goleman, Daniel. 1995. *Emotional Intelligence.* New York: Bantam.

Gordon, Andrew. 1985. *The Evolution of Labor Relations in Japan: Heavy Industry, 1853–1955.* Cambridge, Mass.: Harvard University, Council on East Asian Studies.

———. 1997. "Managing the Japanese Household: The New Life Movement in Postwar Japan." *Social Politics,* Spring: 245–83.

———. 1998. *The Wages of Affluence.* Cambridge, Mass.: Harvard University Press.

Gould, William. 1984. *Japan's Reshaping of the American Labor Law.* Cambridge, Mass.: Harvard University Press.

Graham, Laurie. 1995. *On the Line at Subaru-Isuzu.* Ithaca: Cornell University Press, ILR Press.

Grathoff, Richard H. 1970. *The Structure of Social Inconsistencies: A Contribution to a Unified Theory of Play, Game and Social Action.* The Hague: Martinus Nijhoff.

Greenwood, Ronald, and Robert Ross. 1982. "Early American Influence on Japanese Management Philosophy: The Scientific Management Movement in Japan." In Sang Lee and Gary Schwendiman, eds., *Management by Japanese Systems,* pp. 43–66. New York: Praeger.

Guillen, Mauro. 1994. *Models of Management.* Chicago: University of Chicago Press.

Gunji Kazuo. 1982. *NHK zankoku monogatari* (The cruel story at NHK). Tokyo: Erū shuppansha.

Haden-Guest, Anthony. 1972. *Down the Programmed Rabbit Hole: Travels Through Muzak, Hilton, Coca-Cola, Walt Disney and Other World Empires.* London: Hart-Davis and MacGibbon.

Hagen, Everett. 1965. "Some Implications of Personality Theory for the Theory of Industrial Relations." *Industrial and Labor Relations Review* 18, no. 3: 339–51.

Ham, Heasun. 1991. "An Empirical Examination of Part-time Workers' Organizational Commitment." *Japanese Quarterly of Administrative Science* 6, no. 1: 1–13.

Hamilton, George, and Nicole W. Biggart. 1988. "Market, Culture, and Authority: A Comparative Analysis of Management and Organization in the Far East." *American Journal of Sociology* 94: S52–94.

Hanami Tadashi. 1979. *Labor Law and Industrial Relations in Japan.* Deventer: Kluwer.

———. 1981. *Labor Relations in Japan Today.* Tokyo: Kodansha International.

Handelman, Don. 1986. "Charisma, Liminality and Symbolic Types." In E. Cohen, M. Lissac, and U. Almagor, eds., *Comparative Social Dynamics: Essays in Honour of S. N. Eisenstadt,* Boulder, Colo.: Westview.

———. 1992. "Symbolic Types, the Body, and Circus." *Semiotica* 85, no. 3/4: 205–27.

Hansen, Miriam. 1993. "Of Mice and Ducks: Benjamin and Adorno on Disney." Special issue: The World According to Disney, ed. Susan Willis. *South Atlantic Quarterly* 92, no. 1: 27–63.

Harada Munehiko. 1994. "Towards a Renaissance of Leisure in Japan." *Leisure Studies* 13, no. 4: 277–87.

Hayashi Shūji. 1988. *Culture and Management in Japan.* Trans. Frank Baldwin. Tokyo: University of Tokyo Press.

Hazama Hiroshi. 1964. *Nihon rōmu kanri shi kenkyū* (Research on the history of Japan's personnel management). Tokyo: Daiyamondosha.

———. 1971. *Nihonteki keiei* (Japanese-style management). Tokyo: Nikkei shinsho.

———. 1978. *Nihon ni okeru rōshi kyōchō no teiryū* (Behind labor-management cooperation in Japan). Tokyo: Waseda daigaku shuppanbu.

———. 1989. *Nihonteki keiei no keifu* (The genealogy of Japanese-style management). Tokyo: Bunshindō.

Hazama Hiroshi and Jacqueline Kaminsky. 1979. "Japanese Labor-Management Relations and Uno Riemon." *Journal of Japanese Studies* 5: 91–113.

Hazan, Haim. 1990. *A Paradoxical Community: The Emergence of a Social World in an Urban Renewal Setting.* Greenwich, Conn.: JAI Press.

Hearn, Jeff. 1993. "Emotive Subjects: Organizational Men, Organizational Masculinities and the (De)construction of 'Emotions.'" In Stephen Fineman, ed., *Emotions in Organizations*, pp. 142–67. London: Sage.

Hearn, Lafcadio. 1894. *Glimpses of Unfamiliar Japan.* Boston: Houghton Mifflin.

Heise, Steve. 1994. "Disney Approach to Managing." *Executive Excellence*, Oct. 18: 18–19.

Henkoff, Ronald. 1994. "Finding, Training and Keeping the Best Service Workers." *Fortune*, Oct. 2: 110–15.

Higuchi Yoshio. 1997. "Trends in Japanese Labor Markets." In Mari Sako and Hiroki Satō, eds., *Japanese Labour and Management in Transition*, pp. 27–53. New York: Routledge.

Hill, Benjamin. 1996. "Breaking the Rules in Japanese Schools: Kōsoku Ihan, Academic Competition, and Moral Education." *Anthropology of Education Quarterly* 27, no. 1: 99–110.

Hirschorn, Larry. 1988. *The Workplace Within: Psychodynamics of Organizational Life.* Cambridge, Mass.: MIT Press.

Hochschild, Arlie. 1979. "Emotion Work, Feeling Rules and Social Structures." *American Journal of Sociology* 85: 551–75.

———. 1983. *The Managed Heart: The Commercialization of Human Feelings.* Berkeley: University of California Press.

———. 1991. "Ideology and Emotion Management: A Perspective and Path for Future Research." In T. Kemper, ed., *Research Agendas in the Sociology of Emotions*, pp. 117–42. Albany: SUNY Press.

Hodson, Randy, and Teresa Sullivan. 1992. *The Social Organization of Work.* Belmont, Calif.: Wadsworth.

Hollway, W. 1991. *Work Psychology and Organizational Behaviour.* London: Sage.

Houseman, Susan. 1997. *Temporary, Part-Time, and Contract Employment in the US: New Evidence from an Employer Survey*. Kalamazoo, Mich.: Upjohn Institute for Employment Research.

Howard, Dennis, and John Crompton. 1980. *Financing, Managing and Marketing Recreation and Park Resources*. Dubuque, Iowa: W. C. Brown.

Hunter, Janet, ed. 1993. *Japanese Women Working*. London: Routledge.

Ichino Shōzō. 1989. "Pātotaimu rōdōsha no henbō katei" (The transformation of part-time workers). *Nihon rōdō kenkyū zasshi* 31, no. 5: 16–30.

Imagawa Isao. 1987. *Gendai kimin kō* (Reflections on modern outcasts). Tokyo: Tabata shoten.

Iriye Akira, ed. 1975. *Mutual Images: Essays in American-Japanese Relations*. Cambridge, Mass.: Harvard University Press.

Ishikawa Kaoru. 1985. *What Is Total Quality Control? The Japanese Way*. Trans. David Lu. Englewood Cliffs, N.J.: Prentice-Hall.

Iwao Sumiko. 1992. *The Japanese Woman: Traditional Image and Changing Reality*. New York: Free Press.

Iwata Ryūshi. 1977. *Nihonteki keiei no hensei genri* (The organizational principles of Japanese-style management). Tokyo: Bunshindō.

Jacoby, Sanford. 1993. "Pacific Ties: Industrial Relations and Employment Systems in Japan and the U.S. Since 1900." In Nelson Lichtenstein and Howell J. Harris, eds., *Industrial Democracy in America: The Ambiguous Promise*, pp. 206–49. Washington, D.C.: Woodrow Wilson Center Press and Cambridge University Press.

Jacques, Roy. 1996. *Manufacturing the Employee: Management Knowledge from the 19th to 21st Centuries*. London: Sage.

James, Judi. 1997. *The Office Jungle: The Survivor's Guide to the Nylon Shagpile of Corporate Life*. London: HarperCollins.

Japan. Rōdōshō (Ministry of Labor). 1996. *Joshi koyō kanri kihon chōsa* (Survey on employment and management of women workers). Tokyo: Rōdōshō.

Japan Institute of Labor. 2000. *The Labor Situation in Japan, 2000*. Tokyo: JIL.

Japan Productivity Center for Socio-economic Development. 1999. "Rōshi kankei jōnin iinkai chōsa kenkyū hōkokusho: shokuba to kigyō no rōshikankei no saikōchiku" (Report of the JPC Labor-Management Commission survey: reconstruction of labor-management relations at the workplace). Tokyo: JPC.

Johnson, S. K. 1988. *The Japanese Through American Eyes*. Stanford: Stanford University Press.

Kaigo Tokiomi. 1962. "Shūshin kyōkasho sōkaisetsu" (A comprehensive commentary on the ethics textbooks). In Kaigo Tokiomi, ed., *Nihon kyōkasho taikei: kindaihen* (Collection of Japanese textbooks: modern editions), 3: 616–27. Tokyo: Kodansha.

Kakita Toshizumi. 1984. "Foreign-Capital Enterprises Operating in Japan's Service Industry." *Dentsū Japan Marketing/Advertising Quarterly* 2, no. 1: 4–13.

Kamata Satoshi. 1974. *Rōdō genba no hanran-hachi kigyō ni miru gorika to rōdō no kaitai* (Rebellion on the job: rationalization and the disorganization of labor at eight companies). Tokyo: Daiyamondosha.

———. 1980. *Rōdō genba: zōsenjo de nani ga okotta ka* (The work place: what goes on at the shipbulding yards?). Tokyo: Iwanami shoten.

———. 1982. *Japan in the Passing Lane*. Trans. and ed. Akimoto Tatsuru of *Jidōsha zetsubō kōjō* (The automobile factory with no hope, 1973). New York: Pantheon Books.

Kameda Atsuko. 1986. "Joshi tanki: kyōiku to sekushizumu" (Junior colleges for women: education and sexism). In Amano Masako, ed., *Joshi kōtō kyōiku no zahyō* (The coordinates of women's higher education). Tokyo: Kakiuchi shuppan.

Kanō Yasuhisa. 1986. *Tōkyō dizuniirando no shinsō* (The true story of Tokyo Disneyland). Tokyo: Bungeisha.

Kanter, Rosabeth. 1977. *Men and Women of the Corporation*. New York: Basic Books.

Karthaüs-Tanaka, Nobuko. 1995. *How Japan Views Its Current Labor Market*. Leiden: Leiden University and Netherlands Association of Japanese Studies.

Kawanishi Hirosuke. 1992. *Enterprise Unionism in Japan*. London: Kegan Paul.

Kawashima Mutsuo. 1988a. "The Crumbling Walls of Lifetime Employment." *Tokyo Business Today*, Sept. 28–29.

———. 1988b. "Big Bucks Vs. a Job for Life: Why Top Talent Is Defecting." *Business Week* 9: 58.

Kelsky, Karen. 1994. "Postcards from the Edge: The Office Ladies of Tokyo." *U.S.-Japan Women's Journal* 6: 1–24.

Kemper, T. 1978. *A Social Interactional Theory of Emotions*. New York: Wiley.

Kerr, Clark. 1964. *Labor and Management in Industrial Society*. Garden City, N.Y.: Doubleday, Anchor Books.

Khan Yoshimitsu. 1998. *Japanese Moral Education: Past and Present*. London: Associated University Presses.

Kilduff, Martin; Jeffrey Funk; and Ajay Mehra. 1997. "Engineering Identity in a Japanese Factory." *Organization Science* 8, no. 6: 579–92.

Kinsella, Sharon. 1995. "Cuties in Japan." In L. Skov and B. Moeran, eds., *Women, Media and Consumption in Japan*, pp. 220–55. Richmond, Surrey: Curzon Press.

Kinzley, W. Dean. 1991. *Industrial Harmony in Modern Japan: The Invention of a Tradition*. London: Routledge.

Klein, J. 1984. "Why Supervisors Resist Employee Involvement." *Harvard Business Review* 62: 87–95.

Kling, R., and E. M. Gerson, 1978. "Patterns of Segmentation and Interaction in the Computing World." *Symbolic Interaction* 1: 24–43.

Koike Kazuo. 1988. *Understanding Industrial Relations in Modern Japan.* New York: St. Martin's.

Komuya Kazumeki. 1989. *Tōkyō dizuniirando no keiei majikku* (Tokyo Disneyland's amazing management). Tokyo: Kōdansha.

Kondo, Dorinne. 1990. *Crafting Selves.* Chicago: University of Chicago Press.

Krauss, Ellis; Thomas Rohlen; and Patricia Steinhoff, eds., 1983. *Conflict in Japan.* Honolulu: University of Hawaii Press.

Kuenz, Jane. 1995. "Working at the Rat." In The Project on Disney, comp., *Inside the Mouse: Work and Play at Disney World,* pp. 110–63. Durham: Duke University Press.

Kumazawa Makoto. 1996. *Portraits of the Japanese Workplace.* Boulder, Colo.: Westview Press.

Kume Ikuo. 1998. *Disparaged Success: Labor Politics in Postwar Japan.* Cornell Studies in Political Economy. Ithaca: Cornell University Press.

Kunda, Gideon. 1992. *Engineering Culture.* Philadelphia: Temple University Press.

Kuwahara Yasuo. 2000. "The Future of the Labor Movement in Japan." Paper presented at the Twelfth Congress of the International Industrial Relations Association. Tokyo. May 30.

Laabs, Jennifer. 1999. "Emotional Intelligence at Work." *Workforce* 78, no. 7: 68–81.

Lawler, E., and S. Mohrman. 1985. "Quality Circles After the Fad." *Harvard Business Review* 85: 65–71.

Lazarus, R. 1993. "From Psychological Stress to Emotions: A History of Changing Outlooks." *Annual Review of Psychology* 44: 1–21.

Lebra, Takie S. 1976. *Japanese Patterns of Behavior.* Honolulu: University of Hawaii Press.

Leidner, Robin. 1993. *Fast Food, Fast Talk: Service Work and the Routinization of Everyday Life.* Berkeley: University of California Press.

Leonard, J. 1983. "Can Your Organization Support Quality Circles?" *Training and Development Journal* 37: 67–72.

Levine, Solomon, and Kawada Hishashi. 1980. *Human Resources in Japanese Industrial Development.* Princeton: Princeton University Press.

Levinson, H. 1961. "Industrial Mental Health: Progress and Prospects." *Menninger Quarterly,* Winter.

Lichtenstein, Nelson. 1980. "Auto Worker Militancy and the Structure of Factory Life, 1937–1955." *Journal of American History* 67: 335–53.

Lincoln, James, and Arne Kalleberg. 1990. *Culture, Control, and Commitment: A Study of Work Organization and Work Attitudes in the U.S. and Japan.* Cambridge, Eng.: Cambridge University Press.

Lincoln, James, and Kerry McBride. 1987. "Japanese Industrial Organization in Comparative Perspective." *Annual Review of Sociology* 13: 289–312.

Linhart, Sepp. 1988. "From Industrial to Postindustrial Society: Changes in Japanese Leisure-Related Values and Behavior." *Journal of Japanese Studies* 14, no. 2: 271–307.

Lipp, Douglas. 1994. *Tōkyō dizuniirando daiseikō no shinsō* (The truth about Tokyo Disneyland's great success). Trans. Kuchika Kimundo. Tokyo: NTT shuppan.

Lo, Jeannie. 1990. *Office Ladies, Factory Women.* Armonk, N.Y.: M. E. Sharpe.

Loseke, Doneelin, and Spencer Cahill. 1986. "Actors in Search of a Character: Student Social Workers' Quest for Professional Identity." *Symbolic Interaction* 9: 245–58.

Lutz, Catherine A. 1990. "Engendered Emotion: Gender, Power, and the Rhetoric of Emotional Control in American Discourse." In Catherine Lutz and Lila Abu-Lughood, eds., *Language and the Politics of Emotion*, pp. 69–91. Cambridge, Eng.: Cambridge University Press.

Lutz, C., and J. Collins. 1994. *Reading National Geographic.* Chicago: University of Chicago Press.

Marcus, Alan, and Howard P. Segal. 1989. *Technology in America.* New York: Harcourt Brace Jovanovich.

Marshall, Byron. 1967. *Capitalism and Nationalism in Prewar Japan.* Stanford: Stanford University Press.

Martin, Joanne. 1992. *Cultures in Organizations: Three Perspectives.* Oxford: Oxford University Press.

Martin, Joanne, et al. 1998. "An Alternative to Bureaucratic Impersonality and Emotional Labor: Bounded Emotionality at the Body Shop." *Administrative Science Quarterly* 43, no. 2: 429–69.

Marx, Karl. 1967. *Capital,* vol. 1. Trans. S. Moore and E. Aveling. New York: International Publishers.

Matsumoto, David. 1996. *Unmasking Japan: Myths and Realities About the Emotions of the Japanese.* Stanford, Calif.: Stanford University Press.

Matsumoto, D.; T. Kudō; K. Schere; and H. Wallbott. 1988. "Emotion Antecedents and Reactions in the U.S. and Japan." *Journal of Cross-Cultural Psychology* 19: 267–86.

Matsunaga, Louella. 2000. *The Changing Face of Japanese Retail.* London: Routledge for the Nissan Institute.

Mayo, Elton. 1931. "Economic Stability and the Standard of Living." *Harvard Business School Alumni Bulletin* 7, no. 6: 290–308.

———. 1941. "Research in Human Relations." *Personnel* 17, no 4: 266–275.

———. 1945. *Social Problems of an Industrial Civilization.* Boston: Harvard University, Graduate School of Business, Division of Research.

McVeigh, Brian. 1997. *Life in a Japanese Women's College: Learning to be Ladylike.* London: Routledge.

Mead, George Herbert. 1932. *Mind, Self and Society.* Chicago: University of Chicago Press.

Meyer, Stephen. 1981. *The Five Dollar Day: Labor, Management, and Social Control in the Ford Motor Company, 1908–1921.* Albany: State University of New York Press.

Mick, David, and Susan Fournier. 1998. "Paradoxes of Technology: Consumer Cognizance, Emotions, and Coping Strategies." *Journal of Consumer Research* 25, no. 2: 123–43.

Milkman, Ruth. 1988. "Team Dreams." *Voice Literary Supplement*, Nov.

———. 1991. *Japan's California Factories: Labor Relations and Economic Globalization.* Berkeley: University of California Press.

Miller, Mike. 1999. "Emotional Intelligence Helps Managers Succeed." *Credit Union Magazine* 65, no. 7: 25–26.

Mills, C. Wright. 1951. *White Collar: The American Middle Classes.* Oxford: Oxford University Press.

Mito Tadashi. 1994. *Ie toshite no nihon shakai* (Japanese society as *ie*). Tokyo: Yuhikaku.

Mitsui Company. 1994. *Josei shain no shitsukekata* (How to discipline female workers). Tokyo: Mitsui Bank, Personnel Office.

Miyoshi, M., and H. D. Harootunian, eds. 1988. *Postmodernism and Japan.* Special issue of the *South Atlantic Quarterly.* Durham: Duke University Press.

———. 1991. "Japan in the World." Special issue: Japan in the World. *Boundary 2*, 18: 3: 1–8.

Moeran, Brian. 1989. *Language and Popular Culture in Japan.* Manchester: University of Manchester Press.

Montgomery, David. 1979. *Workers' Control in America.* New York: Cambridge University Press.

Morikawa Hidemasa. 1987. *Nihon keiei shi* (History of Japanese management). Tokyo: Nihon keizai shinbunsha.

Morishima Motohiro and Peter Feuille. 2000. "Effects of the Use of Contingent Workers on Regular Status Workers: A Japan-US Comparison." Paper presented at the 12th World Congress of the International Industrial Relations Association. Tokyo. May 30.

Morita Akio. 1986. *Made in Japan.* New York: E. P. Dutton.

Mouer, Ross, and Yoshio Sugimoto. 1986. *Images of Japanese Society.* London: Routledge and Kegan Paul.

Mumby, Dennis, and Linda L. Putnam. 1992. "The Politics of Emotion: A Feminist Reading of Bounded Rationality." *Academy of Management Review*, 17, no. 3: 465–87.

Murai Minoru. 1990a. *Dōtoku kyōiku genri* (Principles of moral education). Tokyo: Kyōiku shuppan.

————. 1990b. *Dōtoku wa oshierareru ka* (Can morality be taught?). Tokyo: Koku-dosha.

Murakami Yasuaki. 1980. "Ie Society as a Pattern of Civilization." *Journal of Japanese Studies* 10, no. 2: 281–363. (For the original thesis, see Murakami Yasuaki, Kumon Shunpei, and Satō Seizaburō. 1979. *Bunmei to shite no ie shakai* [*Ie* society as civilization]. Tokyo: Chūō kōronsha.)

Murphy, L. R. 1988. "Workplace Intervention for Stress Reduction and Prevention." In C. L. Cooper and R. Payne, eds., *Causes, Coping, and Consequences of Stress at Work.* Chichester: Wiley.

Nakamaki Hirochika. 1992. *Mukashi daimyō ima kaisha* (Once a daimyo, now a corporation). Tokyo: Tankosha.

Nakamaki Hirochika, ed. 1999. *Shasō no keiei jinruigaku* (The anthropology of management: company funerals). Tokyo: Tōhō shuppan.

Nakamaki Hirochika and Hioki Kōichirō, eds., 1997. *Keiei jinruigaku kotohajime* (Toward an anthropology of management). Tokyo: Tōhō shuppan.

Nakamura Osamu, Matsunaga Hideo, and Kitaizumi Mari. 1994. *A Bilingual Guide to the Japanese Economy.* Tokyo: Kodansha.

Nakamura Takafusa. 1981. *The Post-War Japanese Economy: Its Development and Structure.* Tokyo: University of Tokyo Press.

Nakane Chie. 1970. *Japanese Society.* Berkeley: California University Press. Originally published in Japanese in 1967 as *Tate shakai no ningen kankei* (Human relations in a vertical society). Tokyo: Kōdansha.

Nakase Toshikazu. 1993. "The Introduction of Scientific Management in Japan— Case Studies of Companies in the Sumitomo Zaibatsu." In Nakagawa Keiichirō, ed., *Labor and Management,* pp. 171–202. Tokyo: University of Tokyo Press.

Nakayama Ichiro. 1974. *Rōshi kankei no keizai shakaigaku* (The socioeconomic study of labor relations). Tokyo: Nihon rōdō kyōkai.

Nanto, Dick Kazuyuki. 1982. "Management, Japanese Style." In Sang Lee and Gary Schwendiman, eds., *Management by Japanese Systems,* pp. 3–24. New York: Praeger.

National Defense Council for Victims of Karōshi. 1990. *Karōshi: When the Corporate Warrior Dies.* Tokyo.

National Institute of Employment and Vocational Research. 1988. *Women Workers in Japan.* Tokyo: NIEVR.

Nelson, Daniel. 1982. "Origins of the Sit-Down Era: Worker Militancy and Innovation in the Rubber Industry." *Labor History* 23: 198–225.

Nihon nōritsu kyōkai. 1988. "Kigyō no kenkyū shisetsu jittai chōsa" (A survey of company-owned training facilities). *Kigyō to jinzai* 4: 26–35.

Nishimura Hiromichi. 1970. *Nihon no chingin mondai* (The wage problem in Japan). Kyoto: Minerva shobō.

Odaka Kunio. 1984. *Nihonteki keiei* (Japanese-style management). Tokyo: Chūō kōronsha.

Ogasawara Yūko. 1998. *Office Ladies and Salaried Men: Power, Gender, and Work in Japanese Companies.* Berkeley: University of California Press.

Ogawa Masamoto. 2000. "The Case of Mitsuwa Co., Ltd.: Co-partnership Management and the Merchant Spirit." Paper presented at the Twelfth World Conference of the International Industrial Relations Association. Tokyo. May 30.

Okazaki-Ward, Lola. 1993. *Management Education and Training in Japan.* London: Graham and Trotman.

Ōkōchi Kazuo. 1972. *Rōshi kankei ron no shiteki hatten* (The historical development of theories of industrial relations). Tokyo: Yūhikaku.

Okuda Kenji. 1985. *Hito to keiei* (People and management). Tokyo: Manējimentosha.

O'Neill, John. 1985. *Five Bodies: The Human Shape of Modern Society.* Ithaca: Cornell University Press.

Ōno Taiichi. 1978. *Toyota seisan hōshiki* (The Toyota production system). Tokyo: Daiyamondo.

Orii Hyūga. 1973. *Rōmu kanri nijūnen* (Twenty years in worker management). Tokyo: Tōyō keizai shimpōsha.

Ōsuga Hatsuzō. 1994. "Running a Company and Human Beings." *Japanese Personality Psychology Research Association Journal* 1: 1–14.

Ouchi, William. 1981. *Theory Z.* New York: Avon Books.

Owatari Tatsuo. 1989. *Rinrigaku to dōtoku kyōiku* (Ethics schools and morality education). Tokyo: Ibunsha.

Parker, Mike. 1993. "Industrial Relations Myth and Shop-Floor Reality: The 'Team Concept' in the Auto Industry." In Nelson Lichtenstein and Howell J. Harris, eds., *Industrial Democracy in America: The Ambiguous Promise,* pp. 249–75. Washington, D.C.: Woodrow Wilson Center Press and Cambridge University Press.

Pascale, Richard, and Anthony Athos. 1981a. *The Art of Japanese Management.* New York: Warner Books.

———. 1981b. "Winning Through Ambiguity, Vagueness and Indirection—The Secrets of Japanese Management." *Savvy,* July: 53–60.

Peak, Lois. 1991. *Learning to Go to School in Japan: The Transition from Home to Preschool Life.* Berkeley: University of California Press.

Pelzel, J. 1986. "Human Nature in the Japanese Myths." In T. S. Lebra and W. P. Lebra, eds., *Japanese Culture and Behavior: Selected Readings.* Honolulu: University of Hawaii Press.

Perlman, Selig. 1968. *A Theory of the Labor Movement.* New York: Augustus Kelly.

Peters, Tom, and Nancy Austin. 1986. *A Passion for Excellence.* London: Fontana/Collins.

Peters, T., and R. Waterman. 1982. *In Search of Excellence: Lessons from America's Best-Run Companies.* New York: Harper and Row.

Pharr, Susan. 1984. "Status Conflict: The Rebellion of the Tea Pourers." in E. Krauss, T. Rohlen, and P. Steinhoff, eds., *Conflict in Japan,* pp. 214–41. Honolulu: University of Hawaii Press.

Pierce, Jennifer. 1995. *Gender Trials: Emotional Lives in Contemporary Law Firms.* Berkeley: University of California Press.

Piore, Michael, and Charles Sabel. 1984. *The Second Industrial Divide: Possbilities for Prosperity.* New York: Basic Books.

Pringle, Rosemary. 1988. *Secretaries Talk.* London: Verso.

———. 1989. "Bureaucracy, Rationality and Sexuality: The Case of Secretaries." In J. Heran, D. Shepard, T. Tancred-Sheriff, and G. Burrell, eds., *The Sexuality of Organization,* chap. 10. London: Sage.

Project on Disney, The. 1995. *Inside the Mouse: Work and Play at Disney World.* Durham, N.C.: Duke University Press.

Pruette, Lorine, and Douglas Fryer. 1918. "Team System Is Thought to Be the Best Labor Solution." *Electrical World* 72, no. 7: 298.

Rafaeli, Anat, and Robert Sutton. 1989. "The Expression of Emotion in Organizational Life." In L. L. Cummings and B. M. Staw, eds., *Research in Organizational Behavior,* 11: 1–42. Greenwich, Conn.: JAI Press.

———. 1990. "Busy Stores and Demanding Customers: How Do They Affect the Display of Positive Emotion?" *Academy of Management Journal,* 33: 623–37.

Raz, Aviad. 1993. "The Reinherited Self: A Case Study in the Dynamics of a Social World." *Studies in Symbolic Interaction* 14: 43–62.

———. 1999a. *Riding the Black Ship: Japan and Tokyo Disneyland.* Cambridge, Mass.: Harvard University Asia Center.

———. 1999b. "Glocalization and Symbolic Interactionism." *Studies in Symbolic Interaction* 22: 3–16.

Raz, Jacob. 1992. "Self-presentation and Performance in the Yakuza Way of Life." In idem, *Aspects of Otherness in Japanese Culture,* pp. 93–109. Tokyo: Institute for the Study of Languages and Cultures of Asia and Africa.

Raz, Jacob, and Aviad E. Raz. 1996. "'America' Meets 'Japan': A Journey for Real Between Two Imaginaries." *Theory, Culture and Society* 13, no. 3: 157–82.

Rinehart, James; Christopher Huxley; and David Robertson. 1995. "Team Concept at CAMI." In Steve Babson, ed., *Lean Work,* pp. 220–34. Detroit: Wayne State University Press.

———. 1997. *Just Another Car Factory? Lean Production and Its Discontents.* Ithaca: Cornell University Press, ILR Press.

Risu Akizuki. 1980. *OL shinkaron* (The evolution of office ladies). Tokyo: Kōdansha. Trans. Yuriko Tamaki. *The OL Comes of Age.* Tokyo: Kodansha International, 1990.

Ritzer, George. 1996. *The McDonaldization of Society.* Thousand Oaks, Calif.: Pine Forge Press.

Robinson, Michael, and Joel Johnson. 1997. "Is It Emotion or Is It Stress? Gender Stereotypes and the Perception of Subjective Experience." *Sex Roles* 4, no. 4: 235–58.

Roberts, Glenda. 1994. *Staying on the Line: Blue-Collar Women in Contemporary Japan.* Honolulu: University of Hawaii Press.

Robertson, David; James Rinehart; Christopher Huxley; Jeff Wareham; Herman Rosenfeld; Alan McGough; and Steve Benedict. 1993. "Japanese Production Management in a Unionized Auto Plant." Willowdale, Ontario: Canadian Automobile Workers (CAW), Canada Research Department.

Roethlisberger, Fritz, and William Dickson. 1939. *Management and the Worker.* Cambridge, Mass.: Harvard University Press.

Rohlen, Thomas. 1974. *For Harmony and Strength.* Berkeley: California University Press.

—————. 1983. *Japan's High Schools.* Berkeley: California University Press.

Rohlen, T., and G. Letendre, eds. 1996. *Teaching and Learning in Japan.* Cambridge, Eng.: Cambridge University Press.

Romero, Mary. 1992. *Maid in the U.S.A.* New York: Routledge.

Rose, M. 1988. *Industrial Behavior.* Harmondsworth, Eng.: Penguin.

Rosenberg, M. 1990. "Reflexivity and Emotions." *Social Psychology Quarterly* 53, no. 1: 3–12.

Rothschild, J., and A. Whitt. 1986. *The Co-operative Workplace.* Cambridge, Eng.: Cambridge University Press.

Saitō Takenori. 1984. *Ueno Yōichi— hito to gyōseki* (Ueno Yōichi: the man and his achievements). Sangyō nōritsu daigaku shuppanbu.

Sakuta Keiichi. 1967. *Haji no bunka saikō* (Shame culture re-examined). Tokyo: Chikuma shobō.

Salmon, J., et al. 2000. "The Strategic Revival and Renewal of Labour Movements: The Experiences of Britain and Japan." Paper presented at the Twelfth Congress of the International Industrial Relations Association. Tokyo. May 30.

Sandelands, L. E. 1988. "The Concept of Work Feeling." *Journal for the Theory of Social Behavior* 18, no. 4: 437–57.

Sano Yoko. 1995. "Customer-Driven Human Resource Policies and Practices in the Japanese Service Sector." *Human Resource Planning* 17, no. 3: 37–53.

Sasaki Satoshi. 1992. "The Introduction of Scientific Management by the Mitsubishi Electric Company Co. and the Formation of an Organized Scientific Management Movement in Japan in the 1920s and 1930s." *Business History* 34: 12–37.

Saso, Mary, ed. 1990. *Women in the Japanese Workplace*. London: Hilary Shipman.

Schein, Edgar. 1990. "Organizational Culture." *American Psychologist*, Feb.: 109–19.

Scherer, K. R.; D. Matsumoto; H. Wallbott; and T. Kudoh. 1988. "Emotional Experience in Cultural Context: A Comparison Between Europe, Japan, and the USA." In K. Schere, ed., *Facets of Emotion*. Hillsdale, N.J.: Erlbaum.

Schickel, Richard. 1968. *The Disney Version*. New York: Simon and Schuster.

Schilling, Mark. 1988. "When Office Flowers Turn into Weeds." *Japan Times*, Dec. 15.

Schodt, Frederik L. 1983. *Manga! Manga! The World of Japanese Comics*. Tokyo: Kodansha.

———. 1994. *America and the Four Japans: Friend, Foe, Model, Mirror*. Berkeley, Calif.: Stone Bridge Press.

Schooland, Ken. 1990. *Shogun's Ghost: The Dark Side of Japanese Education*. New York: Bergin and Garvey.

Scott, Richard. 1987. *Organizations: Rational, Natural, and Open Systems*. Englewood Cliffs, N.J.: Prentice-Hall.

Selznick, Philip. 1969. *Law, Society, and Industrial Justice*. New York: Russell Sage.

Sengoku Tamotsu. 1985. *Willing Workers: The Work Ethics in Japan, England, and the U.S.* Trans. K. Ezaki and Y. Ezaki. New York: Quorum Books.

Sewell, Graham, and Barry Wilkinson. 1992. "'Someone to Watch Over Me': Surveillance, Discipline, and the Just-In-Time Labour Process." *Sociology* 26, no. 2: 271–89.

Shenhav, Yehouda. 1999. *Manufacturing Rationality: The Engineering Foundations of the Managerial Revolution*. Oxford University Press.

Shibutani, Tamotsu. 1955. "Reference Groups as Perspectives." *American Journal of Sociology* 60: 562–68.

Shields, James, ed. 1989. *Japanese Schooling: Patterns of Socialization, Equality, and Political Control*. University Park: Pennsylvania State University Press.

Shields, S. A. 1991. "Gender in the Psychology of Emotion: A Selective Research Review." In K. T. Strongman, ed., *International Review of Studies on Emotion*. New York: John Wiley and Sons.

———. 1995. "The Role of Emotion, Beliefs and Values in Gender Development." In N. Eisenberg, ed., *Social Development: Review of Personality and Social Psychology*, 15. Thousand Oaks, Calif.: Sage.

Shimamura Mari. 1990. *Fanshii no kenkyū: kawaii ga hito, mono, kane wo sōhai suru* (Research on fancy: cute controls people, objects and money). Tokyo: Nesco.

Shimizu Ikkō. 1995. *The Dark Side of Japanese Business: Three Industry Novels.* Armonk, New York: M. E. Sharpe.

Shinotsuka Eiko. 1982. *Nihon no joshi rōdō* (Female labor in Japan). Tokyo: Tōyō keizai shinpōsha.

Shirai Taishirō. 1979. *Kigyōbetsu kumiai* (The enterprise union). Tokyo: Chūō kōronsha.

————. 1983. *Contemporary Industrial Relations in Japan.* Madison: University of Wisconsin Press.

Shire, Karen. 2000. "Gendered Organization and Workplace Culture in Japanese Customer Service." *Social Science Japan Journal* 3, no. 1: 37–59.

Sievers, Sharon. 1983. *Flowers in Salt: The Beginnings of Feminist Consciousness in Modern Japan.* Stanford: Stanford University Press.

Silverberg, Miriam. 1991. "The Modern Girl as Militant." In G. L. Bernstein, ed., *Recreating Japanese Women, 1600–1945,* pp. 236–67. Berkeley: University of California Press.

Silverman, Laura, ed. 1995. *Bringing Home the Sushi: An Inside Look at Japanese Business Through Japanese Comics.* Tokyo: Mangajin.

Simon, Herbert. 1976. *Administrative Behavior.* New York: Free Press.

————. 1989. "Making Management Decisions: The Role of Intuition and Emotion." In W. H. Agor, ed., *Intuition in Organizations,* pp. 23–39. Newbury Park, Calif.: Sage.

Sinclair, Amanda. 1992. "The Tyranny of Team Ideology." *Organization Studies* 13, no. 4: 611–26.

Smith, R. C., and E. M. Eisenberg. 1987. "Conflict at Disneyland: A Root-Metaphor Analysis." *Communication Monographs* 54: 367–80.

Smith, Thomas C. 1984. "The Right to Benevolence: Dignity and Japanese Workers, 1890–1920." *Journal of Comparative Study of Society and History* 4: 587–613.

Smoodin, Eric, ed. 1994. *Disney Discourse: Producing the Magic Kingdom.* London: Routledge.

Snyder, M. 1974. "Self Monitoring of Expressive Behavior." *Journal of Personality and Social Behavior* 30: 526–37.

Sparks, Leigh. 1995. "Reciprocal Retail Internationalization: The Southland Corporation, Ito-Yokado and 7-Eleven Convenience Stores." *Service Industries Journal* 15, no. 4: 57–69.

Sterle, David, and Mary Duncan. 1973. *Supervision of Leisure Services.* San Diego: San Diego State University.

Stone, Katherine. 1975. "The Origins of Job Structures in the Steel Industry." In R. Edwards, M. Reich, and D. Gordon, eds., *Labor Market Segmentation,* pp. 27–84. Lexington, Mass.: Lexington Books.

Strauss, Anselm. 1978. "A Social World Perspective." In N. K. Denzin, ed., *Studies in Symbolic Interaction,* 1: 119–28. Greenwich Conn.: JAI Press.

———. 1982. "Social Worlds and Legitimation Processes." In N. K. Denzin, ed., *Studies in Symbolic Interaction,* 4: 171–90. Greenwich Conn.: JAI Press.

Sugahara Mariko and Takeuchi Hiroshi. 1982. "Japanese-Style Management and Women's Entry into the Job Market." *The Wheel Extended: A Toyota Quarterly Review* 12, no. 4: 27–32.

Sutton, Robert, and Anat Rafaeli. 1988. "Untangling the Relationship Between Displayed Emotions and Organizational Sales: The Case of Convenience Stores." *Academy of Management Journal* 31, no. 3: 461–87.

Tadokoro Makoto. 1990. *Tōkyō dizuniirando no majikku shōhō* (The magic business of Tokyo Disneyland). Tokyo: Yell Books.

Taira Kōji. 1961. "Japanese Enterprise Unionism and Inter-Firm Wage Structure." *Industrial and Labor Relations Review* 113: 67–83.

———. 1977. "Nihongata kigyōbetsu rōdō kumiai sanbiron" (In justification of the Japanese-style of enterprise unions). *Chūō kōron,* Mar., pp. 114–26.

Takahashi Yasuo. "You Can't Have Green Tea in a Japanese Coffee Shop." In Ueda Atsushi, ed., *The Electric Geisha: Exploring Japan's Popular Culture,* pp. 26–34. Trans. Miriam Eguchi. Tokyo: Kodansha International.

Takezawa Shin-ichi and Arthur Whitehill. 1981. *Work Ways: Japan and America.* Tokyo: Japan Institute of Labor.

TDL. 1995. "TDL Dimensions and Fact Sheet." Maihama, Chiba: OLC Publicity Division.

Tokunaga Shigeyoshi. 1983. "A Marxist Interpretation of Japanese Industrial Relations, with Special Reference to Large Private Enterprises." In Shirai Taishirō, ed., *Contemporary Industrial Relations in Japan,* pp. 313–29. Madison: University of Wisconsin Press.

Tokyo Dome Company. 1995. *Annual Report.* Tokyo: ToDo.

Tomkins, S. 1962, 1963. *Affect, Imagery, Consciousness.* 2 vols. New York: Springer-Verlag.

Tone, Andrea. 1997. *The Business of Benevolence: Industrial Paternalism in Progressive America.* Ithaca: Cornell University Press.

Toyama Takeshi. 2000. Case study presented in the special seminar "Measures Taken by Small and Medium-Scale Companies in the Area of Human Resource Development." Twelfth Congress of the International Industrial Relations Association. Tokyo. May 30.

Tsuromaki Yasuo. 1984. *Tōkyō dizuniirando wo hadaka ni suru* (Stripping Tokyo Disneyland). Tokyo: Tsūshinsha shuppanbu.

Tsurumi, Patricia. 1974. "Meiji Primary School Language and Ethics Textbooks: Old Values for a New Society?" *Modern Asian Studies* 8: 247–61.

————. 1984. "Female Textile Workers and the Failure of Early Trade Unionism in Japan." *History Workshop* 18: 3–27.

Tsutsui, William. 1995. "From Taylorism to Quality Control: Scientific Management in 20th Century Japan." Ph.D. diss., Princeton University.

————. 1998. *Manufacturing Ideology: Scientific Management in 20th-Century Japan.* Princeton: Princeton University Press.

Tu Wei-ming, ed. 1996. *Confucian Traditions in East-Asian Modernity: Moral Education and Economic Culture in Japan and the Four Mini-Dragons.* Cambridge, Mass.: Harvard University Press.

Tung, Rosalie L. 1984. *Key to Japan's Economic Strength: Human Power.* Lexington, Mass.: Lexington Books.

Turner, Lowell. 1991. *Democracy at Work.* Ithaca: Cornell University Press.

Ueno Eishin. 1960. *Chi no tei no waraibanashi* (Funny stories from the underground). Tokyo: Iwanami shinsho.

————. 1985a. *Hanashi no koguchi* (The mine entrance of stories). Tokyo: Keishobō.

————. 1985b. *Naraku no seiun* (The nebula of hell). Tokyo: Keishobō.

————. 1985c. *Moyashitsukusu hibi* (Rekindling the fire everyday). Tokyo: Keishobō.

————. 1985d. *Yami wo sai toshite* (Darkness is the stronghold). Tokyo: Keishobō.

————. 1985e. *Chukon no fu* (A tribute of long-standing hatred). Tokyo: Keishobō.

Uno, Kathleen. 1988. "Good Wives and Wise Mothers in Early 20th-Century Japan." Paper presented at the panel "Women in Prewar Japan." Pacific Coast Branch of the American Historical Association, San Francisco.

————. 1992. "The Death of Good Wife, Wise Mother?" In A. Gordon, ed., *Postwar Japan as History.* Berkeley: University of California Press.

Unruh, David. 1983. *Invisible Life: The Social Worlds of the Aged.* Beverly Hills, Calif.: Sage.

Valentine, James. 1990. "On the Borderlines: The Significance of Marginality in Japanese Society." In Eyal Ben Ari, Brian Moeran, and James Valentine, eds., *Unwrapping Japan: Society and Culture in Anthropological Perspective.* Honolulu: University of Hawaii Press.

Van Maanen, John. 1989. "Whistle While You Work: On Seeing Disneyland as the Workers Do." Paper presented at the panel "The Magic Kingdom." American Anthropological Association Annual Meeting, Washington D.C., Nov. 16.

————. 1991. "The Smile Factory: Work at Disneyland." In P. J. Frost, L. F. Moore, M. R. Louis, C. C. Lundberg, and J. Martin, eds., *Reframing Organizational Culture.* Newbury Park, Calif.: Sage.

————. 1992. "Displacing Disney: Some Notes on the Flow of Culture." *Qualitative Sociology* 15, no. 1: 5–35.

Van Maanen, John, and Gideon Kunda. 1989. "'Real Feelings': Emotional Expression and Organizational Culture." *Research in Organizational Behavior* 11: 43–103.

Wagatsuma Hiroshi and A. Rossett. 1986. "The Implications of Apology: Law and Culture in Japan and the U.S." *Law and Society Review* 20, no. 4: 461–98.

Wakisaka Akira. 1997. "Women at Work." In Mari Sako and Hiroki Sato, eds., *Japanese Labour and Management in Transition*, pp. 130–51. New York: Routledge.

Warner, Malcolm. 1994. "Japanese Culture, Western Management: Taylorism and Human Resources in Japan." *Organization Studies* 15, no. 4: 509–33.

Watanabe Osamu. 1987. "Gendai Nihon shakai no ken'iteki kōzō to kokka" (Authority structures and the nation in contemporary Japanese society). In Fujita Isamu, ed., *Ken'iteki chitsujo to kokka* (The order of authority and the nation), pp. 186–92. Tokyo: Tōkyō daigaku shuppanbu.

Watson, James, ed. 1998. *Golden Arches East*. Stanford: Stanford University Press.

Wever, Kirsten S.. 1998. "International Labor Revitilization: Enlarging the Playing Field." *Industrial Relations* 37, no. 3: 388–407.

White, Merry. 1987. *The Japanese Educational Challenge: A Commitment to Children*. New York: Free Press.

———. 1993. *The Material Child: Coming of Age in Japan and America*. New York: Free Press.

Whitehill, Arthur, and Takezawa Shinichi. 1968. *The Other Worker: A Comparative Study of Industrial Relations in the U.S. and Japan*. Honolulu: East-West Center Press.

Wilensky, J. L., and H. L. Wilensky. 1951. "Personnel Counseling: The Case of Hawthorne." *American Journal of Sociology* 17: 266–80.

Willis, Susan, ed. 1993. *The World According to Disney*. Special issue, *South Atlantic Quarterly* 92, no. 1.

Womack, James; Daniel Jones; and Daniel Roos. 1990. *The Machine That Changed the World*. Boston: Rawson Associates.

Wouters, Cas. 1989. "Commentary: The Sociology of Emotions and Flight Attendants—Hochschild's Managed Heart." *Theory, Culture and Society* 6: 95–123.

Wren, Daniel. 1994. *The Evolution of Management Thought*. New York: John Wiley.

Yano, Christine R. 2002. *Tears of Longing: Nostalgia and the Nation in Japanese Popular Song*. Cambridge, Mass.: Harvard University Asia Center.

Yoshino Kosaku. 1992. *Cultural Nationalism in Contemporary Japan*. Routledge: London.

Yoshimitsu Asano. 1970. *Rejā sangyō* (The leisure industry). Tokyo: Nihon keizai shinbun.

Zuboff, S. 1988. *In the Age of the Smart Machine*. New York: Basic Books.

Index

Harvard East Asian Monographs

(* out-of-print)

Harvard East Asian Monographs

Harvard East Asian Monographs

Harvard East Asian Monographs

Harvard East Asian Monographs

Harvard East Asian Monographs

Harvard East Asian Monographs

Harvard East Asian Monographs

190. James Z. Lee, *The Political Economy of a Frontier: Southwest China, 1250–1850*

191. Kerry Smith, *A Time of Crisis: Japan, the Great Depression, and Rural Revitalization*

192. Michael Lewis, *Becoming Apart: National Power and Local Politics in Toyama, 1868–1945*

193. William C. Kirby, Man-houng Lin, James Chin Shih, and David A. Pietz, eds., *State and Economy in Republican China: A Handbook for Scholars*

194. Timothy S. George, *Minamata: Pollution and the Struggle for Democracy in Postwar Japan*

195. Billy K. L. So, *Prosperity, Region, and Institutions in Maritime China: The South Fukien Pattern, 946–1368*

196. Yoshihisa Tak Matsusaka, *The Making of Japanese Manchuria, 1904–1932*

197. Maram Epstein, *Competing Discourses: Orthodoxy, Authenticity, and Engendered Meanings in Late Imperial Chinese Fiction*

198. Curtis J. Milhaupt, J. Mark Ramseyer, and Michael K. Young, eds. and comps., *Japanese Law in Context: Readings in Society, the Economy, and Politics*

199. Haruo Iguchi, *Unfinished Business: Ayukawa Yoshisuke and U.S.-Japan Relations, 1937–1952*

200. Scott Pearce, Audrey Spiro, and Patricia Ebrey, *Culture and Power in the Reconstitution of the Chinese Realm, 200–600*

201. Terry Kawashima, *Writing Margins: The Textual Construction of Gender in Heian and Kamakura Japan*

202. Martin W. Huang, *Desire and Fictional Narrative in Late Imperial China*

203. Robert S. Ross and Jiang Changbin, eds., *Re-examining the Cold War: U.S.-China Diplomacy, 1954–1973*

204. Guanhua Wang, *In Search of Justice: The 1905–1906 Chinese Anti-American Boycott*

205. David Schaberg, *A Patterned Past: Form and Thought in Early Chinese Historiography*

206. Christine Yano, *Tears of Longing: Nostalgia and the Nation in Japanese Popular Song*

207. Milena Doleželová-Velingerová and Oldřich Král, with Graham Sanders, eds., *The Appropriation of Cultural Capital: China's May Fourth Project*

208. Robert N. Huey, *The Making of 'Shinkokinshū'*

209. Lee Butler, *Emperor and Aristocracy in Japan, 1467–1680: Resilience and Renewal*

210. Suzanne Ogden, *Inklings of Democracy in China*

211. Kenneth J. Ruoff, *The People's Emperor: Democracy and the Japanese Monarchy, 1945–1995*

212. Haun Saussy, *Great Walls of Discourse and Other Adventures in Cultural China*

213. Aviad E. Raz, *Emotions at Work: Normative Control, Organizations, and Culture in Japan and America*

214. Rebecca E. Karl and Peter Zarrow, eds., *Rethinking the 1898 Reform Period: Political and Cultural Change in Late Qing China*

215. Kevin O'Rourke, *The Book of Korean Shijo*